Colonising Egypt

Colonising Egypt

TIMOTHY MITCHELL
New York University

UNIVERSITY OF CALIFORNIA PRESS

BERKELEY • LOS ANGELES • OXFORD

University of California Press
Berkeley and Los Angeles, California
University of California Press, Ltd.
Oxford, England

© Cambridge University Press 1988

First paperback printing 1991

Library of Congress Cataloging-in-Publication Data

Mitchell, Timothy.
Colonising Egypt/Timothy Mitchell.
p. cm.
Reprint. Originally published: Cambridge, Cambridgeshire ; New
York : Cambridge University Press, 1988. With new pref.
Includes bibliographical references and index.
ISBN 0-520-07568-4
1. Egypt—Relations—Europe. 2. Europe—Relations—Egypt.
3. Egypt—Civilization—1798- I. Title.
DT100.M57   1991
303.48'26204—dc20   91-15090 CIP

Printed in the United States of America

9 8 7 6 5 4 3 2

The paper used in this publication meets the minimum require-
ments of American National Standard for Information Sciences—
Permanence of Paper for Printed Library Materials,
ANSI Z39.48–1984. ∞

The fundamental event of the modern age
is the conquest of the world as picture.

Martin Heidegger, 'The age of the world picture'

This order of appearance is *the order of
all appearance*, the very process of appearing
in general. It is the order of truth.

Jacques Derrida, 'The double session'

Contents

Illustrations

Preface to the Paperback Edition

This book is not a history of the British colonisation of Egypt but a study of the power to colonise. While focussing on events in Egypt in the latter part of the nineteenth century, its argument is addressed to the place of colonialism in the critique of modernity. Colonising refers not simply to the establishing of a European presence but also to the spread of a political order that inscribes in the social world a new conception of space, new forms of personhood, and a new means of manufacturing the experience of the real. *Colonising Egypt* analyses in the everyday details of the colonial project the metaphysics of its power.

Chapters 2, 3, and 4 of the book examine the development in Egypt of the power to colonise. Chapter 2 begins by describing a novel attempt in the early nineteenth century to regulate the daily life of rural Egyptians. In the 1820s and 1830s orders were issued from Cairo prohibiting the movement of villagers outside their native districts, prescribing the crops they were to grow and the means of cultivation, distribution, and payment, and stipulating the hierarchy of surveillance, inspection, and punishment by which these rules were to be enforced. Attempting to control from Cairo the agricultural revenue of the Nile valley was nothing new. But earlier forms of control were always porous and uncertain. Typically, a powerful central household imposed levies on less powerful regional households, which in turn imposed obligations on those around them. Revenues flowing towards the center were liable to leak at each juncture and could be increased only by further expansion outward, which weakened the network by adding further points of leakage. The new controls of the nineteenth century attempted not just to appropriate a share of the agricultural surplus but to penetrate the processes of rural production, manipulate its elements, and multiply what John Bowring (an English advisor to the Egyptian government) called 'the productive powers' of the country. The effectiveness of disciplinary methods, as Michel Foucault has termed these modern forms of power, lay not in their weight or extent, but in the localised ability to infiltrate, rearrange, and colonise.

Bowring, the advisor in Cairo, was the friend and assistant of the English reformer Jeremy Bentham, who in turn was the inventor of the Panopticon, the institution in which the use of coercion and commands to control a population was replaced by the partitioning of space, the isolation of individuals, and their systematic yet unseen surveillance. Foucault has suggested that the geometry and discipline of the Panopticon can serve as an emblem of the micro-physical forms of power that have proliferated in the last two centuries and formed the experience of capitalist modernity.

Foucault's analyses are focused on France and northern Europe, yet forms of power based on the re-ordering of space and the surveillance and control of its occupants were by nature colonising in method. Moreover, examples of the Panopticon and similar disciplinary institutions were developed and introduced in many cases not in France or England but on the colonial frontiers of Europe, in places like Russia, India, North and South America, and Egypt. Jeremy Bentham corresponded with local rulers in all these places, including the governor in Cairo, Muhammad Ali Pasha, advocating the introduction of the panoptic principle and other new techniques. For many Europeans—military officers, Saint-Simonist engineers, educationalists, physicians, and others—a place like nineteenth-century Cairo provided the opportunity to help establish a modern state based on the new methods of disciplinary power.

The model for the new forms of power in Egypt, as chapter 2 explains, was the New Order, the Egyptian military reform of the 1820s whose innovative methods of manoeuvering and managing armed men created a military force more than four times the size and strength of previous armies. The creation of this force had both regional and domestic consequences. Regionally, it enabled Cairo to colonise an empire that stretched from Arabia and the Sudan in the south to Greece and Crete and later Palestine and Syria in the north. Local revolt and European intervention forced the empire's dismantling, and military power was subsequently redeployed to set up and police the geographical boundaries that created Egypt as a politico-spatial entity. European commercial and political penetration further weakened the regime in Cairo and brought on its economic collapse, followed in 1882 by the British invasion and occupation.

Domestically, the creation of the new army, as Bowring remarked, 'was in itself the establishment of a principle of order which spread over the entire surface of society.' The spread of this principle is examined in chapters 3 and 4. In agriculture the new controls over movement, production, and consumption were decentralized and intensified by converting the country's 'productive powers'—meaning villagers and their lands—into commodities. The same principle of order was manifested in the rebuilding of Cairo and other Egyptian towns and villages to create a system of regular, open streets, in the supervision of hygiene and public health, and above all in the introduction of compulsory schooling. School instruction seemed to offer a means of transforming every youth in the country into an industrious and obedient political subject. In the second half of the nineteenth century the discipline of schooling came to be considered the defining element in the politics of the modern state. Political order was to be achieved not through the intermittent use of coercion but through continuous instruction, inspection, and control.

Disciplinary methods have two important consequences for an understanding of the colonial and modern state—only the first of which is analysed by Foucault. In the first place, one can move beyond the image of power as a system of authoritative commands or policies backed by force that direct and constrain social action. Power is usually imagined as an exterior restriction: its source is a sovereign authority above and outside society, and it operates by setting limits to behaviour, establishing negative prohibitions, and laying down channels of proper conduct.

Disciplinary power, by contrast, works not from the outside but from within, not at the level of an entire society but at the level of detail, and not by restricting individuals and their actions but by producing them. A restrictive, exterior power gives way to an internal, productive power. Disciplines work within local domains and institutions, entering into particular social processes, breaking them down into separate functions, rearranging the parts, increasing their efficiency and precision, and reassembling them into more productive and powerful combinations. These methods produce the organised power of armies, schools, and factories, and other distinctive institutions of modern nation-states. They also produce, within such institutions, the modern individual, constructed as an isolated, disciplined, receptive, and industrious political subject. Power relations do not simply confront this individual as a set of external orders and prohibitions. His or her very individuality, formed within such institutions, is already the product of those relations.

One should not overstate the coherence of these technologies, as Foucault sometimes does. Disciplines can break down, counteract one another, or overreach. They offer spaces for manoeuver and resistance, and can be turned to counter-hegemonic purposes. Anti-colonial movements have often derived their organisational forms from the military and their methods of discipline and indoctrination from schooling. They have frequently been formed within the barracks, the campus, or other institutions of the colonial state. At the same time, in abandoning the image of colonial power as simply a coercive central authority, one should also question the traditional figure of resistance as a subject who stands outside this power and refuses its demands. Colonial subjects and their modes of resistance are formed *within* the organisational terrain of the colonial state, rather than some wholly exterior social space.

The second consequence of disciplinary power, the one that Michel Foucault does not discuss, yet the more important for understanding the peculiarity of capitalist modernity, is that at the same time as power relations become internal in this way, and by the same methods, they now appear to take the form of external structures. For example, the Egyptian military reforms of the early nineteenth century transformed groups of armed men into what seemed an 'artificial machine.' This military apparatus appeared somehow greater than the sum of its parts, as though it were a structure with an existence independent of the men who composed it. Older armies suddenly looked formless, composed of 'idle and inactive men,' while the new army seemed two-dimensional. It appeared to consist on the one hand of individual soldiers and on the other of the machine they inhabited. Of course this apparatus has no independent existence. It is an effect produced by the organised distribution of men, the coordination of their movement, the partitioning of space, and the hierarchical ordering of units, all of which are particular practices. There was nothing in the new power of the army except this distributing, arranging, and moving. But the order and precision of such processes created the effect of an apparatus apart from the men themselves, whose structure orders, contains, and controls them.

A similar two-dimensional effect can be seen at work in other forms of colonising power. In the nineteenth-century rebuilding of Cairo, for example, the layout of the new streets was designed to give the appearance of a plan. Such a plan was not merely a device to aid the work of urban reconstruction but a principle of order to be represented in the layout of the city's streets and inscribed in the life of its inhabitants. The new city remained, like the old city, simply a certain distributing of surfaces and spaces. But the regularity of the distribution was to create the experience of something existing apart from the physical streets as their non-physical structure. The order of the city was now to be grasped in terms of this relation between the material realisation of things themselves (as one could now say) and their invisible, meta-physical structure.

The precise specification of space and function that characterise modern institutions, the coordination of these functions into hierarchical arrangements, the organisation of supervision and surveillance, the marking out of time into schedules and programmes—all contribute to constructing a world that appears to consist not of a complex of social practices but of a binary order: on the one hand individuals and their activities, on the other an inert structure that somehow stands apart from individuals, preexists them, and contains and gives a framework to their lives. Such techniques have given rise to the peculiar metaphysic of modernity, where the world seems resolved into the two-dimensional form of individual versus apparatus, practice versus institution, social life and its structure—or material reality and its meaning.

The question of meaning or representation is an essential aspect of this structural effect, and is the central theme of the book. The methods of organisation and arrangement that produce the new effects of structure, it is argued, also generate the modern experience of meaning as a process of representation. In the metaphysics of capitalist modernity, the world is experienced in terms of an ontological distinction between physical reality and its representation—in language, culture, or other forms of meaning. Reality is material, inert, and without inherent meaning, and representation is the non-material, non-physical dimension of intelligibility. *Colonising Egypt* explores the power and limits of this ontology by showing the forms of colonising practice that generate it. As a motif exemplifying the nature of representation, the book takes the great nineteenth-century world exhibitions that formed part of Europe's colonising project. Drawing on the work of Martin Heidegger and Jacques Derrida, it refers to this modernist metaphysics as the world-as-exhibition.

Chapter 1 of the book, which precedes the analysis of disciplinary power outlined above, introduces the problem by reading from the accounts of Egyptian and other Arab travellers who visited nineteenth-century Europe. The most common topic of their accounts was the description of the world exhibitions, where they encountered imitation bazaars, Oriental palaces, exotic commodities, colonial natives in their natural habitats, and all the truth of imperial power and cultural difference.

Drawing from the Arabic accounts, the chapter locates the distinctiveness of representation in the ability to set apart a realm of images and signs from the real world they represent. It then shows how this separation, which is analogous to the structural effects just mentioned, lacks the ontological certainty it claims and is no more than an uncertain and unstable effect.

What most surprised the non-European visitors to the exhibitions was the realism of the artificial. The famous Rue du Caire at the 1889 Paris exhibition reproduced an entire street of the Egyptian capital, and imported real Egyptian donkeys and their drivers. By its realism, the artificial proclaims itself to be not the real. The very scale and accuracy of the model assure the visitor that there must exist some original of which this is a mere copy. Such techniques persuade one not that the representation is necessarily exact, but that there is a pure reality out there, untouched by the forms of displacement, intermediation, and repetition that render the image merely an image.

Chapter 1 discusses several features of the exhibitions that reinforce this modernist experience of the real, by generating what seems an unproblematic distinction between reality and its representation. Physical barriers separate the exhibition from the real world outside. The displays inside are arranged to express the European historico-geographic order of culture and evolution, an order reflected and reproduced in the multitude of plans, signposts, and guidebooks to the exhibition. As a result, the exhibition appears not just to mimic the real world outside but to superimpose a framework of meaning over its innumerable races, territories, and commodities. Made to appear an abstract order apart from physical reality, this framework is an effect of structure analogous to those of military order, urban planning, and other colonising practices mentioned above, produced by similar methods of coordination and arrangement.

The technique of representation was not limited to the world exhibitions. Outside the exhibitions visitors to Europe encountered further mechanisms of representation. In museums and Orientalist congresses, the theatre and the zoo, schools and department stores, the very streets of the modern city with their meaningful facades, they found the method of meaning to be the same. Everything seemed to be set up before the observer as a picture or exhibition of something, representing some reality beyond. The visitor to Europe encountered not just exhibitions of the world, but the world itself ordered up as though it were an endless exhibition.

The extent of the processes of representation begins to reveal the elusiveness of their apparently simple structural effect. The structure of meaning in a system of representation arises, it is suggested, from the distinction maintained between the realm of representation and the external reality to which it refers. Yet this real world, outside the exhibition, seems actually to have consisted only of further representations of the real. Just as the imitations in the exhibition were marked with traces of the real (were the natives on display not real people?), so the reality outside was never quite unmediated. *Colonising Egypt* is not concerned so much with this necessary elusiveness, but with the question of how it comes to be overlooked. How does the colonising process extend the world-as-exhibition, supplanting with its powerful metaphysic other less effective theologies?

As a counterpart to the Arab descriptions of Europe with which the book begins, the second half of chapter 1 considers the writings of nineteenth-century Europeans who left the world-as-exhibition and travelled to the Arab world. Their purpose in travelling to the Orient was to experience the reality they had seen so often on exhibit, but what they found there confused them. Although they thought of themselves as moving from exhibits of the Orient to the real thing, they went on trying to grasp the real thing as an exhibit. This was inevitable. To the European, reality meant that which presents itself in terms of a distinction between representation and original; something to be grasped as though it were an exhibit. Unlike London or Paris, however, a place such as Cairo had not yet been rearranged in terms of this absolute distinction and set up as an exhibition before the visitor's gaze.

The Orient refused to present itself like an exhibit, and so appeared simply orderless and without meaning. The colonising process was to introduce the kind of order now found lacking—the effect of structure that was to provide not only a new disciplinary power but also the novel ontology of representation.

In chapters 2, 3, and 4, the discussion of military methods, model villages, urban planning, schooling, and other colonising projects explores the ways in which these methods of order simultaneously inscribed in the social world a new legibility. The disciplined and uniformed soldier would now be clearly distinguishable from civilians, making it possible to identify stragglers and overcome the last major barrier to the development of large armies—the problem of desertion. Model villages were intended to organise and make legible the life of ordinary Egyptians, introducing an architecture that would make even women and their families visible to the 'observation of the police'. The new, open streets of modern Cairo and other Egyptian towns embodied a similar principle of visibility and observation, the principle of the exhibition. The hierarchy of the new primary, secondary, and higher schools constructed over the entire country was designed to give a describable structure to the new nation-state. At the same time, the schools made available a general code of instruction and information, to be mastered prior to embarking on life itself. Without this code, the existence of a nation-state was now considered impossible.

In each of these cases the principle at work was the same. The methods of order and arrangement created the effect of structure. Like the careful layout of an exhibition, this structure appeared as a framework within which activities could be organised, controlled, and observed; and it also appeared as a plan or programme, supplementing the activity with its meaning. The same technologies of order created both a disciplinary power and a seemingly separate realm of meaning or truth.

Chapter 5 of the book explores the relationship between truth and power a step further, by turning to the question of language and drawing a parallel between the creation of linguistic intention or authority and the creation of political authority in the colonial state. Language provides the most far-reaching example of how the distinctive technologies of the colonial age, including new methods of communication, printing, and schooling, create the effect of a structure apart from reality, supplementing it with what is experienced as its order and meaning. Drawing again on the work of Jacques Derrida, the chapter suggests how the modern understanding of language is intertwined with these new technologies. It rests upon the mechanical theory of representation generated by the world-as-exhibition, whose metaphysic was not shared by pre-modern Arab scholarship.

Arabic writing was transformed by the new technologies. Textual practices designed to protect the meaning or intention of writing were made obsolete by the metaphysics of representation. Textual intention was analogous in nature and method to the intention or authority of political power, and in fact had always formed an important part of such power. The new effect of meaning—as an abstract frame constituted in opposition to the real—offered at the same time a new effect of political authority. Like meaning in the world-as-exhibition, authority was now to appear as a generalised abstraction, with names like law or the state. Like meaning, it would now appear as a framework standing outside the real world. The colonial transformations that introduced the effects of representation tended at the same time to create this new effect of authority.

To make its argument about the metaphysics of Western writing, chapter 5 sketches an account of some of the practices surrounding the art of writing in the pre-colonial Arab world. This account resembles parts of other chapters that discuss pre-colonial methods of building, of organising space, of learning, and of producing meaning and social order. These passages are deliberately fragmentary and incomplete. They do not pretend to represent a pre-colonial past. For reasons that lie at the core of the argument of this book, such a representation would not be possible. Rather, they are intended as commentaries on the book's account of the colonising project, to suggest the possibility of thinking about language, meaning, and political order in ways that are not governed by the metaphysic of representation. The passages should also be read as arguments with the work of the contemporary theorists to whom they refer, such as Pierre Bourdieu and Jacques Derrida. The aim is to advance a more radical critique of modernity than their theories are usually allowed to support.

T.P.M.
New York
June 1991

Acknowledgements

Most of this book was written in the spring and summer of 1986 at St. Antony's College, Oxford. Derek Hopwood, Albert Hourani, and Roger Owen facilitated my stay there, and together with the staff and other members of the Middle East Centre at St. Antony's, made it extremely enjoyable. I was supported financially during those months by a Presidential Fellowship from New York University, for which I owe particular thanks to Farhad Kazemi.

Chapter 3 of the book, half each of chapters 2 and 4, and certain other sections are based on my doctoral dissertation, supervised by Manfred Halpern and Charles Issawi of Princeton University. To both of them I am grateful for their interest in my work and their support. Part of the research for the dissertation and book was done in Egypt, in the reference room and the periodicals room at Dar al-Kutub, the Egyptian national library, where the staff were always friendly and efficient. My trips to Egypt were funded first by a grant from the Program in Near Eastern Studies at Princeton and on two subsequent occasions by fellowships from the American Research Center in Egypt. I want to thank the many individuals at both institutions who gave me help, including James and Susan Allen, Carl Brown, May Trad, and Paul Walker.

Many of the arguments made in this book were first born, developed, or stolen from conversations with friends. For its major themes I have learned and taken most from Stefania Pandolfo. Her discussions of my work first decided its direction, and her reading of subsequent versions improved it at every point. Among many other friends and colleagues who have helped, I owe special thanks to Michael Gilsenan, Uday Mehta, Brinkley Messick, Roy Mottahedeh, and Helen Pringle. I am also grateful to Elizabeth Wetton of Cambridge University Press for her patient work overseeing the editing and production of the book, and to Charlene Woodcock of the University of California Press for the paperback edition.

I owe my greatest debt, for her intellectual support, her criticism, her encouragement, and her care, to Lila Abu-Lughod. I might possibly have

Acknowledgements

finished this book without her presence. But neither the book nor the rest of life would have been the same. Finally I want to thank my family, for whom these pages are no doubt insufficient excuse for my ten-year absence from England.

The book is dedicated to my mother, and to the memory of my father.

Chapter 1

Egypt at the exhibition

The Egyptian delegation to the Eighth International Congress of Orientalists, held in Stockholm in the summer of 1889, travelled to Sweden via Paris and paused there to visit the World Exhibition. The four Egyptians spent several days in the French capital, climbing twice the height (as they reported) of the Great Pyramid in Alexandre Eiffel's new tower, and exploring the city laid out beneath. They visited the carefully planned parks and pavilions of the exhibition, and examined the merchandise and machinery on display. Amid this order and splendour there was only one thing that disturbed them. The Egyptian exhibit had been built by the French to represent a winding street of Cairo, made of houses with overhanging upper stories and a mosque like that of Qaitbay. 'It was intended', one of the Egyptians wrote, 'to resemble the old aspect of Cairo.' So carefully was this done, he noted, that 'even the paint on the buildings was made dirty'.[1]

The Egyptian exhibit had also been made carefully chaotic. In contrast to the geometric lines of the rest of the exhibition, the imitation street was laid out in the haphazard manner of the bazaar. The way was crowded with shops and stalls, where Frenchmen dressed as Orientals sold perfumes, pastries, and tarbushes. To complete the effect of the bazaar, the French organisers had imported from Cairo fifty Egyptian donkeys, together with their drivers and the requisite number of grooms, farriers, and saddlemakers. The donkeys gave rides for the price of one franc up and down the street, resulting in a clamour and confusion so life-like, the director of the exhibition was obliged to issue an order restricting the donkeys to a certain number at each hour of the day.

The Egyptian visitors were disgusted by all this and stayed away. Their final embarrassment had been to enter the door of the mosque and discover that, like the rest of the street, it had been erected as what the Europeans called a façade. 'Its external form as a mosque was all that there was. As for the interior, it had been set up as a coffee house, where Egyptian girls performed dances with young males, and dervishes whirled.'[2]

After eighteen days in Paris, the Egyptian delegation travelled on to Stockholm to attend the Congress of Orientalists. Together with other non-European delegates, the Egyptians were received with hospitality – and a

1

great curiosity. As though they were still in Paris, they found themselves something of an exhibit. '*Bona fide* Orientalists', wrote a European particip-ant in the congress, 'were stared at as in a Barnum's all-world show: the good Scandinavian people seemed to think that it was a collection of *Orientals*, not of *Orientalists*.' Some of the Orientalists themselves seemed to delight in the role of showmen. At an earlier congress, in Berlin, we are told that 'the grotesque idea was started of producing natives of Oriental countries as illustrations of a paper: thus the Boden Professor of Sanskrit at Oxford pro-duced a real live Indian Pandit, and made him go through the ritual of Brahmanical prayer and worship before a hilarious assembly . . . Professor Max Müller of Oxford produced two rival Japanese priests, who exhibited their gifts; it had the appearance of two showmen exhibiting their monkeys.'[3] At the Stockholm congress the Egyptians were invited to partici-pate as scholars, but when they used their own language to do so they again found themselves treated as exhibits. 'I have heard nothing so unworthy of a sensible man', complained an Oxford scholar, 'as . . . the whistling howls emitted by an Arabic student of El-Azhar of Cairo. Such exhibitions at Congresses are mischievous and degrading.'[4]

The exhibition and the congress were not the only examples of this Euro-pean mischief. Throughout the nineteenth century non-European visitors found themselves being placed on exhibit or made the careful object of European curiosity. The degradation they often suffered, whether intended or not, seemed nevertheless inevitable, as necessary to these spectacles as the scaffolded façades or the curious crowds of onlookers. The façades, the onlookers and the degradation seemed all to belong to the organising of an exhibit, to a particularly European concern with rendering things up to be viewed. I will be taking up this question of the exhibition, examining it through non-European eyes as a practice that exemplifies the nature of the modern European state. But I want to reach it via a detour, which explores a little further the mischief to which the Oxford scholar referred. This mischief is a clue, for it runs right through the Middle Eastern experience of nineteenth-century Europe.

To begin with, Middle Eastern visitors found Europeans a curious people, with an uncontainable eagerness to stand and stare. 'One of the characteristics of the French is to stare and get excited at everything new', wrote an Egyptian scholar who spent five years in Paris in the 1820s.[5] It was perhaps this staring he had in mind when he explained in another book, dis-cussing the manners and customs of various nations, that 'one of the beliefs of the Europeans is that the gaze has no effect'.[6] An Ottoman envoy who stopped at Köpenick on his way to Berlin in 1790 reported that 'the people of Berlin were unable to contain their impatience until our arrival in the city. Regardless of the winter and the snow, both men and women came in

1 Exposition Universelle, Paris, 1889: the Egyptian exhibit.

carriages, on horseback, and on foot, to look at us and contemplate us.'[7] Where such spectacles were prevented, it seemed necessary to recreate them artificially. The members of an Egyptian student mission sent to Paris in the 1820s were confined to the college where they lived and allowed out onto the streets only every second Sunday. But during their stay in Paris they found themselves parodied in vaudeville on the Paris stage, for the entertainment of the French public. 'They construct the stage as the play demands', explained one of the students. 'For example, if they want to imitate a sultan and the things that happen to him, they set up the stage in the form of a palace and portray him in person. If for instance they want to play the Shah of Persia, they dress someone in the clothes of the Persian monarch and then put him there and sit him on a throne.'[8]

Even Middle Eastern monarchs who came in person to Europe were liable to be incorporated themselves into its theatrical events. When the Khedive of Egypt visited Paris to attend an earlier Exposition Universelle in 1867, he found that the Egyptian exhibit had been built to simulate medieval Cairo in the form of a royal palace. The Khedive stayed in the imitation palace during his visit and became a part of the exhibition, receiving visitors with medieval hospitality.[9] His father, Crown Prince Ibrahim of Egypt, had been less fortunate. Visiting the manufactories and showrooms of Birmingham in June 1846, he insisted wearily to the press after his experiences elsewhere with the British public that 'he should be regarded merely as a private gentleman'. But he was unable to escape becoming something of an exhibit. He went out for a stroll incognito one evening and slipped into a showtent to see on display the carcass of an enormous whale. He was recognised immediately by the showman, who began announcing to the crowd outside that 'for the one price they could see on display the carcass of the whale, and the Great Warrior Ibrahim, Conqueror of the Turks, into the bargain'. The crowd rushed in, and the Crown Prince had to be rescued by the Birmingham police.[10]

This sort of curiosity is encountered in almost every Middle Eastern description of nineteenth-century Europe. Towards the end of the century, when one or two Egyptian writers began to compose works of fiction in the realistic style of the novel, they made the journey to Europe their first topic. The stories would often evoke the peculiar experience of the West by describing an individual surrounded and stared at, like an object on exhibit. 'Whenever he paused outside a shop or showroom,' the protagonist in one such story found on his first day in Paris, 'a large number of people would surround him, both men and women, staring at his dress and appearance.'[11] Such stories could be multiplied, but for the time being I want to indicate only this, that for the visitor from the Middle East, Europe was a place where one was liable to become an object on exhibit, at which people gathered and stared.

I should make clear my own interest in this mischief, because the tendency of Europeans to stand and stare has sometimes been noted before. In fact words such as those quoted from the Ottoman envoy on his way to Berlin have been offered as part of the evidence for an essential historical difference between Europeans and other people, the difference between the curiosity of the European concerning strange places and people, and the 'general lack of curiosity' of others. The difference is said to go back to, and to illustrate, the great blossoming of European intellectual curiosity at the beginning of the modern age. We are told that it is to be understood, essentially, as a 'difference of attitude'.[12] Many people, myself included, would find it implausible that such staring could help to serve as evidence within a group for the presence or absence of intellectual curiosity. But there is also the implication that this 'attitude' – if that is how it should be understood – was in some sense natural. Such curiosity, it seems to be suggested, is simply the unfettered relation of a person to the world, emerging in Europe once the 'loosening of theological bonds' had brought about 'the freeing of human minds'. Fewer people would question this assumption. In fact I would argue that the notion of 'theological bonds' that loosen or become broken, leaving the individual confronted by the world, continues to govern our understanding of the historical encounter of the Middle East with the modern West, and even of political struggles in the Middle East today. The reason for my detour through this mischief is because I want to examine the way of addressing the world that Middle Eastern writers found in Europe as something not natural but mischievous – dependent, so to speak, on a certain theology of its own.

Objectness

Accepting for the moment this curious attitude of the European subject, we can note first of all that the non-European visitor also encountered in Europe what might have seemed a corresponding 'objectness'. The curiosity of the subject was called forth by a diversity of mechanisms for rendering things up as its object. Ibrahim Pasha's encounter with the whale and the students' experience of being parodied on the Paris stage were only minor beginnings. The student from that group who published an account of their stay in Paris devoted several pages to the Parisian phenomenon of *le spectacle*, a word for which he knew of no Arabic equivalent. Besides the Opéra and the Opéra-Comique, among the different kinds of spectacle he described were 'places in which they represent for the person the view of a town or a country or the like', such as 'the Panorama, the Cosmorana, the Diorama, the Europorama and the Uranorama'. In a panorama of Cairo, he explained in illustration, 'it is as though you were looking from on top of the minaret of Sultan Hasan, for example, with al-Rumaila and the rest of the city beneath you'.[13]

The panoramas were the forerunners of the world exhibitions, which were organised on an ever increasing scale as Europe entered its imperial age. Along with other public and political spectacles, including the increasingly lavish international congresses of Orientalists, the first of which was held in Paris in 1873, these events became the major subject of Arabic accounts of the modern West. By the last decade of the nineteenth century, more than half the descriptions of journeys to Europe being published in Cairo were written to describe visits to a world exhibition or an international congress of Orientalists.[14] These accounts devote hundreds of pages to describing the peculiar order and technique of such spectacles – the curious crowds of spectators, the device of the exhibit and the model, the organisation of panoramas and perspectives, the display of new discoveries and merchandise, the architecture of iron and glass, the systems of classification, the calculation of statistics, the lectures, the plans and the guide books – in short the entire machinery of what I am going to refer to as 'representation': everything collected and arranged to stand for something, to represent progress and history, human industry and empire; everything set up, and the whole set-up always evoking somehow some larger truth.

Spectacles like the world exhibition and the Orientalist congress set up the world as a picture. They ordered it up before an audience as an object on display, to be viewed, experienced and investigated. The Great Exhibition of 1851 in London claimed to present to its six million visitors 'a living picture' of the development of mankind.[15] Orientalism, it was claimed in the same way at the inauguration of the Ninth International Congress in London in 1892, had 'displayed before us the historical development of the human race'.[16] An earlier Orientalist, the great French scholar Sylvestre de Sacy, had envisioned this process of display in a manner very similar to the future world exhibitions. He had planned to establish a museum, which was to be 'a vast depot of objects of all kinds, of drawings, of original books, maps, accounts of voyages, all offered to those who wish to give themselves to the study of [the Orient]; in such a way that each of these students would be able to feel himself transported as if by enchantment into the midst of, say, a Mongolian tribe or of the Chinese race, whichever he might have made the object of his studies'.[17]

By the later decades of the century, almost everywhere that Middle Eastern visitors went they seemed to encounter this rendering up the world as a picture. They visited the museums, and saw the cultures of the world portrayed in objects arranged under glass, in the order of their evolution.

They were taken to the theatre, a place where Europeans portrayed to themselves their history, as several Egyptian writers explained. They spent afternoons in the public gardens, carefully organised 'to bring together the trees and plants of every part of the world', as another Arab writer put it. And inevitably they took trips to the zoo, a product of nineteenth-century colonial penetration of the Orient, as the critic Theodor Adorno wrote, 'which paid symbolic tribute in the form of animals'.[18]

These symbolic representations of the world's cultural and colonial order, continually encountered and described by visitors to Europe, were the mark of a great historical confidence. The spectacles set up in such places of modern entertainment reflected the political certainty of a new age. 'England is at present the greatest Oriental Empire which the world has ever known', proclaimed the president of the 1892 Orientalist Congress. 'She knows not only how to conquer, but how to rule.'[19] Exhibitions, museums and other spectacles were not just reflections of this certainty, however, but the means of its production, by their technique of rendering history, progress, culture and empire in 'objective' form. They were occasions for making sure of such objective truths, in a world where truth had become a question of what Heidegger calls 'the certainty of representation'.[20]

Such certainty of representation has a paradoxical quality, which I want to try and bring to light. By reading from some of the Arabic accounts of the world exhibition, it may be possible to understand a little further the strange objectness, and the strangely objective truths, that visitors from outside Europe encountered. The strangeness, I am going to suggest, did not arise as one might suppose from the 'artificial' quality of the endless exhibitions, displays and representations. It arose from the effect of an 'external reality' to which such seeming artificiality lays claim. The source of objective truths was the peculiar distinction maintained between the simulated and 'the real', between the exhibition and the world. This was a peculiarity which non-European visitors, finding themselves so often not just visitors but objects on exhibit, might have found a little more noticeable.

Representation

At first sight, the distinction between representation and 'external reality' seemed very clearly determined. There are three features of the world exhibitions I will mention in order to illustrate how this distinction was set up: the apparent realism of the exhibits, their organisation around a common centre, and the position of the visitor as the occupant of this central point. First, it was remarkable how perfectly the exhibitions seemed to model an external world. As the Egyptian visitor noticed, on the buildings representing a Cairo street even the paint was made dirty. It was precisely this kind of accuracy of detail that created the certainty, the effect of a determined correspondence between model and reality. Very often some of the most realistic exhibits were models of the city in which the exhibition was held, or of the world of which it claimed to be the centre. The realism with which these models were calculated and constructed always astonished the visitor. The 1889 exhibition, for example, included an enormous globe housed in a special building. An Arab writer described its extraordinary resemblance to reality:

Ordinary maps do not resemble the world perfectly, no matter how perfectly they are made, because they are flat while the earth is spherical. Conventional globes are very small, and the countries are not drawn on them clearly. This globe, however, is 12.72 metres in diameter and 40 metres in circumference. One millimetre on its surface corresponds to one kilometre on the surface of the earth. A city such as Cairo or Alexandria appears on it clearly. It is made of iron bars covered in thick paper shaped according to the form of the earth. It is mounted on a pivot on which it rotates with ease. Above it there is a large dome. Mountains, valleys and oceans are moulded on it, with the mountains raised proud of the surface. A mountain of 20,000 feet protrudes more than 6 millimetres, which makes it clearly visible. The globe turns on its axis one complete revolution every 24 hours, and rotates half a millimetre every second.[21]

Equally accurate representations were made of the city where the exhibition was held. At the centre of the 1878 Paris exhibition visitors had found the Pavillon de la Ville de Paris, which included exhibits and models of 'everything connected with the city's functions: schools, sewers, pumping stations, urban rebuilding' as well as plans of the city in three-dimensional relief.[22] This was surpassed at the next Paris exhibition, in 1889, where one of the most impressive exhibits was a panorama of the city. As described by the same Arab writer, this consisted of a viewing platform on which one stood, encircled by images of the city. The images were mounted and illuminated in such a way that the observer felt himself standing at the centre of the city itself, which seemed to materialise around him as a single, solid object 'not differing from reality in any way'.[23]

Secondly, the clearly determined relationship between model and reality was strengthened by their sharing of a common centre. A model or panorama of the city stood at the centre of the exhibition grounds, which were themselves laid out in the centre of the real city. The city in turn presented itself as the imperial capital of the world, and the exhibition at its centre laid out the exhibits of the world's empires and nations accordingly. France, for example, would occupy the central place on the Champs de Mars surrounded by the exhibits of the other industrialised states, with their colonies and other nations surrounding them in the proper order. ('It is not on the Champs de Mars that one should look for the Egyptian exhibit', we are told in a didactic guide entitled *L'Egypte, la Tunisie, le Maroc et l'exposition de 1878*. 'This is easily explained, for the country has no industry at all, properly speaking . . . ')[24] The common centre shared by the exhibition, the city and the world reinforced the relationship between representation and reality, just as the relationship enabled one to determine such a centre in the first place.

Finally, what distinguished the realism of the model from the reality it claimed to represent was that this central point had an occupant, the figure on the viewing platform. The representation of reality was always an exhibit set up for an observer in its midst, an observing gaze surrounded and set apart by the exhibition's careful order. If the dazzling displays of the exhibition could evoke some larger historical and political reality, it was because they were arranged to demand this isolated gaze. The more the exhibit drew in and encircled the visitor, the more the gaze was set apart from it, as the mind is set apart from the material world it observes. The separation is suggested in a description of the Egyptian exhibit at the Paris Exhibition of 1867:

A museum inside a pharaonic temple represented Antiquity, a palace richly decorated in the Arab style represented the Middle Ages, a caravanserai of merchants and performers portrayed in real life the customs of today. Weapons from the Sudan, the skins of wild monsters, perfumes, poisons and medicinal plants transport us directly to the tropics. Pottery from Assiut and Aswan, filigree and cloth of silk and gold invite us to touch with our fingers a strange civilisation. All the races subject to the Viceroy were personified by individuals selected with care. We rubbed shoulders with the fellah, we made way before the Bedouin of the Libyan desert on their beautiful white dromedaries. This sumptuous display spoke to the mind as to the eyes; it expressed a political idea.[25]

The remarkable realism of such displays made a strange civilisation into an object the visitor could almost touch. Yet to the observing eye, surrounded by the display but distinguished from it by the status of visitor, it remained a mere representation, the picture of some strange reality. Thus there were, in fact, two parallel pairs of distinctions, between the visitor and the exhibit, and between the exhibit and what it expressed. The representation was set apart from the real political reality it claimed to portray as the observing mind was set apart from what it observed.

Despite these methods of creating the determined distinction between representation and reality, however, it was not always easy in Paris to tell where the exhibition ended and the world itself began. It is true that the boundaries of the exhibition were clearly marked, with high perimeter walls and monumental gates. But, as the Egyptian delegation had begun to discover, there was much about the real world outside, in the streets of Paris and beyond, that resembled the world exhibition; just as there was more about the exhibition that resembled the world outside. It was as though, as we will see, despite the determined efforts within the exhibition to construct perfect representations of the real world outside, the real world beyond the gates turned out to be rather like an extension of the exhibition. This extended exhibition would continue to present itself as a series of mere representations, representing a reality outside. Thus we should think of it as not so much an exhibition as a kind of labyrinth, the labyrinth which includes in itself its own exits.[26] But then, perhaps the sequence of exhibitions became so accurate and so extensive, no one ever realised that the 'real world' they promised was not there. Except perhaps the Egyptians.

The world as an exhibition

To examine this paradox, I will begin again inside the exhibition, back at the Egyptian bazaar. Part of the shock of the Egyptians came from just how 'real' the street claimed to be. Not simply that the paint was made dirty, that the donkeys were from Cairo, and that the Egyptian pastries on sale claimed to taste like the real thing. But that one paid for them, as we say, with real money. The commercialism of the donkey rides, the bazaar stalls and the dancing girls was no different from the commercialism of the world outside. This was the real thing, in the sense that what commercialism offers is always the real thing. The commercialism of world exhibitions was no accident, but a consequence of the scale of representation they attempted and of the modern, consumer economy that required such entertainment. Beginning with the 1867 Exposition Universelle in Paris, which was four times the size of any previous exhibition, the expense of the event was offset by charging each exhibitor for the costs of furnishing the exhibit, and by including throughout the exhibition-ground shops and places of entertainment.[27]

As a result, the exhibitions came to resemble more and more the commercial machinery of the rest of the city. This machinery, in turn, was rapidly changing in places like London and Paris, as small, individually owned shops, often based on local crafts, gave way to the larger apparatus of shopping arcades and department stores. The Bon Marché opened in 1852 (and had a turnover of seven million francs by the end of the next decade), the Louvre in 1855, and Printemps in 1865.[28] The size of the new stores and arcades, as well as their architecture, made each one almost an exhibition in itself. The *Illustrated Guide to Paris* offered a typical description:

These arcades, a recent invention of industrial luxury, are glass-roofed, marble-walled passages, cut through whole blocks of houses, whose owners have combined in this speculation. On either side of the passages, which draw their light from above, run the most elegant shops, so that an arcade of this kind is a city, indeed a world in miniature.[29]

The Egyptian accounts of Europe contain several descriptions of these mechanical worlds-in-miniature, where the real world, as at the exhibition, was something created in the representation of its commodities. The department stores were described as 'large and well organised', with their merchandise 'arranged in perfect order, set in rows on shelves with everything symmetrical and precisely positioned'.[30] Non-European visitors would remark especially on the panes of glass, inside the stores and along the gas-lit arcades, which separated the observer from the goods on display. 'The merchandise is all arranged behind sheets of clear glass, in the most remarkable order . . . Its dazzling appearance draws thousands of onlookers.'[31] The glass panes inserted themselves between the visitors and the goods on display, making the former into mere onlookers and endowing the goods with the distance that is the source of their objectness. Just as exhibitions were becoming more commercialised, the machinery of commerce was becoming a means of creating an effect of reality, indistinguishable from that of the exhibition.

Something of the experience of the strangely organised world of modern commerce and consumers is indicated in the first fictional account of Europe to be published in Arabic. Appearing in 1882, it tells the story of two Egyptians who travelled to France and England in the company of an English Orientalist. On their first day in Paris, the two Egyptian protagonists wander accidentally into the vast, gas-lit premises of a wholesale supplier. Inside the building they find long corridors, each leading into another. They walk from one corridor to the next, and after a while begin to search for the way out. Turning a corner they see what looks like an exit, with people approaching from the other side. But it turns out to be a mirror, which covers the entire width and height of the wall, and the people approaching are merely their own reflections. They turn down another passage and then another, but each one ends only in a mirror. As they make their way through the corridors of the building, they pass groups of people at work. 'The people were busy setting out merchandise, sorting it and putting it into boxes and cases. They stared at the two of them in silence as they passed, standing quite still, not leaving their places or interrupting their work.' After wandering silently for some time through the building, the two Egyptians realise they have lost their way completely and begin going from room to room looking for an exit. 'But no one interfered with them', we are told, 'or came up to them to ask if they were lost.' Eventually they are rescued by the manager of the store, who proceeds to explain to them how

11

it is organised, pointing out that the merchandise being sorted and packed represents the produce of every country in the world.[32]

On the one hand this story evokes a festival of representation, a celebration of the ordered world of objects and the discipline of the European gaze. At the same time, the disconcerting experience with the mirrors undermines this system of representational order. An earlier Egyptian writer recalled a similar experience with mirrors, on his very first day in a European city. Arriving at Marseilles, he had entered a café, which he mistook at first for some sort of 'vast, endless thoroughfare'. 'There were a lot of people in there,' he explained, 'and whenever a group of them came into view their images appeared in the glass mirrors, which were on every side. Anyone who walked in, sat down, or stood up seemed to be multiplied. Thus the café looked like an open street. I realised it was enclosed only when I saw several images of myself in the mirrors, and understood that it was all due to the peculiar effect of the glass.'[33] In such stories, it is as though the world of representation is being admired for its dazzling order, and yet the suspicion remains that all this reality is only an effect. Perhaps the world remains inevitably a labyrinth, rather than an interior distinguished from – and defined by – its exterior.

At any rate the unusual and sometimes discomforting experiences of the world exhibition seem to be repeated, in such stories, in the world outside, a world of passages ending in one's own reflection, of corridors leading into a labyrinth of further corridors, of objects ordered up to represent every country in the world, and of disciplined, staring Europeans. It was not just in its commercialism, in other words, that all this resembled the world exhibition. Characteristic of the way Europeans seemed to live was their preoccupation with what the same Egyptian author described as *intizam al-manzar*, the organisation of the view. The Europe one reads about in Arabic accounts was a place of discipline and visual arrangement, of silent gazes and strange simulations, of the organisation of everything and everything organised to represent, to recall like the exhibition some larger meaning. Outside the world exhibition, it follows paradoxically, one encountered not the real world but only further models and representations of the real. Beyond the exhibition and the department store, everywhere that non-European visitors went – the museum and the Orientalist congress, the theatre and the zoo, the countryside encountered typically in the form of a model farm exhibiting new machinery and cultivation methods, the very streets of the modern city with their deliberate façades, even the Alps once the funicular was built – they found the technique and sensation to be the same.[34] Everything seemed to be set up before one as though it were the model or the picture of something. Everything was arranged before an observing subject into a system of signification (to use the European jargon), declaring itself to be the signifier of a signified.

The exhibition, perhaps, could be read in such accounts as epitomising the strange character of the West, a place where one was continually pressed into service as a spectator by a world ordered so as to represent. In exhibitions the traveller from the Middle East could describe the curious way of setting up the world encountered more and more in modern Europe, a particular arrangement between the individual and an object-world which Europeans seemed to take as the experience of the real. This reality-effect, let me provisionally suggest, was a world more and more rendered up to the individual according to the way in which, and to the extent to which, it could be set up before him or her as an exhibit. Non-Europeans encountered in Europe what one might call, echoing a phrase from Heidegger, the age of the world exhibition, or rather, the age of the world-as-exhibition.[35] World exhibition here refers not to an exhibition of the world but to the world conceived and grasped as though it were an exhibition.

There are three features of this world, each of them already introduced, that are going to provide themes I want to explore in this book. First, its remarkable claim to certainty or truth: the apparent certainty with which everything seems ordered and organised, calculated and rendered unambiguous – ultimately, what seems its political decidedness. Second, the paradoxical nature of this decidedness: its certainty exists as the seemingly determined relation between representations and 'reality'; yet the real world, like the world outside the exhibition, despite everything the exhibition promises, turns out to consist only of further representations of this reality. Third, what I will refer to as its colonial nature: the age of the exhibition was necessarily the colonial age, the age of world economy and global power in which we live, since what was to be rendered as exhibit was reality, the world itself.

The colonial order

To explore these themes, in the final pages of this chapter I am going to return with the Egyptian travellers to Cairo, and examine Middle Eastern life through the eyes of nineteenth-century European scholars, writers and tourists. If Europe was becoming the world-as-exhibition, I am going to ask, what happened to Europeans who left and went abroad? How did they experience a life not yet lived, so to speak, as though the world were a picture of something set up before an observer's gaze? Part of the answer, I will suggest, is that they did not realise they had left the exhibition. How could they, if they took the world itself to be an exhibition? Reality was that which presents itself as exhibit, so nothing else would have been thinkable. Living within a world of signs, they took semiosis to be a universal condition, and set about describing the Orient as though it were an exhibition.

We will remain in the Middle East for the rest of the book, mostly in Egypt of the later nineteenth century. My aim is to examine this combination of order and certainty that I have referred to as the world-as-exhibition, in the attempts to construct Egypt as a modern or colonial state. (Britain's colonial occupation of Egypt occurred late in the nineteenth century, in 1882. I will be using the word colonial, however, to refer beyond this event to the 'colonising' nature of the kind of power that the occupation sought to consolidate, a power which began to develop around the beginning of the century if not earlier.) The book is not intended as a history of this process, which remains even today something unaccomplished and incomplete. Instead I will examine certain exemplary projects, writings, and events which can suggest how such order and certainty were to be achieved, and illuminate something, I hope, of their strange nature.[36]

In chapters 2 and 3 I am going to begin by examining parallels between three characteristic practices in which a modern political method came into being: the formation of a new army, the introduction of organised schooling and the rebuilding of Egyptian villages and towns. The new processes that I examine – taking peasants for the first time to be drilled and disciplined into an army, pulling down houses to construct model villages or to open up the streets of a modern city, putting children into rows of desks contained within schools laid out like barracks – all replicated one another as acts of what was now called *nizam*, order and discipline. Such acts of order, which I contrast with other, older notions of order, all worked to create the appearance of a structure, a framework that seemed to exist apart from, and prior to, the particular individuals or actions it enframed. Such a framework would appear, in other words, as order itself, conceived in no other terms than the order of what was orderless, the coordination of what was discontinuous, something suddenly fundamental to human practice, to human thought. This effect was something new. It was the effect, I will argue, of a world that would now seem divided in two, into the material realm of things in themselves, as could now be said, and an abstract realm of their order or structure.

In chapters 4 and 5 I will try to connect this appearance of order with the 'order of appearance' I am calling the world-as-exhibition. To the world divided in two, I argue first of all, there corresponded a new conception of the person, similarly divided into a physical body and a non-physical entity to be called the mind or mentality. I examine how the new political practices of the colonial period were organised around this distinction, with the aim of making the individual body disciplined and industrious, and how the

14

same distinction became the subject of a large literature, concerned in particular with the Egyptian mind or 'character', whose problematic trait was its lack of the same habit of industry. The political process was conceived, in other words, according to this novel dichotomy between a material and a mental world, an object and a subject world. Its purpose, in turn, was to create both a material order and a conceptual or moral order. The new name for this moral order was 'society'.

In chapter 5, in the context of the military occupation of Egypt by the British, I will deal with the problem of political certainty or meaning. I want to consider how the new methods and new conception of order, examined in the preceding chapters, brought about the effect of a realm of meaning and authority. I propose to explore this by drawing a parallel from the same period with the question of meaning and authority in written texts, arguing that a new kind of distinction between the material and the mental also came to govern the nature of writing. I will use this parallel to argue that it was in terms of this strange distinction that the nature and authority of the modern state were to be conceived and achieved. Finally in chapter 6 I will try to connect together these parallel themes, returning to the question of the world as exhibition.

The globe

Before moving on to the Middle East, I want to outline briefly some of the more general aspects of Egypt's relation to the Europe of department stores and world exhibitions. This outline will provide both a historical itinerary and a further indication of the direction in which my own path leads off. The world exhibitions and the new large-scale commercial life of European cities were aspects of a political and economic transformation that equally affected Egypt. The new department stores were the first establishments to keep large quantities of merchandise in stock, in the form of standardised textiles and clothing. The stockpiling, together with the introduction of advertising (the word was coined at the time of the great exhibitions, Walter Benjamin tells us) and the new industry of 'fashion', on which several Egyptian writers commented, were all connected with the boom in textile production.[37] The textile boom was an aspect of other changes, such as new ways of harvesting and treating cotton, new machinery for the manufacture of textiles, the resulting increase in profits, and the reinvestment of profit abroad in further cotton production. At the other end from the department store, these wider changes extended to include places like the southern United States, India, and the Nile valley.

Since the latter part of the eighteenth century the Nile valley too had been undergoing a transformation, associated principally with the European

15

textile industry.[38] From a country which formed one of the hubs in the commerce of the Ottoman world and beyond, and which produced and exported its own food and its own textiles, Egypt was turning into a country whose economy was dominated by the production of a single commodity, raw cotton, for the global textile industry of Europe. By the eve of the First World War, cotton was to account for more than ninety-two per cent of the total value of Egypt's exports.[39] The changes associated with this growth and concentration in exports included an enormous growth in imports, principally of textile products and food, the extension throughout the country of a network of roads, telegraphs, police stations, railways, ports and permanent irrigation canals, a new relationship to the land, which became a privately owned commodity concentrated in the hands of a small, powerful and increasingly wealthy social class, the influx of Europeans, seeking to make fortunes, find employment, transform agricultural production or impose colonial control, the building and rebuilding of towns and cities as centres of the new European-dominated commercial life, and the migration to these urban centres of tens of thousands of the increasingly impoverished rural poor. No other place in the world in the nineteenth century was transformed on a greater scale to serve the production of a single industry.

It was exactly this kind of global transformation that world exhibitions were built to promote. The Saint-Simonists, believers in the new religion of 'social science' who had travelled to Cairo in the 1830s to begin from within Egypt their project for the industrialisation of the earth, and had miserably failed, were subsequently among the first to turn to the idea of world exhibitions. Michel Chevalier, editor of the Saint-Simonist journal *Globe*, advocated exhibitions for the same reason he advocated constructing canals at Panama and Suez: to open up the world to the free movement of commodities.[40] 'The Great Exhibition of the Works of Industry of All Nations' was the full title of the first of them, the Crystal Palace Exhibition of 1851. In place of the industrial exhibitions exclusive to one nation that had become popular during the first half of the century, all foreign nations and manufacturers were invited to exhibit at the Crystal Palace, reflecting the desire to promote unrestricted international trade on the part of British industrialists. What was on exhibit was the conversion of the world to modern capitalist production and exchange, and to the movements of communication and the processes of inspection on which these were thought to depend. The purpose of the exhibition was to

bring the leading men in manufactures, commerce and science into close and intimate communication with each other – establish an intelligent supervision of every branch of production by those most interested and most likely to be informed – have annual reports made in each department, and let the whole world be invited to assist in carrying forward the vast scheme of human labour which has hitherto been prosecuted at random and without any knowledge or appreciation of the system which pervaded it.[41]

The 'whole world' was to be invited in to see a fantastic and yet systematic profusion of material goods, all the new necessities and desires that modern capitalism could order up and display. 'Europe is on the move to look at merchandise', wrote the French historian Taine, when France responded to the Crystal Palace Exhibition with its first Exposition Universelle in 1855.[42] The first Arabic account of a world exhibition, describing the next Paris exposition in 1867, was entitled simply and accurately enough, *The Universal Exhibition of Commodities*.[43]

It was the representatives of these commercial and manufacturing interests who organised the participation of non-European nations at the exhibitions, to draw them into modern capitalism's 'vast scheme of human labour'. The government of Ottoman Turkey, for example, received the encouragement and assistance of local European consuls and businessmen, and of organisations such as the Manchester Cotton Association, in gathering together samples of all the marketable commodities that might be produced in the Empire and shipping them to Europe for the exhibitions. The Manchester Cotton Association even promoted local exhibitions in Istanbul and Izmir, to encourage Turkish landowners to convert their fields to cotton growing. After the success of the Paris exhibition of 1855, an international exhibition was organised in Istanbul itself, to promote capitalist production and marketing.[44] Egypt followed a decade later, after the Paris exhibition of 1867. The occasion of the Egyptian exhibition was an international celebration to mark the opening of the Suez Canal, built under the Saint-Simonist engineer de Lesseps, which confirmed Egypt's new importance to European world trade. The exhibition took the form of a new Europeanised city, its façades hastily constructed alongside the existing quarters of Cairo, and in some cases cutting right through them, complete with public gardens, a vaudeville theatre, and an opera house for the performance of Verdi's *Aïda*. The Khedive returned the favour of the imitation medieval palace that had been constructed for his use at the Paris exhibition two years earlier, by having a palace specially built on the Nile for the Empress Eugénie, in which the rooms were made exact replicas of her private apartments in the Tuilleries.[45]

The rebuilding of Cairo and other Middle Eastern cities according to the principle of the exhibition was intended, therefore, like the construction of exhibitions and exhibition-like cities in Europe, to promote the global economic and political transformation I have just outlined, and to symbolise its accomplishment. In other words the new façades of the city, like the display of commodities at the exhibition, could be taken as a series of signs or representations, as we say, of the larger economic changes 'underneath'. The problem, however, is that the sort of thing I want to understand is this very distinction between what we see as a realm of signs or representations, and an outside or an underneath. The economic and political transformations, I shall argue, were themselves something dependent on the working of this peculiar distinction.

Objective people

The new world of façades and exhibits, models and simulations, is certainly to be understood in relation to the wider capitalist transformation I have been describing. 'World exhibitions are sites of pilgrimages to the commodity fetish', wrote Benjamin, associating them with that 'theological' effect through which Marx understood power to operate in capitalist societies.[46] The effect occurs when production for the market causes the ordinary things people produce to be treated as commodities – objects, that is, whose diverse meanings or values are made comparable and exchangeable, by supposing them each to represent the result of a certain quantity of an identical and abstract process that we call 'production'. As a commodity, Marx explained, an object is treated as a mysterious 'social hieroglyphic' representing this imaginary productive process. It no longer represents to people the real labour and the real social lives of those who actually made it.[47]

Marx's analysis of commodity fetishism already suggested the central role that events like world exhibitions – and the whole industry of entertainment, the media, advertising, packaging and popular education which followed – were to play in modern, consumer capitalism. Exhibitions 'open up a phantasmagoria that people enter to be amused', wrote Benjamin. 'They submit to being manipulated while enjoying their alienation from themselves and others.'[48] The theory of commodity fetishism rests, however, on revealing such representations to be misrepresentations. Marx opposed to the imaginary productive processes represented by these misunderstood hieroglyphics the 'transparent and rational form' in which the practical relations of everyday life should present themselves.[49] To the mechanism of misrepresentation by which power operates, Marx opposed a representation of the way things intrinsically are, in their transparent and rational reality.

The problem with such an explanation was that, in revealing power to work through *mis*representation, it left representation itself unquestioned. It accepted absolutely the distinction between a realm of representations and the 'external reality' which such representations promise, rather than examining the novelty of continuously creating the effect of an 'external

18

reality' as itself a mechanism of power. The working of this mechanism is what I will be examining in later pages of this book, but the weakness of accepting the distinction already begins to appear as soon as one asks what the 'transparent and rational' reality, which capitalist representation mis-represents, really is. The answer in Marx's case, once one lifts the veil of the commodity, or the earlier veils of religion or 'the ancient worship of nature', was of course 'material production'. Material production, wrote Marx, is 'a process in which both man and Nature participate, and in which man of his own accord starts, regulates and controls the material reactions between himself and Nature . . . thus acting upon the external world and changing it'.[50] Such an account, however useful, is only a particular description. As Jean Baudrillard points out, it remains itself a language, a social hiero-glyphic, no less a representation, and thus no more a transparency, than the commodity fetish or the ancient worship of nature.[51]

The language is problematic not just because it can be shown to be a par-ticular description, rather than reality itself. It also happens to be the very language which world exhibitions were constructed to promote, and which was to be introduced into nineteenth-century Egypt. As I will try to show, the political and economic transformation that was to be attempted in places such as Egypt required, not a Marxist conception of the human person, but a conception which shared with Marx certain common assumptions. To prepare for the trip we will be taking to Egypt for the rest of this book, it may help to end this section by considering briefly what modern Europeans had come to think a person was.

The person was now thought of as something set apart from a physical world, like the visitor to an exhibition or the worker attending a machine, as the one who observes and controls it. His own nature (I will say 'his' when dealing, here as elsewhere, with male-centred notions) was realised in being 'industrious' – in maintaining the same steady observation and control over his own physical body and will. In the labour process, wrote Marx, the worker 'opposes himself to Nature as one of her own forces, setting in motion arms and legs, head and hands, the natural forces of his body . . . and compels them to act in obedience to his sway . . . This subordination is no mere momentary act. Besides the exertion of the bodily organs, the process demands that, during the whole operation, the workman's will be steadily in consonance with his purpose. This means close attention.'[52] Separated in this way from a physical world and from his own physical body, the true nature of the human person, like that of the observer at the exhibition, was to learn to be industrious, self-disciplined, and closely attentive.

In the middle of the nineteenth century, a new term came into vogue for characterising this combination of detachment and close attentiveness – the word 'objective'. 'Just now we are an objective people', *The Times* wrote in the summer of 1851, on the occasion of the Great Exhibition. 'We want to place everything we can lay our hands on under glass cases, and to stare our fill.'[53] The word denoted the modern sense of detachment, both physical and conceptual, of the self from an object-world – the detachment epitomised, as I have been suggesting, in the visitor to an exhibition. At the same time, the word suggested a passive curiosity, of the kind the organisers of exhibitions hoped to evoke in those who visited them. Despite their apprehension about allowing enormous numbers of the lower classes to congregate in European capitals so soon after the events of 1848, the authorities encouraged them to visit exhibitions. Workers were given permission to leave their shops and factories to attend, and manufacturers and benevolent societies subsidised the cost of their travel and accommodation. The result was an example of mass behaviour without precedent. 'Popular movements that only a few years ago would have been pronounced dangerous to the safety of the State', it was reported after the 1851 exhibition, ' . . . have taken place not only without disorder, but also almost without crime.'[54] The article on 'objective people' in *The Times* was commenting on the reassuring absence of 'political passions' in the country during the exhibition. The objective attitude of the exhibition visitor, in other words, seemed to suggest not only the true nature of the modern individual, but the model of behaviour for the modern political subject.

I want to recall, finally, from my earlier discussion of the exhibition that this 'objective' isolation of the observer from an object-world, in terms of which personhood was understood, corresponded to a distinction that was now made between the material world of exhibits or representations and the meaning or plan that they represented. This too the authorities and organisers seemed to understand. In order to encourage the proper objective attitude among visitors, they made a concerted effort to provide the necessary catalogues, plans, sign-posts, guidebooks, instructions, educational talks and compilations of statistics. (Thus the Egyptian exhibit at the 1867 exhibition was accompanied by a guidebook containing an outline of the country's history – divided clearly, as was the exhibit to which it referred, into the ancient, the medieval and the modern – together with a 'notice statistique sur le territoire, la population, les forces productives, le commerce, l'effective militaire et naval, l'organisation financière, l'instruction publique, etc. de l'Egypte' compiled, appropriately enough, by the Commission Impériale in Paris.)[55] Such outlines, guides, tables and plans mediated between the visitor and the exhibit, by supplementing what was displayed with a structure and meaning. The seemingly separate text or plan, one might say, was what confirmed the separation of the person from the things themselves on exhibit, and of the things on exhibit from the meaning or external reality they represented.

Marx himself, although he wanted none of the accompanying political passivity, conceived of an essential separation between the person and an object-world in the same way, in terms of a structure or plan existing apart from things themselves. What distinguished man from 'external' nature was his ability to make an interior mental map. Like the architect, as Marx explained in a well-known phrase, man 'raises his structure in imagination before he erects it in reality'.[56] Like the visitor to the exhibition, that is, his separation from an external object-world was something mediated by a non-material plan or structure.

This notion of an 'imaginary structure' that exists before and apart from something called 'external reality', in the same way as an exhibit or a plan stands apart from the real world it represents, is what gives shape to the experience and understanding of objective people. It governs, in other words, the strange anthropology in which we inhabitants of the world-as-exhibition believe. In order to anthropologise a little further our thinking about the person and the world, I am now going to move on to consider what happened to the nineteenth-century European who travelled to the Middle East. The Orient, after all, was the great 'external reality' of modern Europe – the most common object of its exhibitions, the great signified. By the late 1860s Thomas Cook, who had launched the modern tourist industry by organising excursion trains with the Midland Railway Company to visit the Crystal Palace exhibition, was offering excursions to visit not exhibits of the Orient but the real thing.[57] Yet as we will see, European visitors would arrive in the Orient looking for the same kind of structure 'raised in the imagination'. They would come expecting to find a world where a structure or meaning exists somehow apart, as in an exhibition, from the 'reality' of things-in-themselves.

The East itself

'So here we are in Egypt', wrote Gustave Flaubert, in a letter from Cairo in January 1850. 'What can I say about it all? What can I write you? As yet I am scarcely over the initial bedazzlement . . . each detail reaches out to grip you; it pinches you; and the more you concentrate on it the less you grasp the whole. Then gradually all this becomes harmonious and the pieces fall into place of themselves, in accordance with the laws of perspective. But the first days, by God, it is such a bewildering chaos of colours . . . '[58] Flaubert experiences Cairo as a visual turmoil. At first it is indescribable, except as disorder. What can he write about the place? That it is a chaos of colour and detail, which refuses to compose itself as a picture. The disorienting experience of a Cairo street, in other words, with its arguments in unknown languages, strangers who brush past in strange clothes, unusual colours, and unfamiliar sounds and smells, is expressed as an absence of pictorial order. There is no distance, this means, between oneself and the view, and the eyes are reduced to organs of touch: 'each detail reaches out to grip you'. Without a separation of the self from a picture, moreover, it becomes impossible to grasp 'the whole'. The experience of the world as a picture set up before the subject is linked, as we will see, to the unusual conception of the world as a limited totality, something that forms a bounded structure or system. Subsequently, coming to terms with this disorientation and recovering one's self-possession is expressed again in pictorial terms. The world arranges itself into a picture and achieves a visual order, 'in accordance with the laws of perspective'.

If Europe, as I have been suggesting, was the world-as-exhibition, what happened to Europeans who went abroad – to visit places whose images invariably they had already seen in pictures and exhibitions? How did they experience the real world such images had depicted, when the reality was a place whose life was not yet lived as if the world were an exhibition? They were confused of course, but perhaps the key to their confusion was this: although they thought of themselves as moving from the pictures to the real thing, they went on trying – like Flaubert – to grasp the real thing as a picture. How could they do otherwise, since they took reality itself to be a picture? The real is grasped in terms of a distinction between a picture and what it represents, so nothing else would have been, quite literally, thinkable. Brought up within what they thought of as a representational world, they took representation to be a universal condition. Thus they set about trying to describe the Orient as though it were an exhibition – a delapidated and mismanaged one of course, indeed an exhibition of its own delapidation and mismanagement. What else could it be taken to represent?

Among European writers who travelled to the Middle East in the middle and latter part of the nineteenth century, one very frequently finds the experience of its strangeness expressed in terms of the problem of forming a picture. It was as though to make sense of it meant to stand back and make a drawing or take a photograph of it; which for many of them actually it did. 'Every year that passes', an Egyptian wrote, 'you see thousands of Europeans travelling all over the world, and everything they come across they make a picture of.'[59] Writers from Europe wanted to make pictures in the same way. They wanted to portray what they saw in words with the same chemically-etched accuracy, and the same optical detachment, as the daguerreotype or the photographic apparatus, that 'instrument of patience' as Gérard de Nerval described it, ' . . . which, destroying illusions, opposes to each figure the mirror of truth'.[60] Flaubert travelled in Egypt on a photographic mission with Maxime du Camp, the results of which were expected to be 'quite special in character', it was remarked at the Institut de France, 'thanks to the aid of this modern travelling companion, efficient, rapid, and always scrupulously exact'.[61] The exact correspondence of the image to reality would provide a new, almost mechanical kind of certainty. The publication in 1858 of the first general collection of photographs of the Middle East, Francis Frith's *Egypt and Palestine, Photographed and Described*, would be 'an experiment in Photography . . . of surpassing value', it was announced in the *Art Journal*, 'for we will *know* that we see things exactly as they are'.[62]

Like the photographer, the writer wanted to reproduce a picture of things 'exactly as they are', of 'the East itself in its vital actual reality'.[63] Flaubert and Nerval were preceded in Egypt by Edward Lane, whose famous *Account of the Manners and Customs of the Modern Egyptians* was published in 1835. The book's 'singular power of description and minute accuracy' made it, in the words of his nephew, the Orientalist Stanley Poole, 'the most perfect picture of a people's life that has ever been written'. 'Very few men', added his great-nephew, the Orientalist Stanley Lane-Poole, 'have possessed in equal degree the power of minutely describing a scene or a monument, so that the pencil might almost restore it without a fault after the lapse of years . . . The objects stand before you as you read, and this not by the use of imaginative language, but by the plain simple description.'[64] Lane, in fact, did not begin as a writer but as a professional artist and engraver, and had first travelled to Egypt in 1825 with a new apparatus called the camera lucida, a drawing device with a prism that projected an exact image of the object on to paper. He had planned to publish the drawings he made with this device and the accompanying descriptions in an eight-volume work entitled 'An Exhaustive Description of Egypt', but had been unable to find a publisher whose printing techniques could reproduce the minute and mechanical accuracy of the drawings. Subsequently, he published the part dealing with contemporary Egypt, rewritten as the ethnographic description of the modern Egyptians.[65]

The point of view

Besides the apparent accuracy of representation of these mechanical 'mirrors of truth', writers also sought their optical detachment. Like the exhibition, the daguerreotype or photograph presented the world as a panorama, a picture-world set apart from its observer. The predecessor of the photographer was in many cases the panorama painter, men like David Roberts and Robert Ker Porter who travelled to the Middle East in the first three decades of the nineteenth century. They returned to produce not just prints or easel pictures but enormous panoramic paintings, often with moving shadows and mechanical animations, which the general public came to see in places of entertainment such as the Leicester Square Panorama.[66] Daguerre himself, the inventor of the photographic process, was a panorama painter in Paris (where he had pioneered the technique of changing shadows known as the diorama). In 1839 his diorama burnt down, and it was that year that he announced the invention of the daguerreotype.[67]

The problem, then, for the daguerreotypist visiting the Middle East, or for the writer who desired the same accuracy of representation, was to separate oneself from the world and thus constitute it as a panorama. This required what was now called a 'point of view', a position set apart and outside. Edward Lane lived while he was in Cairo near one of the city's gates, outside which there was a large hill with a tower and military telegraph on top. This elevated position commanded 'a most magnificent view of the city and suburbs and the citadel', Lane wrote. 'Soon after my arrival I made a very elaborate drawing of the scene, with the camera lucida. From no other spot can so good a view of the metropolis . . . be obtained.'[68] Such spots, however, were difficult to find. Besides the military observation tower used by Lane, visitors to the Middle East would appropriate whatever buildings and monuments were available in order to obtain the necessary viewpoint. The Great Pyramid at Giza had now become a viewing platform. Teams of Bedouin were organised to heave and push the writer or tourist to the top, where two more Bedouin would carry the European on their shoulders to all four corners, to observe the view.[69] At the end of the century an Egyptian novel satirised the westernising pretensions among members of the Egyptian upper middle class, by having one such character spend a day climbing the pyramids at Giza, to see the view.[70] The minaret presented itself similarly to even the most respectable European as a viewing tower, from which to sneak a panoptic gaze over a Muslim town. 'The mobbing I got at *Shoomlo*', complained Jeremy Bentham on his visit to the Middle East, 'only for taking a peep at the town from a thing they call a *minaret* . . . has cancelled any claims they might have had upon me for the dinner they gave me at the *divan*, had it been better than it was.'[71]

Bentham can remind us of one more similarity between writer and camera, and of what it meant, therefore, to grasp the world as though it were a picture or exhibition. The point of view was not just a place set apart, outside the world or above it. It was ideally a position from where, like the authorities in the panopticon, one could see and yet not be seen. The photographer, invisible beneath his black cloth as he eyed the world through his camera's gaze, in this respect typified the kind of presence desired by the European in the Middle East, whether as tourist, writer or indeed, as we will see, as colonial power.[72] The ordinary European tourist, dressed (according to the advice in Murray's *Handbook for Travellers in Lower and Upper Egypt*, already in its seventh edition by 1888) in either 'a common felt helmet or

2 Giza: climbing the Great Pyramid.

wide-awake, with a turban of white muslin wound around it' or alternatively a pith helmet, together with a blue or green veil and 'coloured-glass spectacles with gauze sides', possessed the same invisible gaze, the same ability to see without being seen.[73] It was no wonder that an Egyptian writer had to explain, as I mentioned, that one of the beliefs of the European was that the gaze had no effect. To see without being seen confirmed one's separation from the world, and corresponded at the same time to a position of power. Certain of the more Europeanised members of the country's Turkish ruling elite, such as Adham Pasha, whom we will encounter in a later chapter as the man who introduced into Egypt a modern system of schooling based on constant surveillance, began to wear green- or blue-coloured spectacles with gauze sides when they went on tours of inspection.[74] By the 1860s even the Khedive himself travelled the country wearing coloured glasses. When the first satirical political journal appeared in Egypt in 1877, attacking the power of the Europeans in the country and ridiculing their Turkish collaborators, it was shut down almost immediately by the government and its editor deported. It had called itself *Abu al-nazzara al-zarqa'*, the man in blue-coloured spectacles.[75]

The writer shared with the authorities this desire to see without being seen. The representation of the Orient, in its attempt to be detached and objective, would seek to eliminate from the picture the presence of the European observer. Indeed to represent something as Oriental, as Edward Said has argued, one sought to excise the European presence altogether. 'Many thanks for the local details you sent me', wrote Gautier to Nerval in Cairo, who was supplying him with first-hand material for his Oriental scenarios for the Paris Opéra. 'But how the devil was I to have included among the walk-on's of the Opéra these Englishmen dressed in raincoats, with their quilted cotton hats and their green veils to protect themselves against ophthalmia?'[76] Representation was not to represent the voyeur, as the Algerian scholar Malek Alloula has described the colonial presence in a study of colonial postcards, the seeing eye that made representation possible. To establish the objectness of the Orient, as something set apart from the European presence, required that the presence itself, ideally, become invisible.

On the other hand, however, while setting themselves apart in this way from a world-as-picture, Europeans also wanted to experience it as though it were the real thing. Like the visitor to an exhibition, travellers wanted to immerse themselves in the Orient and 'touch with their fingers a strange civilisation'. Edward Lane wrote in his journal of wanting 'to throw myself entirely among strangers, . . . to adopt their language, their customs, and their dress'.[77] This kind of immersion was to make possible the profusion of ethnographic detail in writers such as Lane, and produce in their work the effect of a direct and immediate experience of the Orient. In Lane, and even more so in writers like Flaubert and Nerval, the desire for this immediacy of the real became a desire for direct and physical contact with the exotic, the bizarre, and the erotic.

There was a contradiction, therefore, between the need to separate oneself from the world and render it up as an object of representation, and the desire to lose oneself within this object-world and experience it directly; a contradiction which world exhibitions, with their profusion of exotic detail and yet their clear distinction between visitor and exhibit, were built to accommodate and overcome. The problem in a place like Cairo, which had not been built as an exhibition, was to fulfil this double desire. On his first day in Cairo, Gérard de Nerval met a 'painter' equipped with a daguerreotype, who 'suggested that I come with him to choose a point of view'. Agreeing to accompany him, Nerval decided 'to have myself taken to the most labyrinthine point of the city, abandon the painter to his tasks, and then wander off haphazardly, without interpreter or companion'. But within the labyrinth of the city, where Nerval hoped to immerse himself in the exotic and finally experience 'without interpreter' the real Orient, they were unable to find any point from which to take the picture. They followed one crowded, twisting street after another, looking without success for a suitable viewpoint, until eventually the profusion of noises and people subsided and the streets became 'more silent, more dusty, more deserted, the mosques fallen in decay and here and there a building in collapse'. In the end they found themselves outside the city, 'somewhere in the suburbs, on the other side of the canal from the main sections of the town'. Here at last, amid the silence and the ruins, the photographer was able to set up his device and portray the city.[78]

It was Edward Lane who found the ideal device for meeting this double demand, to immerse oneself and yet stand apart. The device was that of hiding beneath a deliberate disguise, rather like the tourist in coloured spectacles or the photographer beneath his cloth. In order 'to escape exciting, in strangers, any suspicion of . . . being a person who had no right to intrude among them', Lane explained, he adopted the dress and feigned the religious belief of the local Muslim inhabitants of Cairo. The dissimulation allowed him to gain the confidence of his Egyptian informants, making it possible to observe them in their own presence without himself being observed. His ethnographic writing seems to acquire the authority of this presence, this direct experience of the real. But at the same time, as Said points out, in a preface to his ethnography Lane carefully explains the deception to the European reader, thus assuring the reader of his absolute distance from the Egyptians. The distance assured by the deception is what gives his description its 'objectivity'.[79]

Egypt at the exhibition

The curious double position of the European, as participant-observer, makes it possible to experience the Orient as though one were the visitor to an exhibition. Unaware that the Orient has not been arranged as an exhibition, the visitor carries out the characteristic cognitive manoeuvre of the modern subject, who separates himself from an object-world and observes it from a position that is invisible and set apart. From there, as Pierre Bourdieu says of the modern anthropologist or social scientist, one transfers into the object the principles of one's relation to the object and 'conceives of it as a totality intended for cognition alone'. The world is grasped, inevitably, as though it were 'a representation (in the sense of idealist philosophy, but also as used in painting or the theatre)', and people's lives appear as no more than 'stage parts . . . or the implementing of plans'.[80] I would add to what Bourdieu says that the anthropologist, like the tourist and the Orientalist writer, had come to the Middle East from Europe, a world as we have seen that had been set up more and more to demand this kind of cognitive manoeuvre, a world where objectivism was increasingly built-in. They came from a place, in other words, in which ordinary people were learning to live as tourists or anthropologists, addressing an object-world as the representation of something, and grasping personhood as the playing of a cultural stage part or the implementation of a plan.

Traces of the East

With this in mind, I want to introduce what will seem at first a contradictory argument. The Europeans, I have said, arrived in the Middle East without realising that they had left the world-as-exhibition. On the other hand, however, they came looking for a reality which invariably they had already seen in an exhibition. They thought of themselves in other words as actually moving from the exhibit to the real thing. This was literally the case with Théophile Gautier, who lived in Paris writing his Orientalist scenarios for the Opéra-Comique and championing the cause of Orientalist painting. He finally set off for Egypt in 1869 after being inspired to see the real thing by a visit to the Egyptian exhibit at the 1867 Exposition Universelle.[81] But in this respect Gautier was no exception. Europeans in general arrived in the Orient after seeing plans and copies – in pictures, exhibitions and books – of which they were seeking the original; and their purpose was always explained in these terms.

Edward Lane, for example, was inspired to travel to Egypt after seeing the replicas and paintings on display at the Egyptian Hall in Piccadilly. David Roberts, who had begun his career as a set designer at the Drury Lane Theatre, went to the Orient as an accomplished panorama painter and aspiring artist in search of the originals of theatre sets and panoramas he had already produced. Both Roberts and Lane were also inspired to visit Egypt by the famous *Description de l'Egypte*, the twenty-two volume work of French artists and scholars who had set up camp with the French army during Napoleon's occupation of Egypt, published by the French government between 1809 and 1822. And both of them set off declaring that their purpose was to correct the 'inaccuracies' of the *Description*, which somehow they knew to exist before even seeing the 'original' it claimed to represent.[82] So, I am arguing that on the one hand Europeans in the Middle East were unaware they had left the world-as-exhibition, but on the other they conceived of themselves as having moved from a mere representation to the real thing.

The contradiction can be resolved, I think, by recalling the paradoxical nature of the world-as-exhibition. The exhibition persuades people that the world is divided into two fundamental realms – the representation and the original, the exhibit and the external reality, the text and the world. Everything is organised as if this were the case. But 'reality', it turns out, means that which can be represented, that which presents itself as an exhibit before an observer. The so-called real world 'outside' is something experienced and grasped only as a series of further representations, an extended exhibition. Visitors to the Orient conceived of themselves as travelling to 'the East itself in its vital actual reality'. But, as we saw, the reality they sought there was simply that which could be photographed or accurately represented, that which presented itself as a picture of something before an observer. A picture here refers not just to a visual illustration, but to what stands apart as something distinct from the subject and is grasped in terms of a corresponding distinction between representation and reality. In the end the European tried to grasp the Orient as though it were an exhibition of itself.

There were two kinds of consequence. First, as I have already suggested, since the Middle East had not yet been organised representationally, Europeans found the task of representing it almost impossible and the results disappointing. 'Think of it no more!' wrote Nerval to Théophile Gautier, of the Cairo they had dreamed of describing. 'That Cairo lies beneath the ashes and dirt, . . . dust-laden and dumb.' Nothing encountered in those Oriental streets quite matched up to the reality they had seen represented in Paris. Not even the cafés looked genuine. 'I really wanted to set the scene for you here', Nerval explained, in an attempt to describe the typical Cairene street, 'but . . . it is only in Paris that one finds cafés so Oriental.' His disappointment resulted from the failure to construct representations of the city that were to serve, as so often, very practical purposes. As I mentioned, he was supplying Gautier with descriptions that could be reproduced as stage sets and pantomime acts for the Paris Opéra. Nerval finally despaired completely of finding 'real Egypt', the Cairo that could be represented. 'I will find at the Opéra the real Cairo, . . . the Orient that escapes me.' In the end only the Orient one finds in Paris, the simulation of what is itself a series of representations to begin with, can offer a satisfying spectacle. As he moved on towards the towns of Palestine, Nerval remembered Cairo as something no more solid or real than the painted scenery of a theatre set. 'Just as well that the six months I spent there are over; it is already nothing, I have seen so many places collapse behind my steps, like stage sets; what do I have left from them? An image as confused as that of a dream: the best of what one finds there, I already knew by heart.'[83]

The second consequence was that the Orient more and more became a place that one 'already knew by heart' on arrival. 'Familiar to me from days of early childhood are the forms of the Egyptian pyramids', wrote Alexander Kinglake in *Eōthen*. 'Now, as I approached them from the banks of the Nile, I had no print, no picture before me, and yet the old shapes were there; there was no change: they were as I had always known them.' Gautier, for his part, wrote that if the visitor to Egypt 'has long inhabited in his dreams' a certain town, he will carry in his head 'an imaginary map, difficult indeed to erase even when he finds himself facing the reality'. His own map of Cairo, he explained, 'built with the materials of *A Thousand and One Nights*, arranges itself around Marilhat's *Place de l'Ezbekieh*, a remarkable and violent painting . . . ' The attentive European, wrote Flaubert in Cairo, '*re*discovers here much more than he discovers.'[84]

The Orient was something one only ever rediscovered. To be grasped representationally, as the picture of something, it was inevitably to be grasped as the reoccurrence of a picture one had seen before, as a map one already carried in one's head, as the reiteration of an earlier description. The 'traces of travel brought home from the East', as Kinglake called such reiterations, were in such profusion by mid-century that a reviewer in *Tait's Edinburgh Magazine* complained in 1852 about 'these all but daily Oriental productions . . . There they are; the same Arabs, camels, deserts, tombs and jackals that we journeyed with, rode on, traversed, dived into, and cursed respectively, only a week ago, with some other traveller.'[85] And besides the books there were the paintings, the photographs, the spectacles, the panoramas and the exhibitions. To describe the Orient, which refused to provide a point of view and to present itself, became more and more a process of redescribing these representations. How far this process went was illustrated by Gautier, the champion of Orientalist art, when he was finally inspired by the world exhibition, as I mentioned, to leave Paris and visit Cairo to see the real thing.

The account of Egypt he then published began with a long chapter entitled 'Vue génerale'. This took the form of a description, in great detail, not of Egypt but of the Egyptian exhibit at the 1867 Paris exhibition.[86]

The representation of the Orient obeyed, inevitably, this problematic and unrecognised logic, a logic determined not by any intellectual failure of the European mind but by its search for the certainty of representation – for an effect called 'reality'. Europeans like Edward Lane had begun the drawing up of their 'exhaustive description of Egypt', already determined to correct the earlier work of the French scientific mission's *Description de l'Egypte*. Later writers would then take themselves to the library of the French Institute in Cairo, and draw from and add to this body of description. Gérard de Nerval, collecting the material in Egypt he later published as *Voyage en Orient*, his life's major prose work, saw more of the library than of the rest of the country. After two months in Cairo, more than half way through his stay, he wrote to his father that he had not even visited the pyramids. 'Moreover I have no desire to see any place until after I have adequately informed myself from the books and memoires', he explained. 'At the Société Egyptienne I have found a collection of almost all the works, ancient and modern, that have been published on the country, and as yet I have read only a very small part of them.' Six weeks later he wrote again, saying that he was leaving the country even though he had not yet ventured outside Cairo and its environs.[87]

As a result the bulk of *Voyage en Orient*, like so much of the literature of Orientalism, turned out to be a reworking or direct repetition of earlier descriptions, in Nerval's case mostly from Lane's *Manners and Customs of the Modern Egyptians*. Such repetition and reworking is what Edward Said has referred to as the citationary nature of Orientalism, its writings added to one another 'as a restorer of old sketches might put a series of them together for the cumulative picture they implicitly represent'. The Orient is put together as this 're-presentation', and what is represented is not a real place but 'a set of references, a congeries of characteristics, that seems to have its origin in a quotation, or a fragment of a text, or a citation from someone's work on the Orient, or some bit of previous imagining, or an amalgam of all these'.[88] The 'East itself' is not a place, despite the exhibition's promise, but a further series of representations, each one reannouncing the reality of the Orient but doing no more than referring backwards and forwards to all the others. It is the chain of references that produces the effect of the place. Robert Graves remarks wryly on this effect in *Goodbye to All That*, when he disembarks at Port Said in the 1920s to take up a job at the Egyptian University and is met by an English friend: 'I still felt seasick', he writes, 'but knew that I was in the East because he began talking about Kipling.'[89]

No plan, no anything

There is an ambiguity here, which must be cleared up –or at least acknowledged – before we can move on into the following chapters and begin to consider the politics of nineteenth-century Egypt. In claiming that the 'East itself' is not a place, am I saying simply that Western representations created a distorted image of the real Orient; or am I saying that the 'real Orient' does not exist, and that there are no realities but only images and representations?[90] My answer is that the question is a bad one, and that the question itself is what needs examining. We need to understand how the West had come to live as though the world were divided in this way into two: into a realm of mere representations and a realm of 'the real'; into exhibitions and an external reality; into an order of mere models, descriptions or copies, and an order of the original. We need to understand, in other words, how these notions of a realm of 'the real', 'the outside', 'the original', were in this sense effects of the world's seeming division into two. We need to understand, moreover, how this distinction corresponded to another division of the world, into the West and the non-West; and thus how Orientalism was not just a particular instance of the general historical problem of how one culture portrays another, but something essential to the peculiar nature of the modern world. Finally we need to understand the political nature of these kinds of division, by understanding them as techniques both of order and of truth.

Herman Melville, who visited the Middle East in the winter of 1856–57, felt the usual need to find a point of view and experienced the usual difficulties. Rather than an exhibition of something, Cairo seemed like some temporary market or carnival – 'one booth and Bartholomew Fair', he called it. Like Gérard de Nerval and others before him, Melville wrote of wanting to withdraw from the 'maze' of streets, in order to see the place as a picture or plan. Visiting Constantinople, he complained in his journal that there was 'no plan to streets. Perfect labyrinth. Narrow. Close, shut in. If one could but get *up* aloft . . . But no. No names to the streets . . . No numbers. No anything.'[91] Like Nerval, Melville could find no point of view within the city, and therefore no picture. What this meant, in turn, was that there seemed to be no plan. As I suggested earlier when discussing world exhibitions, the separation of an observer from an object-world was something a European experienced in terms of a code or plan. He expected there to be something that was somehow set apart from 'things themselves' as a guide, a sign, a map, a text, or a set of instructions about how to proceed. But in the Middle Eastern city nothing stood apart and addressed itself in this way to the outsider, to the observing subject. There were no names to the streets and no street signs, no open spaces with imposing façades, and no maps.[92] The city refused to offer itself in this way as a representation of something, because it had not been built as one. It had not been arranged, that is, to effect the presence of some separate plan or meaning.

Already in the 1830s, however, Emile-T. Lubbert, former director of the Paris Opéra and Opéra-Comique, had been appointed by the Egyptian government as director of *fêtes et divertissements*.[93] Entertainments alone, of course, were not enough. 'What Egypt like the rest of the Levant has never possessed is order', explained Charles Lambert, a Saint-Simonist social scientist and engineer who set up and directed an Ecole Polytechnique in Cairo modelled on the great school in Paris, in a report to Muhammad Ali Pasha, the Governor of Egypt.[94] 'You have acquired great power', wrote Jeremy Bentham approvingly in his own letter to the Pasha in 1828. ' . . . but it remains to determine the plan.'[95]

To colonise Egypt, to construct a modern kind of power, it would be necessary 'to determine the plan'. A plan or framework would create the appearance of objectness that Melville found lacking, by seeming to separate an object-world from its observer. This sort of framework is not just a plan that colonialism would bring to Egypt, but an effect it would build in. As the following chapters will show, the colonial process would try and re-order Egypt to appear as a world enframed. Egypt was to be ordered up as something object-like. In other words it was to be made picture-like and legible, rendered available to political and economic calculation. Colonial power required the country to become readable, like a book, in our own sense of such a term.

A framework appears to order things, but also to circumscribe and exclude. As we will see later on, like the perimeter walls that seemed to exclude the 'real world' from the world exhibition, a framework sets up the impression of something beyond the picture-world it enframes. It promises a truth that lies outside its world of material representation. To 'determine the plan' is to build-in an effect of order and an effect of truth.

Chapter 2

Enframing

In the second quarter of the nineteenth century the people of Egypt were made inmates of their own villages. A government ordinance of January 1830 confined them to their native districts, and required them to seek a permit and papers of identification if they wished to travel outside. 'It was scarcely possible', we are told, 'for a fellah to pass from one village to another without a written passport.' The village was to be run like a barracks, its inhabitants placed under the surveillance of guards night and day, and under the supervision of inspectors as they cultivated the land – and surrendered to the government warehouse its produce.[1]

No one before had thought to organise Egypt as one would barrack and discipline an army. The acts of confinement, regulation, and supervision of the population dawned suddenly. Wherever people looked, they were to be inspected, supervised, or instructed. If they left the village, it was generally under guard, forcibly drafted into the still harsher discipline of the corvée or the military camp – unless they were 'absconders' who abandoned their homes and fled, as tens of thousands began to do. If they were guards rather than those who were guarded, they still did not escape surveillance. Spies were placed at every point, and the hierarchy of supervision and inspection was to ascend from the field and the shop, through the levels of village, district, regional and provincial supervision, to the central Bureaux of Inspection (*dawawin al-taftish*) under the direct supervision of the Governor.[2]

The attempt to control from Cairo the agricultural wealth of the Nile valley was in itself nothing new. Fifty years before, a single powerful household had defeated all other centres of power in the country and established, for a decade, uncontested control over its agricultural and commercial revenues – encouraging, as a result, Cairo's gradual incorporation into European world trade.[3] What was new in the nineteenth century was the nature of control. Earlier kinds of power, however centralised, were never continuous. They operated intermittently, typically in the form of levies, obligations and extortions imposed upon certain less powerful households, which in turn imposed levies on those less powerful around them, and so on. The irregular flows of revenue towards the centre were always weakened by the inevitable leakage at each juncture, the need to expand outwards, and the centrifugal tendency to disintegrate.[4] From the nineteenth century for the first time political power sought to work in a manner that was continuous, meticulous and uniform. The method was no longer simply to take a share of what was produced and exchanged, but to enter into the process of production. By supervising each of its aspects separately and without interruption, political power attempted to discipline, coordinate and increase what were now thought of as the 'productive powers' of the country. The tendency of disciplinary mechanisms, as Michel Foucault has called these modern strategies of control, was not to expand and dissipate as before, but to infiltrate, re-order, and colonise.[5]

Foucault's analyses are focussed on France and northern Europe. Perhaps this focus has tended to obscure the colonising nature of disciplinary power. Yet the panopticon, the model institution whose geometric order and generalised surveillance serve as a motif for this kind of power, was a colonial invention. The panoptic principle was devised on Europe's colonial frontier with the Ottoman Empire, and examples of the panopticon were built for the most part not in northern Europe, but in places like colonial India.[6] The same can be said for the monitorial method of schooling, also discussed by Foucault, whose mode of improving and disciplining a population, as we will see, came to be considered the model political process to accompany the capitalist transformation of Egypt.

In this and the following chapter I will examine the introduction of these disciplinary mechanisms in modern Egypt, turning later to consider their connection to the methods of order and meaning I have referred to as the world-as-exhibition. Their introduction began under a single Turkish ruling household, that of Muhammad Ali, which acquired authority over Egypt (and increasing independence from Istanbul) after the Napoleonic occupation of 1798–1801. This authority subsequently came to be shared and exercised among a new landowning class, with the ruling family as the largest single landowners, together with European creditors and commercial interests and, from 1882, a European colonial regime.[7] The original strategies of disciplinary control on which such authority came to rest were found in the creation of a new Egyptian army.

From the year 1822, Egyptians had found themselves being taken in tens of thousands and turned, for the first time in memory, into soldiers.[8] The military forces of Ottoman Egypt had previously been formed out of foreigners conscripted from abroad, together with native Egyptians who inherited or purchased the right to military salaries. These small, part-time garrisons in the major towns, mostly of only one or two thousand men and with loyalties to competing political factions, controlled urban affairs only with difficulty and the countryside even less.[9] Such small bodies of foreigners were now to be replaced with an enormous military force – up to two hundred thousand men or more according to some sources – drafted from the villages and towns of Egypt.[10] Barracks and training camps were ordered to be built near major towns along the length of the Nile, from Aswan to Cairo and out across the Delta, with 'each of the barracks to hold one thousand trainees and soldiers, and to be placed a quarter of an hour's distance from the town'.[11] The men were drafted into the army not for single campaigns but for several years and eventually for life. Their families often accompanied them where they went, building their own 'mud barracks' up against the walls of the camps.[12] The country's new regimentation can be said to begin with this event, the sudden spreading among the villages of the Nile of a new type of settlement, the barracks, and the drafting of ordinary Egyptians to populate them. The plan to turn the peasantry into soldiers by confining them and training them in barracks introduced a new kind of military practice, a new idea of what an army was and how it could be formed.

The new forms of practice were referred to as the 'new order' or *nizam jadid*. 'New order' was the Ottoman name for a plan introduced a little before in the Ottoman Empire, threatened by Russia's continued colonisation of its northern frontier, to reorganise the imperial soldiery and the system of taxation that supported it.[13] The name referred more specifically to the object at the heart of this plan: a new infantry corps, to be trained and organised according to the new techniques developed by the Prussians and the French. 'New order' was also the name used by Ottoman writers to refer to the Napoleonic regime in France.[14] After the fall of the Empire in 1815, defeated officers and engineers of the French armies made their way to Egypt, where the new order was to be established with their help. Egypt was the first province of the Ottoman Empire to introduce successfully the new kind of army.[15] The barracks and the training camps were built, and in April 1822 regulations were issued bringing all the barracks, military schools, and training camps under a common code of discipline and instruction.[16] The confinement to barracks, the discipline, and the instruction were all innovations.

An artificial machine

The new army, it was explained in an official Ottoman pamphlet, 'should not, like the rest of our forces, be composed of sellers of pastry, boatmen, fishermen, coffee-house keepers, baccals, and others who are engaged in the thirty-two trades, but of well disciplined men'.[17] An army was no longer to be thought of as an occasional body, brought together for seasonal campaigns. It was to be an organised force, created out of men compelled to live permanently together as a distinct community, continuously under training even when not at war. The troops, in this new practice, 'should remain night and day in their quarters, applying themselves daily to military exercises, and keeping their arms, cannon, muskets, and warlike implements of every description necessary for immediate service; thus practising a discipline suitable to their appellation of soldiers of the new regulation'.[18]

Discipline of this sort was a new invention, adopted in most European countries only a generation or so before the *nizam jadid*, following the dramatic Prussian victories in the Seven Years War (1756–63).[19] The Prussians had introduced revolutionary techniques of precise timing, rapid signalling, and rigorous conformity to discipline, out of which an army could be manufactured as what the Prussian military instructions called an 'artificial machine'. Other armies in comparison would now seem like collections of 'idle and inactive men', a perception that was to change the way not just an army but any human group was viewed – as the ordinary Egyptian was to discover.[20] Such a 'machine' could fire with a rapidity three times that of other armies, making it three times as destructive, and could be expanded, wheeled, and withdrawn with mechanical ease.[21]

The Prussian military regulations were adopted in the decades after the Seven Years War by all the major armies of Europe, and improved upon by the French in new regulations of 1791. The new techniques of drill, discipline and command were the first thing upon which an Egyptian commented when describing the French troops that invaded his country in 1798. 'They make signs and signals among themselves', wrote the historian al-Jabarti, 'that they follow and never deviate from.'[22] The Ottoman pamphlet described more fully the careful control of sound and gesture that a system of discipline would achieve. 'The whole body, consisting of many thousand men, observe attentively the signals given them by the two fuglemen who explain by signs the commands of the officers, and not one dares so much as to turn his head. Thus the orders of the officers being communicated without the least noise, they stand firm, and lend an attentive ear, whilst not a word issues from their mouths.' Each movement and each moment, every sound, glance, and word, the angle of the head and the posture of the body, can all be controlled. 'If, for instance, the officer whose business it is to give the command, makes the signal for attention, the whole body are ready in an instant, and not one of them dares to stand idle, or to make any noise, or to look another way.'[23] The exact discipline and coordination of individuals makes it possible to build with them the artificial machine.

The ponderous warfare of the seventeenth and eighteenth centuries, in which ever greater numbers of men were amassed to face each other head-on, was now to seem like the foolish clashing of mere crowds.[24] The old troops, observed the Ottoman pamphlet, 'when in the presence of the enemy, do not remain drawn up in a line, but stand confusedly and promiscuously like a crowd in a place of diversion. Some load their muskets, and fire once, some twice, or oftener, just as they think proper, whilst others being at their wits' end, and not knowing what they are about, turn from side to side like fabulous story-tellers.' The troops of the new discipline in contrast 'remain drawn up in a line as if at prayers, the rear ranks being exactly parallel with the front, and consisting of the same number of companies, neither more nor less, so that, when it is necessary, they turn with as much precision as a watch'.[25] The parallel lines and mechanical precision present themselves as a new conception of order. Such order was not a harmony, balance or correspondence between the forces of the world – an older kind of order whose nature I will try to evoke more carefully below – but order itself, a state defined in no other terms than the ordering of what was orderless, the coordinating of what was discontinuous. In the new order, the disordered was transformed, the dispersed was articulated, forming a unity or whole whose parts were in mechanical and geometric coordination.

In the military, this produced a piece of machinery that could be 'turned with the precision of a watch'. It could be made to perform what the French officers in Egypt now called 'manoeuvres', to rotate, discharge weapons, contract, or expand on command. The officers of the new order, it was explained, could 'dispose a large body of men in a circular form, and then cause them to march round in such a manner, that as the circle turns the soldiers incessantly discharge their muskets on the enemy and give no respite to the combat, and having prepared their guns for a fresh discharge before they return to the same place, they fire the moment they arrive in the face of the enemy. The result of this circular formation is, that the fire and slaughter do not cease for an instant.' In such a machine, every individual occupied a position, a space, created (as with the cog of a wheel) by the identity of interval between each one. The interval or space was what men now controlled, contracting or enlarging it on command. 'Sometimes, when it is judged necessary, several thousand men being crowded into a narrow space, form a solid mass for the purpose of appearing to the enemy to be few in number, then by opening out, they can execute any manoeuvre that they please, and sometimes, ten thousand men deploying, appear to consist of fifty or sixty thousand.'[26] Order was a framework of lines and spaces, created out of men, in which men could be distributed, manoeuvred and confined.

With the new order, finally, efficient means were now available to control desertion, breaking the major technical barrier to the management of large human groups. Soldiers were confined when not at war to the camp or barracks, where they were guarded, drilled, and 'kept closely to the pitch of discipline'.[27] They were also to be set apart from the civilian community, by their confinement and by the wearing of a uniform dress. 'The soldiers of our ancient corps', it was explained, 'are not at all clothed alike; from this diversity of garment, the following bad effect results: if, in times of war, any of them should desert from the army, as there are no marks by which we can distinguish whether the deserters belong to the troops, or whether they are tradesmen, or servants, they have thereby the opportunity of escaping without being known. Whereas the new troops have a particular uniform of their own, so that the stragglers would soon be discovered. Hence it results, that in a large camp of the new troops, every man will be forced to remain fixed in his company, and steady in the performance of his duty.'[28]

The whole surface of society

Besides the barracks and the training camps, the new military order included more than a dozen schools for training specialised military cadres – including cavalry, artillery, infantry, and naval officers, signalmen, doctors and veterinarians, regimental bands, and engineers.[29] The schools were to employ the same disciplinary methods, based on 'the confinement of the students' and 'a regime of surveillance and constraint'.[30] Most of them were administered by French and Egyptian military engineers and scholars, many of whom had been trained at the Ecole Polytechnique in Paris, including several disciples of Saint-Simon and of his secretary Auguste Comte.

In the middle of the 1830s these men were responsible for drawing up a more comprehensive military training policy. The new plans called for the improved drill and training of the troops (February 1835), and a year later for the reorganisation of the military training schools. The latter plan called for a system of fifty primary schools for military recruitment, four in Cairo and the rest in the provincial towns. It laid down uniform rules governing discipline, physical fitness, curriculum, exams, clothing, rations, teaching staff, administration, and inspection. Students were to be under continuous supervision, not only in class but during their walks outside the school, during recreation, and in the dormitories. 'Discipline was to be strictly military and punishments were to be graded according to the misdemeanour; a student could be reprimanded in the presence of the whole school, confined to school, imprisoned and given bread and water, beaten with the *kurbaj*, or dismissed from school.'[31]

The plan further called for two preparatory schools, one in Cairo for 1,500 students and the other in Alexandria. These were 'essentially military establishments; the students were to be barracked like soldiers; they were to form three battalions in the Cairo school, each battalion consisting of four companies with one hundred and twenty-five students in each company; the junior officers and corporals were to be chosen from among the students, the assistant masters were to command the companies, and the prefects the battalions.' Conduct was to be monitored continuously, and regulated by a careful hierarchy of disciplinary acts. 'Punishments were of twelve different degrees, which ranged from public reprimand to dismissal from school; a student could lose his rank if he were a junior officer or a corporal or be withheld from promotion by way of punishment.'[32]

The new order introduced a new mode of authority, which operated by the physical confinement of groups, the continuous monitoring of behaviour, the control of movements and gestures, and the careful construction of hierarchies. As the new schoolrooms already began to indicate, this order was to extend far beyond the barracks and the battlefield. 'The introduction of western organization into the armies of the Levant', wrote John Bowring, the friend and biographer of Jeremy Bentham who served as an advisor to Muhammad Ali and produced a report on Egypt for the British government,

brought with it other important results, for the appliances of mechanical art, of education, of knowledge, and a general system of dependence and subordination, were the needful companions of the new state of things. The transfer of the military power from unruly and undisciplined hordes to a body of troops regularly trained through the various grades of obedience and discipline, was in itself the establishment of a principle of order which spread over the whole surface of society.[33]

In the barracks, in the training camps and schools, and in battle, this principle of order made it possible to 'fix' men in place, to keep them 'steady in the performance of their duty', and to coordinate them as the separate parts of a single military machine. In the village and the cotton fields, the application of the same principle 'over the whole surface of society' made it suddenly conceivable to confine the population to their native districts, and (as the government was said to claim) 'to initiate people to an industry far superior to their own'.[34]

Watched over night and day

In order to fix the rural population in their place and induce them to begin producing cotton and other commodities for European consumption, it was necessary to have their places carefully marked out, their duty or quota exactly specified, and their performance continuously monitored and reported. The daily record, or *jurnal* (the word was borrowed from Europe), was the administrative practice with which the regimentation of rural Egypt began in the mid 1820s, when the government established regional and central Bureaux of Inspection, to receive the reports of its local inspectors (*jurnalji's*).[35] The 'general system of dependence and subordination' was more fully elaborated in a sixty-page booklet issued in December 1829, *La'ihat zira`at al-fallah wa-tadbir ahkam al-siyasa bi-qasd al-najah* (Programme for Successful Cultivation by the Peasant and the Application of Government Regulations), which prescribed in detail how peasants were to work in the fields, the crops they were to cultivate, their confinement to the village, and the duties of those who were to guard and supervise them. The booklet was the outcome of a meeting of four hundred provincial administrators and military and government officers, called in Cairo in 1829 to address the problem of declining revenues and increasing desertion of the land.[36] It included at the end fifty-five paragraphs stipulating in hierarchical detail the punishments for over seventy separate failures of duty by peasants or their supervisors.[37]

The peasants were to be monitored in the performance of their tasks, as laid out in the Programme, working in the fields under the supervision of the *mishadd* and *ghafir*. 'These officers checked the *fallahin* daily, and watched them night and day to prevent them from abandoning the village.' Any peasant failing to perform his task was reported to the government-appointed head of the village, *shaykh al-balad*. 'If the *shaykh* discovered that a *fallah* had failed to cultivate his fields as required, he punished him by whipping him twenty-five times with the *kurbaj*. Three days later the *shaykh* inspected the *fallah*'s fields once again and if the peasant had not yet completed the necessary cultivation the *shaykh* was authorised to whip him fifty times. An inspection took place after another three days and this time the negligent *fallah* received one hundred lashes.' The head of the village was under the supervision of a district official, *hakim al-khutt*. If he was negligent in the supervision of the peasants, he was to be chastised on the first offence, punished with two hundred lashes on the second, and with three hundred on the third. The *hakim* was himself supervised by a regional official, the *ma'mur*, and his negligence was to be punished with a warning on the first offence and fifty strokes of the cane on the second. The *ma'mur* was responsible to the provincial official, the *mudir*, who was to submit his report each week to the central Bureau of Inspection. A similar hierarchy of duty, supervision, and discipline was instituted for the distribution of crops, the collection of taxes, the provision of men for the army and corvée, and the reporting, questioning, and seizure of any person found outside his village district without a permit and papers of identity.[38]

It is not the severity or frequency of punishment that makes this different from anything preceding it. Indeed regulation was intended to remove the harsh abuse of power. The change was in the meticulous elaboration of task, surveillance, and penalty. Each separate act was stipulated and supervised, to coordinate every individual in a single economy of crops, money, and men. It was an attempt to achieve the new order of the barracks and the battlefield, with its hierarchy of signal, movement, and supervision, inscribed and enforced in the life of village and peasant.

There is no need to recount in detail the way in which these practices failed, or the devastation they caused.[39] Throughout the period there had been political uprisings in the provinces, which the new government troops systematically put down, and enormous numbers had absconded from their villages and fled. Such uprisings were nothing new; what was new was the power of the troops to put them down, for the methods of regimentation, as Bowring reported, had made the soldiery 'protectors instead of destroyers of property; they formed part of a structure of social improvement . . .'[40] Yet in the 1830s even this structure of improvement seemed to some of the European experts to be weakening from within. 'One of the causes of the exhaustion of the pacha's army is the prevalence of nostalgia or homeache,' reported Bowring to the British government, 'a disease alike mysterious and incurable.'

A medical man in the service of the pacha reported to me that the number of persons who pined to death, sinking under the influence of this unmedicable malady, was very considerable . . . 'I cannot keep them alive,' said a physician to me, 'when they begin to think of home.' And long before they die they sink into a listless, careless inanity.[41]

In the 1840s, after Egypt's growth into a regional military power had been halted by British intervention and its army reduced to 18,000 men, the government was still using its troops internally to gather up peasants not in their place of origin and return them forcibly to their native villages.[42] In April 1844 a government minister issued a notice to district officials, which announced 'that Tillage and Agriculture are the foundation of the comfort, happiness and prosperity of the Egyptian population, and in order to obtain the same it is found absolutely necessary that all those who have absented themselves from their primitive homes should return back to their native villages'. The notice was to be made known to the general public, and went on to order, as had frequently been ordered before, death by hanging for anyone harbouring peasants who had absconded from their villages 'in order to drop the word absconder entirely hereafter'. It described as a warning to others the fate of Suliman Badruddin, native of Minyat al-Sarig, who had been found giving refuge to absconders and 'was gibbeted in the Public Market of that place'.[43]

Despite such examples, peasants continued to desert their lands; and those sent for military service would mutilate themselves to avoid conscription. 'Some draw their teeth, some blind themselves, and others maim themselves, on their way to us,' complained the Governor of Egypt in a circular to his district officials issued in March 1833, 'and for this reason we send back the greater part . . . I will take from the family of every such offender men in his place, and he who has maimed himself shall be sent to the galleys all his life; I have already ordered this to the Sheiks in writing.'[44] The weaknesses of the military order are evident from the increasing severity of its methods of conscription, which began to rival those of Europe in their brutality.[45]

The nature of the problem emerges from the very contradiction of these texts. There is a conflict between the unprecedented penetration of the new methods of power, and the need to make them more acceptable, more unnoticed, more effective against diseases like 'nostalgia', and thereby more efficient. On the one hand, to escape conscription the greater part of the peasants were prepared to maim or mutilate themselves. Public hangings and other uses of violence had failed to deter entire populations from abandoning their villages and fleeing. The regimentation of the 'productive powers' of the country had made cultivation and forced labour a duty almost as oppressive as conscription into the army. The only relief for peasant families was to abandon their homes and 'abscond'. On the other hand, the state had already begun to search for a new language, 'in order to drop the word absconder entirely hereafter'. It announces, as widely as possible, 'that Tillage and Agriculture are the foundation of the comfort, happiness, and prosperity of the Egyptian population'. In the same way, Muhammad Ali had written in 1836 to the Inspector General of the military factories, in response to news that workers were being interned there and deprived of their wages, warning that the ordinary Egyptian ('the peasant') was to be properly treated, to ensure the government its income. 'Attend to his comfort, increase his pay, so that he applies himself to his work with complete satisfaction.'[46] The new methods of power were to seek to work through the very language and process of improvement.

After failing in the 1830s, when the attempt to penetrate and control the processes of production was made again in the 1840s a new method was used. The method this time was to place groups of villages in the custody of individual officials, beginning with members of the ruling family, and of European merchants. The villages were to be organised as personal estates, employing the same regime of spatial confinement, discipline and supervision.[47] These estates can be taken to mark the origin of a system of private landownership in modern Egypt, on which production for the European market would now depend.[48] On the private estates power as a localised process of order and discipline could now emerge and become entrenched, to the benefit of a new class of largely urban-based landowners and commercial landowning interests. As with the new army, this process of order would appear not as an arbitrary arrangement, but as order itself. The peculiar nature of such order can be further illustrated by examining what was to become a common feature of the new estates: the 'model village'.

Model housing

The village of Kafr al-Zayat in the Nile Delta was part of an estate placed under the control of Muhammad Ali's son Ibrahim (the man whose unfortunate encounter with a Birmingham whale was mentioned in chapter 1). In 1846 its inhabitants were instructed to draw up a list of the families of the village, their animals, and the different 'industries' in which they were engaged. In accordance with this list the village was then rebuilt, under the supervision of French engineers charged with what was called 'the reconstruction of the villages of Egypt'. The inhabitants were moved into new houses, with each family allotted rooms according to its size and its social rank (ordinary, well-to-do, rich, or foreign). The 'model house' for an ordinary family consisted, in the description of one of the French engineers,

(1) of a courtyard of which the floor is raised 0.10 m above the level of the street, 8 m long by 4.34 m wide and thus able to accommodate, at night, at least three large animals and three small . . . (2) of a room on ground level, of which the floor is raised 0.10 m above the floor of the courtyard, and thus 0.20 m above the level of the street, 4.35 m long by 3.70 m wide, illuminated by two windows: one high up, barred, overlooking the street, the other plain, overlooking the courtyard; containing at the rear a *divan*, large enough for two beds end-to-end . . . (3) of a room on the first floor, with a small covered balcony overlooking the courtyard . . . [49]

The same plans were used to rebuild several other Egyptian villages, including Neghileh, eleven miles to the south, and Ghezaier in the province of Menufiyya. At Neghileh, 'the wretched mass of huts formerly piled together without plan' was removed altogether, and replaced with a new village which an English traveller found to be 'very neat, laid out in streets crossing one another at right angles'.[50]

Projects of improvement of this kind contain less of the harshness of the methods of military order I have been describing. But the order they seek to achieve is a similar one. Such projects, no less than the military innovations, typify the new way in which the very nature of order was to be conceived. In modern Egypt, as in every modern state, order of this kind was to claim to be order itself, the only real order there has ever been.

The essence of this kind of order is to produce an effect I am going to call enframing. Enframing is a method of dividing up and containing, as in the construction of barracks or the rebuilding of villages, which operates by conjuring up a neutral surface or volume called 'space'. (It is no accident that the beginnings of this method in rural Egypt coincide with origins of private landownership, in which space becomes a commodity.) In reconstructing the village, the spacing that forms its rooms, courtyards, and buildings is specified in exact magnitudes, down to the nearest centimetre. Rather than as an occurrence of walls, floors, and openings, this system of magnitudes can be thought of apart, as space itself. The plans and dimensions introduce space as something apparently abstract and neutral, a series of inert frames or containers.[51]

Within these containers, items can then be isolated, enumerated, and kept: three large animals and three small per courtyard; two beds end to end (and hence two persons) per room; even the positioning of pots, water jars and food supplies was specified in the French plans. The dividing up of such items is also the breaking down of life into a series of discrete functions – sleeping, eating, cooking, and so on – each with a specific location. The order of the reconstructed village was to be achieved by reducing its life to this system of locations and the objects and functions contained there, of a framework and what was enframed. The apparent neutrality of space, as the dimension of order, is an effect of building and distributing according to the strict distinction between container and contained.

The system of containers was easily represented in plans. Those for the reconstruction of Egyptian villages as far as I know have not survived, but in the same period French administrators drew up similar plans for the reconstruction of villages in Algeria. In the Algerian case the rebuilding of villages was more directly connected with achieving military control. Enormous numbers of Algerians had their villages destroyed and were moved to the new settlements, in order to depopulate areas where it was proving difficult to establish colonial control, and to bring the population under closer surveillance.[52] With the drawing of such plans, the achievement of order could be thought of in a particular way: as the relationship between the village and the plans. It could be achieved accordingly, with the conformity of village to plan reproduced in village after village, resulting in an ordered countryside of containers and contained.

Such a method of order offered the possibility of a remarkable standardisation, between houses, between families and between villages. As in the army, such uniformity would be a hallmark of the new order. But as with the invention of a system of military rank, the new methods of spatial order also worked by producing and codifying a visible hierarchy. The distinction was to be made, as was mentioned, between four different ranks of housing. Besides the model house for the ordinary peasant, there were dwellings for the well-to-do, for the rich, and for foreigners. The distribution of families according to these four categories would generate, or at least enfix and make certain, these distinctions among them, tending both to fix and make legible a determined social hierarchy. In any case, rebuilding made the village itself something legible, in the sense of the lists of households, livelihoods and livestock that were drawn up. This information could then be compiled into statistics revealing the country's 'productive powers', at the same time as it was being inscribed in the unambiguous architecture of its new villages.

Such legibility, which is the mark of the world-as-exhibition, had a larger importance. The European experts were anxious to organise the production of statistical knowledge of this sort concerning Egypt (just as world exhibitions, as we saw in the last chapter, were designed to produce the same statistical legibility for the globe), gathering information on 'her population, her productions . . . and generally speaking on all the questions which have a statistical character, and a bearing, directly or indirectly, on the development of her resources'.[53] The production of statistical information was already well under way with the publication of the *Description de l'Egypte* mentioned in the previous chapter, the work compiled by the French scholars who had accompanied Napoleon's military occupation of Egypt. The parts of the *Description* dealing with the *état moderne* included the calculation, in exact magnitudes, of such statistical questions as 'the average power of Egyptian men'; it was such powers, after all, that the new methods of order were seeking to penetrate, colonise, police and multiply.[54] The mechanical production of this knowledge, however, was impeded by the difficulties of colonial penetration and policing; not only, as the engineers would find, was there 'no machinery in existence to collect and classify facts', but the peculiar architecture and way of life of the Egyptian village made such 'facts' concerning the population and its productive power particularly inaccessible. As Bowring explained to the British government,

the difficulties of making anything like a correct estimate of the population are much heightened by the state of the Mahomedan laws and usages, which exclude half of society from the observation of the police. Every house has its harem, and every harem is inaccessible.[55]

The legible order of the model village would overcome this kind of inaccessibility, this problem of a population and a way of life invisible to 'the observation of the police'. As Foucault has written, in such ways the architecture of distribution and the art of policing can acquire a hold over individuals not simply by confining them but by opening up and inscribing what is hidden, unknown and inaccessible.

And yet, as Foucault also points out, this new kind of order was not in itself anything fixed or rigid. As a method of containment, its strength lay in its flexibility. 'The system of construction', the French account of the model village explains, 'is arranged so that one can install in the houses a family of any number of individuals (people as well as animals).' This was possible because the system of partition made the rooms into individual cells, which could be interconnected in any combination. Larger families were to be contained simply by 'opening up a doorway in one of the dividing walls', which could be done 'without damage to the harmony between rooms or build-ings'. Thus the network of cellular containers could be expanded, con-tracted, and made to communicate, without ever losing the character of composing a system, a whole whose separate parts were in 'harmony'.

This harmony of parts enabled a reconstructed village to offer not just a better knowledge and control of its inhabitants, but the possibility of coordinating them together in order to increase their productivity as a unit. Like the army, the new village could be thought of as a machine, generating effort out of the interaction of its individual parts. 'The mode of construction will greatly facilitate industry (*le travail*) and will become in addition a valuable benefit to the future transactions of the inhabitants.'[56] Effort,

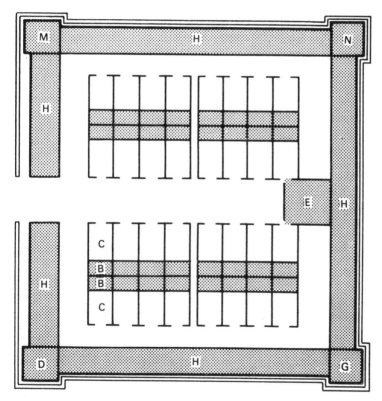

3 Plan of a government village, Algeria, 1848. Key: B house; C courtyard; D guest-house; E residence of village head; G guardhouse; H storerooms, stables; M mill; N mosque.

productivity and interaction, these methods of rebuilding seemed to suggest, were individual forces which, like the village itself, could now be measured, re-assembled, multiplied, and controlled.

Cultural beings

The connection between the techniques of enframing and the possibility of coordinating and increasing individual effort is to be explored further in the following chapter, where I will examine parallels between the rebuilding of Cairo and the introduction of organised civilian schooling. But to make it clearer what was new about the process of enframing, it may help at this point to say something first about the kinds of housing and the ways of living that the reconstruction of towns and villages attempted to replace; and at the same time to begin connecting the question of enframing, as a technique of order, to the question of meaning or representation. I propose to do so by discussing in the remainder of this chapter certain features of pre-modern Middle Eastern (or rather, Mediterranean) towns, combining this with some more recent examples drawn from Pierre Bourdieu's account of the

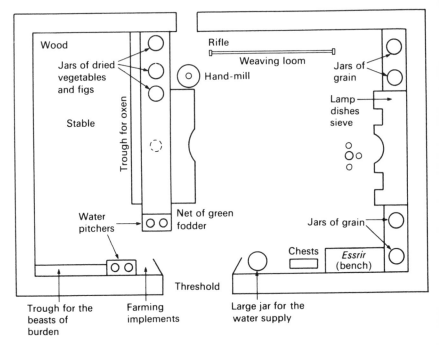

4 Plan of a Kabyle house.

housing of Kabyle villagers, a Berber-speaking community in Algeria.[57] I have two reservations about what follows. First, because the purpose of such examples is to make visible our own assumptions about the nature of order by contrasting them with a kind of order whose assumptions are different, I run the risk of setting up this other as the very opposite of ourselves. Such an opposite, moreover, would appear inevitably as a self-contained totality, and its encounter with the modern West would appear, again inevitably, as its rupturing and disintegration. These sorts of self-contained, pre-capitalist totalities acquire the awful handicap, as Michael Taussig has remarked, of having to satisfy our yearning for a lost age of innocence.[58] Such consequences, though perhaps inevitable, are undesired and unintended.

Second, my attempt to describe the kind of building that colonial villages and towns were to replace involves a particular difficulty: to describe a way of dwelling that did not reduce order to a question of the relationship between things and their plan, between the world and a map. Yet I will have to begin with a plan. The Kabyle house can be described as follows. It is rectangular in shape, and a double door gives access from the courtyard. Inside there is a low wall, dividing the interior into two parts. One part, slightly larger than the other and raised slightly higher, is reserved for human use. The fireplace is at its far end, and a weaving loom is assembled by the side wall opposite the doorway, the source of daylight; the other side wall, in which the door is set, is called the wall of darkness. The smaller, lower part of the house, occupied by the animals, has a loft above it where tools and animal fodder are stored, and where women and children usually sleep, especially in winter.

Thus described, the particular layout of the house could be given what we and the French engineers would call a functional explanation. But Bourdieu suggests that distinctions between the different parts of the house and the different places where things are kept or activities carried out correspond to a series of associations and oppositions, which are not to be dismissed as 'merely symbolic', as they would be in a functional explanation.

The lower, dark, nocturnal part of the house, the place of damp, green or raw objects – water jars set on benches on either side of the stable entrance or against the wall of darkness, wood, green fodder – the place too of natural beings – oxen and cows, donkeys and mules – and natural activities – sleep, sex, birth, and also death, is opposed to the light-filled, noble, upper part: this is the place of humans and especially the guest, of fire and fire-made objects, such as the lamp, kitchen utensils, the rifle – the attribute of the male point of honour (*nif*) which protects female honour (*hurma*) – and of the loom, the symbol of all protection.[59]

The house is organised, Bourdieu explains, according to a set of homologous oppositions: between fire and water, cooked and raw, high and low, light and shade, day and night, male and female, *nif* and *hurma*, fertilising and able to be fertilised. But to say 'the house is organised' in this way is misleading for two kinds of reason. First, the house is not in that sense a neutral space in which items or persons are arranged. The space itself is polarised, according to the oppositions Bourdieu describes, and the polar oppositions invest every activity of the house, including even the way in which the house is built. Considered, moreover, in relation to the rest of the village, the house becomes just one polarity, the 'female', in a larger world: 'The same oppositions are established between the house as a whole and the rest of the universe, that is, the male world, the place of assembly, the fields, and the market.'[60] The oppositions are not fixed categories into which items and spaces can be organised; they are an effect not of spatial coordinates but of polar forces. Second, as we will see, such polar forces occur themselves not as a structure of oppositions but as an unstable play of differences. The male, the light or the dry is each nothing more than the process of excluding or deferring the female, the dark or the wet. In a sense, therefore, the male includes the female, the light includes the dark, the dry includes the wet, and vice versa, for each term occurs only as the uncertain disappearance or postponement of what it differs from. Difference, as Derrida would tell us, is not a pattern of distinctions or intervals between things, but an always unstable deferring or differing within.

The remarkable order generated from the playing of these forces of difference must not mislead us into explaining it as just a 'different order' from the kind the French engineers envisioned; still less into explaining this difference in terms of the mythical beliefs of its North African inhabitants compared with the rational, disenchanted thought of the European; or even in terms of beliefs or cultural patterns that, again, are simply different from the cultural patterns of the modern European. Such explanations all continue to explain order in terms of a structure, pattern or mental plan conceived as existing apart from 'things themselves'.

Unlike the order envisioned by French engineers (and the builders of world exhibitions), the ordering of the North African house is not concerned with a relationship between things and a pattern or plan. Using the Algerian example and introducing some historical evidence alongside, I am going to try to characterise this kind of order in a number of ways. First, I will argue, it is not concerned with order as a framework, whose lines would bring into existence a neutral space in terms of which things were to be organised. Second, such ordering does not work by determining a fixed boundary between an inner world and its outside. Third, it is not concerned with an order set up in terms of an isolated subject, who would confront the world as his or her object. Nor, finally, is it concerned with meaning as a problem

50

for this individual subject of fixing the relation between the world and its plan or representation; or with truth as the certainty of such representation. Or rather, to put the emphasis differently for a moment, what we inhabitants of the world-as-exhibition would ordinarily take for granted as the elements of any order – framework, interior, subject, object, and an unambiguous meaning or truth – remain problematised and at play in the ordering of the Kabyle world. In my re-reading of Bourdieu's account of the Kabyle house, I want to suggest how much our own exhibition-world is enchanted with certain beliefs about structure, subjectivity and truth.

Rather than in terms of a structure, first of all, it may help to begin by thinking of the Kabyle house in terms of a balancing or tending. In the Kabyle world, everything that presents itself – darkness and sunlight, fire and water, men and women, animals and seeds, roofbeams and pillars – presents itself not as a mere object, as we would say, but no less reasonably, as a certain force or potential. The life of the house is a tending to the play of these differential forces, an attending to their potential for plenitude or barrenness.

Grain, to take just one example, is not a thing to be consumed, but a potential fullness (of the fields or of the stomach) whose necessary and contradictory relations with both fire and water determine how it is to be handled. The grain set aside for consumption is kept, we are told, in large earthenware jars against the end wall of the upper part of the house, near the fireplace, whereas grain intended for sowing is stored in the dark part of the house, 'in sheepskins or wooden chests placed at the foot of the wall of darkness, sometimes under the conjugal bed; or else in chests placed under the bench against the dividing wall, where the woman, who normally sleeps at a lower level, by the stable entrance, comes to join her husband'. Thus whereas the grain which must feed the household and ensure its wellbeing is associated with the fire that will transform it into bread, the grain set aside as seed corn, which must swell in the soil to provide next year's food, is associated with the dampness and water on which such swelling depends, and also with the woman, and by analogy with the swelling of the pregnant woman's belly.[61]

The order of the Kabyle house, or what we would call the organisation of its space (none of these terms is sufficient or appropriate) can better be thought of as this kind of attentiveness to the world's fertility or potential fullness. Such potential or force plays as the rhythm of life, a life made up not of inert objects to be ordered but of demands to be attended to and respected, according to the contradictory ways in which they touch and affect each other, or work in harmony and opposition, or resemble and oppose one another. Thinking of the life of the house in these terms, which have little to do with magic or myth in the pejorative sense of such words, enables us to begin to see the limits of the French engineers' provocative technique of order, and the political mythology to which it gives rise.

The filling of the house

In the first place, then, there is nothing, strictly speaking, in the North African house made to stand apart as a frame. Its order is not achieved by effecting an inert structure that contains and orders a contents. Not even its roof and sides form such a framework. The pillars, walls and beams of the house all carry their own charge, so to speak. They all exist only in exerting a continuous force or maintaining a certain balance, implicating them in the same patterns of resemblance and difference. 'At the centre of the dividing wall, between the "house of the human beings" and the "house of the animals" stands the main pillar, supporting the "master beam" . . . [This beam], which connects the gables and extends the protection of the male part of the house to the female part, is explicitly identified with the master of the house, whereas the main pillar, a forked tree trunk . . . upon which it rests, is identified with the wife.' The interlocking of the beam and the pillar, we are told, 'symbolises sexual union'.[62] The word symbol here suggests merely a conceptual representation, but the connection is nothing conceptual. Since the building of a house always takes place when a son is married, the interlocking of its parts is a direct reenactment and repetition of the union that forms the new household. The sexual union and the assembling of the house echo and resemble one another. Neither is a mere symbol of the other. I will come back to this question of representation and the symbolic a little later.

In this and similar ways the parts of the house are implicated in the life of the household. What exists is this life, in its cycles of birth, growth and death. The house is a process caught up in this life-and-death, not an inert framework that pretends to stand apart. A simple parallel can illustrate this from within the house, in the form of the weaving loom. We would tend to think of the loom in the way we think of a house, as a frame, within whose framework an object, the textile, is formed and given shape. But in North Africa, we are told, the loom is not thought of as a mere frame in this sense. Its parts are never assembled except in the process of weaving, and have no single name except as an aspect of the weaving. The parts brought together in weaving are conceived as male and female, and the textile formed out of them is a 'life' that is tended and grown, in a manner that imitates the growth of the house.[63] Moving back to the house, one could say in the same way that there is no mere house, but rather an active housing, engendered in the forming of a household and sustained as an aspect of its vigour, never as a neutral framework. Housing is not an object or container but a charged process, an inseparable part of a life that grows, flourishes, decays and is reborn.

In the Berber and Arabic languages there are several words for this life, in the sense of what builds and flourishes. To indicate some of the larger significance of this discussion of houses, I will mention briefly the use of one such term, taken from a relatively well-known historical source, the work of Ibn Khaldun, who lived in North Africa in the fourteenth century. Ibn Khaldun's major work, the *Muqaddima*, is an extended study of `umran, a word usually translated in this context as 'civilisation' or 'culture'. The book examines the political and historical conditions under which `umran appears, flourishes, and declines. Ibn Khaldun discusses such political conditions not in terms of some abstract framework such as 'the state', but in terms of the rise and decline of the built environment. Political life is examined as the building and decay of cities. The word to build, in this context, is `amar (the ` here refers to the Arabic letter `ayn), a word which for Ibn Khaldun can mean to live, prosper, flourish, be full, fill with life, inhabit, raise, be in good repair, build, and rebuild. It is from this word that is produced the term `umran, with the same kinds of meaning: activity, bustling life, fullness (of a market well-stocked with goods, for example, or a harbour frequented by ships and merchants), prosperity, building.[64] Ibn Khaldun's study of `umran is a study of the conditions that can bring about this building, this fullness, which we awkwardly translate as culture. Building is an active, undetermined process, marked in cycles of abundance and decay, rather than simply the material realisation of a predetermined 'plan'.

Nowhere in the *Muqaddima* does building, or `umran, involve the notion of a plan. Consequently in Ibn Khaldun the word `umran never means culture in the modern senses of the term, which are inseparable from the idea of a plan. The modern term establishes its meaning in contradistinction to an inert 'materiality' of the city, by designating an ideality of shared meanings or social patterns. The meaning of Ibn Khaldun's term, whatever its technical senses, remains rooted in a process of growth and fullness. It does not derive its force from any distinction between materiality versus meaning, the city versus its plan.[65] Without reference to Ibn Khaldun, and in the rather different context of the Berber village, Bourdieu draws attention to a very similar notion of fullness. In the housing he studied, the practices demanded of the peasant follow a pattern of emptying and filling. Analogies are drawn, as we saw, between the fullness of the fields, the fullness of the stomach and the fullness of the pregnant woman. In general, the processes of social and agricultural life seek 'the filling of the house' (*la`mmara ukham*), where the Berber word for filling corresponds to the Arabic terms `amar and `umran.[66]

53

The notion of cyclical growth and fullness apprehends the processes of the world without dividing it into a material realm and a conceptual, and is connected to an entire understanding of history and politics in the writing of Ibn Khaldun. A proper discussion of his ideas lies beyond the scope of this work, but it is in these sorts of terms that one might approach the question of order in the pre-colonial Middle Eastern or Mediterranean town. Discussions of the so-called Islamic city have tended to acknowledge none of the peculiarity of the methods of order and meaning that characterise cities since the industrial age, sometimes making do instead with a reference to the 'organic' nature of pre-modern cities and then examining the consequent problem of their 'order'. But there was no problem of order, in our own sense of a framework or plan, in such cities, just as there was no word naming such a thing in Ibn Khaldun. There was instead a cycle of fullness and emptiness, a continuous life which includes death (whereas order can never include disorder), a continuous building and rebuilding amid the forces of decay.

What this amounted to, then, was a way of building and living that refused to resolve itself into the appearance of a frame and what is enframed. A Middle Eastern town never affected a distinction between the 'materiality' of building and other practices and the 'ideality' of their structure and representational meaning. A town was not built as a series of structures located in space. The spacing was the building, and such spacing, in the city as much as in the village, was always polarised.

In the case of pre-modern Cairo, for example, building usually involved opening up an enclosure, such as a courtyard enclosed by rooms or columns, polarised in many cases according to the direction of Mecca. This was so not only with mosques, but with ordinary housing as well, at least up until after the Ottoman conquest. In fact it has been shown, for Cairo, that the orientation of building, of worshipping, and of receiving guests, the direction of Mecca, the path of the sun, the forces of the zodiac and the properties of the prevailing winds were all precisely correlated.[67] With larger houses, the interior space carved out as courtyard and rooms was aligned precisely with such 'polar' directions and forces, rather than with the street or with neighbouring buildings.[68] The house, or the shared housing in the case of poorer dwellings, then expanded around this enclosure, in whatever shape and size the presence of neighbouring buildings allowed. Its generally blank and irregular exterior seldom corresponded to the shape, or represented the purpose, of its carefully oriented interior. In this sense there were no exteriors, and the city was never a framework of streets on which structures were placed. As we will see, streets too were enclosures. The city was the spacing of intervals or enclosures forming a continuous materiality. Its order was a question of maintaining, within such enclosures, the proper relationships between directions, forces and movements, not its ability to reveal in material form the determining presence of a non-material plan or meaning. It was an order without frameworks.

The outside

A second, related way of characterising the modern kind of order I have called enframing is that it works by determining a fixed distinction between outside and inside. There appears to be an unambiguous line along which an exterior frames an interior. The new colonial and European cities of the nineteenth century made their clearest principle the fixed divide between the bourgeois interior and the public exterior. There has been no difficulty since then in discovering a similar division in the traditional Middle Eastern town; similar but in fact more rigid, between the interior world of women and the family and the public, male world of the marketplace and mosque.

At first sight the Kabyle village seems to exemplify this fundamental division. The walls of each house certainly separate an inside from an outside, the one corresponding to a female world and the other the male. But if we look at the house more closely, or rather situate ourselves within it (for the method of building provides no place for an outside observer to stand), this fixed division begins to invert itself and collapse. First, as we saw, the female interior is itself composed out of a 'male' upper part and a 'female' lower part. But this, Bourdieu tells us, is really only at night, and especially in the winter when the men sleep indoors. In the summer, when they sleep outside in the courtyard, the house as a whole forms a 'female' interior. During the daytime, however, the courtyard is made temporarily a women's space by the exclusion of the men, who are confined to the gateway, the place of assembly, or the fields. (Women can only be said to be confined to the interior in the sense that men, for example, are also confined to the fields.) So the dividing of male and female space, outside and inside, varies with the time, the season, the work to be done, and other forces and demands. It is such unstable forces and demands that polarise space, and each polarity occurs only as the temporary exclusion or postponement of its own opposite.

If we turn from the village to the town, things at first seem rather different. André Raymond's work on the great Arab cities of the eighteenth century stresses the distinction between the public world of the mosques and markets on the main thoroughfares, and the private world enclosed around the courtyards of the houses, which opened not on to the street but on to blind alleyways whose gates to the street were always closed at night. In Ottoman Cairo, these impasses leading to courtyards are said to have formed almost half the total length of the city's streets.[69] The market streets were distinguished from such impasses as public places where strangers to the city could enter and do business. Disputes involving strangers required the intervention of public officials, who would never intervene in the piivate disputes of the courtyard or alley.

But again the distinction between the public exterior and the domestic enclosure was not some fixed boundary. The market streets were lines of penetration from outside the city, where external routes extended into the urban interior. They too formed only a 'hollow enclosure' like the courtyard, as Roberto Berardi has written, stretched out in linear form to contain the visiting stranger. They too had gates, separating the city into quarters. At night, the gates of the city would close upon the world outside, those of the impasses upon the streets and lanes, of these upon the main thoroughfare, and of the thoroughfare upon the neighbouring quarters. The city, writes Berardi, is 'a network made up of enclosures, of prohibitions and accorded rights. There is no more than a sliding between its moment of permission and its moment of prohibition. It is in fact this sliding between degrees of opening and accessibility, of closure and exclusion, that in everyday practice is lived.'[70] Rather than a fixed boundary dividing the city into two parts, public and private, outside and inside, there are degrees of accessibility and exclusion determined variously by the relations between the persons involved, and by the time and the circumstance.

The vie intérieure

The dynamic relation between openness and closure was the corollary of an urban life that refused to make something stand apart as its framework. Without the urban effect of a framework there could be no fixed division into outside and inside. To this division there corresponds, in turn, a question of the city's 'meaning'. A city with no fixed exteriors, after all, is a city generally without façades. The significance of this can be drawn from the experience of the European visitor. Whether tourist or scholar, the European expected to find an order in the form of an unambiguous line which, like the gates of the exhibition or the cover of a book, separates what is inside from what is outside. This separation was how Europeans made sense of something, how they read it. Take the following reading of the city of Algiers, seen from the sea, by Alexis de Tocqueville in 1841.

Le tout présent l'aspect de la vie intérieure au plus haute degré. L'architecture peinte les besoins et les moeurs: celle-ci résulte seulement pas de la chaleur du climat, elle peint à merveille l'état social et politique des populations musulmanes et orientales: la polygamie, la séquestration des femmes, l'absence de toute vie politique, un gouvernement tyrannique et ombrageux qui force de cacher sa vie et rejette toutes les affectations du coeur du côté de la famille.[71]

Algiers, unlike Cairo as we saw, was a town that happened to be clearly visible to an external observer, from a ship at sea. So clearly, in fact, that in 1830 entrepreneurs from Marseilles had converted a steamer into a floating hotel and taken tourists to watch the city's bombardment and occupation by the French. (Thus from its opening act of violence, European colonisation of the Middle East began to involve the new tourist industry.) It was to examine the progress of this occupation a decade later that Tocqueville arrived. He was already within France an 'expert' on Algeria, and one of the most articulate spokesmen in the Chamber of Deputies for the completion of the country's conquest and colonisation.[72]

From outside and from a distance Tocqueville sees the city as a 'whole', which is to say as a picture or representation. He interprets this picture by

L'Exposition algérienne. — Maison kabyle; cour intérieure.

5 Exposition Universelle, Paris, 1889: the Kabyle house.

assuming the city is constructed out of the opposition between an exterior and an interior, the one visible, the other invisible. The visible exterior, or 'architecture', is taken to be a representation of the invisible *vie intérieure*. The architecture 'portrays the necessities and customs' of this interior life, indeed of Muslim and Oriental life in general. In a characteristic intellectual gesture, life is read as an invisible internal meaning made visible in an external material form. The meaning is something made visible only to the outside observer, who stands apart and sees the world as a representation.

The problem with this is not that Tocqueville has misread. A misreading implies that there would be a correct reading of what Algiers was built to represent. Algiers, however, like Cairo, was not built according to the easy mythology of representation, and did not offer an 'architecture' or external framework pretending to 'portray' its interior life. Its understanding would require other gestures than those of the intellectual tourist viewing the city from the sea. But Tocqueville is unable to escape the tourist's objectifying habit. The characteristics of the life he then sees, so convenient to the colonisation he defends, that it is secretive, suspicious, and without a political or public life, are no more than the effects of reading it as though it were a representation.

Western students of Middle Eastern societies since Tocqueville have generally not brought up this problem of representation. Instead they have often taken what are considered its distinctive urban forms, or indeed the lack of such forms, as one of the most characteristic features of Middle Eastern culture. The *Cambridge History of Islam* has described urban life as a model or ideal at the centre of Islam, but an ideal whose strange material embodiment in actual Middle Eastern towns becomes a 'paradox' of Islamic society:

The urban ideal of Islam created no forms, no urban structure . . . It replaced the solidarity of a collective community with an anomalous disorganised heap of disparate quarters and elements. By a really very remarkable paradox, this religion endowed with the ideal of urban life produced the very negation of urban order.[73]

The complaint to be made about these kinds of descriptions of the Middle East is not that they are distorted, by the ordinary intellectual assumptions of their authors, or that they are misrepresentations. These words imply the simple existence of an original object, of which an accurate representation might be made. They remain oblivious to the peculiar, historical nature of this absolute distinction between representation and original. It is this obliviousness which produces Islam's so-called paradoxes. The 'urban order' or the 'urban structures' such accounts find missing are assumed to be order or structure itself, rather than the effects, as we saw in Paris, of a technique of building that seems to divide the world into imaginary structures and their material realisation, into representations and simple originals. There are no such simple originals, but only the process of deciding to pretend that there are, and of forgetting this decision.

What this anomalous urban life lacked in particular, we are sometimes told, is formal institutions – the 'inner structure' of the 'material' city.[74] When we speak of an institution, somewhere in our thinking there often lurks the picture of a building or a street. The building stands for an institution, giving a visible exterior to the invisible 'inner structure', and it is remarkably difficult to think of a public institution without thinking of the building or street that represents it. Middle Eastern cities that 'lacked institutions' lacked more especially the imposing public buildings which might contain an institution, and represent it. It is perhaps worth thinking of our assumptions about urban structure in terms of this simple question. Further help can be sought in the writings of Ibn Khaldun and other Arab historians and geographers. In such works, and even in the everyday documents and correspondence that have survived from the pre-modern past of a city such as Cairo, official activities are never indicated by reference to or in terms of an imposing building; in manuscript illustrations, we are told, 'there does not seem to be an identifiable architectural vision of the publicly accessible official building'. Urban life was understood and referred to in written sources 'by function, never by location'.[75] Or rather, since we saw in the model village that the notion of function itself depends on the partitions of a system of frameworks, the life of the city was understood in terms of the occurrence and reoccurrence of practices, rather than in terms of an 'architecture' – material or institutional – that stands apart from life itself, containing and representing the meaning of what was done.

A transcendental presupposition

The example from Tocqueville has recalled the third aspect of enframing I want to mention, namely the way it provides a place from which the individual can observe. As we saw in chapter 1, the new nineteenth-century capitals of Europe, like the world exhibitions at their centre, were deliberately constructed around the individual observer. Haussmann laid out the boulevards of Paris to create a precise perspective in the eye of the correctly positioned individual, who was given an external point of view by the enframing architecture. The observer 'perceives himself at the centre of the city', wrote a Tunisian visitor, 'surrounded by its buildings, its streets and its gardens'.[76] But it was not just the particular position that was new; it was the very effect of having a position. Its strange novelty was the novelty of modern subjectivity, which is not a 'natural' relation of the person to the world but a careful and curious construction. The subject was set up outside the façades, like the visitor to an exhibition, and yet was surrounded and contained by them. It was a position at once both outside and inside. In contrast, the Kabyle village or the pre-colonial Middle Eastern town provided no such position. The architectural feint of façades and viewpoints was not at work. The individual did not stand outside an object world as the one addressed by it, nor at its centre as the one in terms of whom, as it seems to us, there is an order and a meaning.

The techniques of enframing, of fixing an interior and exterior, and of positioning the observing subject, are what create an appearance of order, an order that works by appearance. The world is set up before an observing subject as though it were the picture of something. Its order occurs as the relationship between observer and picture, appearing and experienced in terms of the relationship between the picture and the plan or meaning it represents. It follows that the appearance of order is at the same time an order of appearance, a hierarchy. The world appears to the observer as a relationship between picture and reality, the one present but secondary, a mere representation, the other only represented, but prior, more original, more real. This order of appearance is what might be called the hierarchy of truth.[77] As we saw in the first chapter with the European visitors to the Orient, it is in terms of such a hierarchical division, between a picture and what it stands for, that all reality, all truth is to be grasped. The methods of ordering, distributing and enframing that create the division, therefore, are the ordinary way of effecting what the modern individual experiences as the really real. The construction of ordered villages and towns in the Middle East was one particular manner of introducing this effect into Middle Eastern politics, just as it had been introduced in the modern age into the politics of Europe.

In what ways was the order of appearance something new? I will try to explain this, again, using the example of the Kabyle house. Whatever happens or presents itself in the world Bourdieu describes, happens, I suggested, as a potential for fertility or barrenness, for the fullness of life or its emptiness. Practical life is lived as an attending to this potential. It demands an attentiveness to the practical ways in which one thing could affect or excite another, the ways in which things that are juxtaposed could displace or intermingle with one another, how something could produce strength in one thing and weakness in another, how things penetrate or allow penetration. In other words one needs to understand the relations of sameness or sympathy between things, and of antipathy and disagreement. One needs to understand the homology between the bitterness of gall and the bitterness of wormwood, or between the seed that swells in the ground and that which swells in the woman's womb. Such relations are not the relations between an object and its meaning, as we would say, or between a symbol and the idea for which it stands.

There is nothing symbolic in this world. Gall is not associated with worm-wood because it symbolises bitterness. It occurs itself as the trace of bitter-ness. The grain does not represent fertility, and therefore the woman. It is itself fertile, and duplicates in itself the swelling of a pregnant woman's belly. Neither the grain nor the woman is merely a sign signifying the other and neither, it follows, has the status of the original, the 'real' referent or meaning of which the other would be merely the sign. These associations, in consequence, should not be explained in terms of any symbolic or cultural 'code', the separate realm to which we imagine such signs to belong. They arise entirely from their particular context, in the difference and similarity that produces context, and are as many and as varied as such contexts might be. This is something the notion of code, which by definition stands apart from context, can never contain. Thus gall, Bourdieu tells us, is associated with bitterness and therefore equivalent to wormwood, but also to oleander and to tar (and opposed, with these, to honey); in other contexts it is associated with greenness, and thus equivalent to lizards and to the colour green; and in still other contexts with anger (a quality inherent in the other two). Lizards, in turn, are associated with toads and thus with further qualities, and so on. Such resemblances and differences do not form a separate realm of meaning, a code apart from things themselves; hence this very notion of 'thing' does not occur. For the same reason, there is no 'nature' – in our own sense of the great referent, the signified in terms of which such a code is distinguished. There are, rather, the necessary relations at work in a world where nothing occurs except as something that resembles, differs from, duplicates or re-enacts something else.[78]

This vibration of echoes and repetitions always carries the paradox of such repetition – what occurs is always the same as and yet different from what it duplicates. In the face of this paradox, moreover, nothing is decided, no simple hierarchy of truth is accepted. Where everything occurs as the trace of what precedes and follows it, nothing is determined as the original. Nothing stands apart from what resembles or differs, as the simple, self-identical original, the way a real world is thought to stand outside the exhi-bition. There is no hierarchical order of the imitator and the imitated, as in an exhibition or any other system of representation. Everything both imitates and is imitated. There is no simple division into an order of copies and an order of originals, of pictures and what they represent, of exhibits and reality, of the text and the real world, of signifiers and signifieds – the simple, hierarchical division that for the modern world is 'what constitutes order'. The order of this world is not an order of appearance.[79]

The European visitor arrived in this world, let us recall in conclusion, contained by an unshakeable habit of thought, a habit nurtured in the world of the exhibition. He arrived with a metaphysical belief, a theology, or what

Max Weber was to call in his essay on 'Objectivity in social science' a 'transcendental presupposition', namely 'that we are *cultural beings*'. Weber meant by this that we are the kind of beings who 'take up a deliberate posture towards the world and lend it *significance*'.[80] Thanks to this peculiar posture, such 'significance' can appear as something apart from the 'meaningless infinity', as Weber could now say, of the world outside. Significance resides in the space opened up, in the grounds of the world exhibition and in the similar ordering of the world beyond, between a human subjectivity and the world's inert facticity. 'There are no mysterious incalculable forces that come into play', Weber tells us. '. . . One can, in principle, master all things by calculation. This means that the world is disenchanted. One need no longer have recourse to magical means in order to master or implore the spirits, as did the savage, for whom such mysterious powers existed.'[81]

Believing in an 'outside world', beyond the exhibition, beyond all process of representation, as a realm inert and disenchanted – the great signified, the referent, the empty, changeless Orient – the modern individual is under a new and more subtle enchantment. The inert objectness of this world is an effect of its ordering, of its setting up as though it were an exhibition, a set-up which makes there appear to exist apart from such 'external reality' a transcendental entity called culture, a code or text or cognitive map by whose mysterious existence 'the world' is lent its 'significance'. Hence the European visitors to the Middle East, no longer savage but tamed into scholars and soldiers and tourists, as docile and as curious as the millions who visited the exhibition, take up their deliberate posture towards its towns and its life, and implore the spirits of significance to speak.

Chapter 3

An appearance of order

In the winter of 1867–68 Ali Mubarak, an accomplished Egyptian administrator, teacher and engineer, travelled to Paris on financial business for the Egyptian government, and to visit the Exposition Universelle. He stayed several weeks, as he later described in some detail, studying the new Parisian systems of education and of sewerage. He examined the buildings, the books, and the curricula of the new schools, and walked with other visitors along the enormous tunnels of the sewage system built beneath the boulevards of Haussmann's new city. On his return to Egypt he was appointed Minister of Schools and Minister of Public Works, and over the following decade he laid out and began building the modern city of Cairo and the modern system of education.[1]

Laying out the streets of a city and planning institutions of learning did not come together only by accident, by some chance in the career of an exceptional individual. Ali Pasha Mubarak's career indicated the concerns of his age. Streets and schools were built as the expression and achievement of an intellectual orderliness, a social tidiness, a physical cleanliness, that was coming to be considered the country's fundamental political requirement. The new order of the army and the model village was to be extended to include the city and the civilian. In this process came into being the politics of the modern state. The nature of the new politics, as they emerged in the five decades between the 1860s and the First World War, will be the subject of this and the following chapter. In this chapter, beginning with the rebuilding of the city and then concentrating on the introduction of schooling, I want to explore the links between the methods of ordering that I have called enframing and a new kind of political discipline among the population.

In a work of fiction written during this period, intended for people's instruction and improvement in unfilled moments of their day (such moments were now visible, and in need of being filled), Ali Mubarak illustrated the connection between spatial order and personal discipline through a comparison of the condition of life in Egypt and France. The protagonists in his story journeyed by steamer from Egypt to France. Arriving in Marseilles, the visitors remarked on the enormous quantity and variety of ships, merchandise, traffic, and production, and on how the people of Marseilles went about their business with 'industry, initiative, and earnestness about making wealth'. The distinctive character of life in the French city lay in the order of its streets and the discipline of those who moved through them. What astounded the travellers most was 'seeing an enormous crowd of humanity and not hearing them yell and shout as is the custom with Egyptians . . . Rather, each person was occupied with his own business, proceeding on his way, taking care not to harm or interfere with anyone else. Despite the great variety of activity and occupation and the enormous number of people involved, there was not a single fight or argument. It was as though they were gathering together for prayer, or to listen to some announcement from a ruler. Nothing was heard from them except the words necessary to do business.'[2]

Similarly when they continued on to Paris, their first reaction to the city was 'astonishment at how well it is organised, at the number of people there, the breadth of its streets and their order, the vigour of its commerce and the elegance and tidiness of its commercial establishments'. Inside the shops, they were 'amazed at how well they were organised', and how business was done without having to talk and argue and raise voices. They also visited the public gardens of Paris and Versailles, where even the play of children was clean, orderly, and quiet. The calm, the diligence, and the order of life on the street and in public places were the very characteristics that indicated and made possible the material prosperity of the French and the progress of their society. All this bore no resemblance to the streets of Cairo and Alexandria, where 'hardly an hour can pass without people being interfered with and disturbed, with the amount of shouting and yelling and cursing and foul language'.[3]

From the noise and confusion in the streets of Cairo, Mubarak's protagonist moved directly to the root of the problem: discipline and education. 'The Egyptian considered the origin and cause of this great difference, and found that it stemmed from elementary rules of discipline and methods of educating the young, to which everything else goes back.'

Doing what now had to be done

If an event should be chosen that marks the appearance of the new politics of the modern state, it would be in the winter of 1867–68 when Ali Mubarak, on his return from Paris, acquired a palace on Darb al-Gamamiz in the heart of Cairo and established there his office and his schools.[4] 'I rolled up my sleeves', he wrote, 'and set about doing what had to be done . . . After having some necessary alterations carried out, I set up the Bureau of Schools in the reception rooms, and placed the schools themselves in each of the palace wings. I also brought to the palace the Bureau of Endowments and the Bureau of Public Works, where I could easily attend to them.'[5]

He had brought to the palace the new government Preparatory and Engineering schools, and opened there the same year a School of Administration and Languages and a School of Surveying and Accounting, and the following year a School of Ancient Egyptian Language and a School of Drawing, adding later on an infirmary, a Royal Library, an amphitheatre for public lectures and exams, and a school for the training of teachers. In the same location he had put the Bureau of Public Works, the office which would be responsible for the rebuilding of the city, and the Bureau of Endowments (*Diwan al-awqaf*), the office which supervised much of the property and income that would be destroyed to build new streets through the city, or requisitioned to build village and provincial schools.

There followed the greatest period of construction and demolition in the city since the growth of Mamluk Cairo in the 1300s.[6] A new structure was laid out between the northern and western edges of the existing city and its new gateway from Alexandria and Europe, the railway station, with plots made available to anyone who would construct a building with a European façade. 'The transformation of the city of Cairo from an aesthetic point of view', as it was described by one of those responsible, required 'the filling in and levelling of the waste land around the city, the opening up of main streets and new arteries, the creation of squares and open places, the planting of trees, the surfacing of roads, the construction of drains, and regular cleaning and watering'. This spatial ordering in turn required 'the removal of certain human agglomerations from the interior', for as the map overleaf shows the new streets did not leave the existing city intact.[7] From Khedive Isma`il's new palace of Abdin, close to the palace on Darb al-Gamamiz housing the new schools, the Boulevard Muhammad Ali was ploughed diagonally through the old city. It was two kilometres long, and in its path stood almost four hundred large houses, three hundred smaller ones, and a great number of mosques, mills, bakeries and bath-houses.[8] These were all destroyed, or cut in half and left standing like dolls' houses with no outer wall, so that when the road was completed the scene resembled 'a city that has recently been shelled – houses in all stages of delapidation, though still inhabited, giving most odd views of domestic interiors, frowning down upon you'.[9]

If such measures seem heartless, it must be remembered that, like the educational policies I will be examining later on, they conformed with prevailing medical and political theory. The disorder and narrowness of the streets that open boulevards eliminated were considered a principal cause of physical disease and of crime, just as the indiscipline and lack of schooling among their inhabitants was the principal cause of the country's backward-

6 Plan of Cairo, showing the new streets.

ness. The medical argument was made according to the miasmic theory of contagion, which in nineteenth-century Europe had temporarily superseded the rival germ theory as an explanation of the transmission of diseases.[10] Contagion would not be checked, it was now thought, by quarantine and confinement, practices common throughout the Mediterranean world including Egypt, against the tyranny of which English liberals had in recent decades campaigned. What was required was the elimination from the city of sites from which the foul vapours of disease were given off, such as 'cemeteries . . . as well as sewers, cess pools and all places of rottenness and decomposition', and the demolition of houses to allow the unobstructed passage of air and light. The new theories made this an urgent matter. Indeed there were questions raised, considering the number of buried human corpses alone, whether the ground all over Egypt had not become so saturated with putrifying material that it was unable further to decompose.

With such urgent medical and political reasons in favour of open towns, there happened to coincide economic and financial arguments. Open, well-lit streets were a benefit not only to health but to commerce, for they embodied the principles of visibility and inspection whose commercial usefulness was demonstrated at world exhibitions. The dark 'interior' of the city, cleared of its human agglomerations, would become easier to police, and artificial lighting would enable the new shops and places of entertainment to do business into the night. Financially, the need for cleanliness in the streets reflected the newly envisaged relationship between the city as a place of consumption and the countryside as a place of production. By organising a system of sewage disposal, it was said, the government would realise the value per capita of human excrement. 'The towns must restore to the countryside in the form of fertiliser the equivalent of what they receive in the form of items of consumption.' In these exchanges of a new consumer economy, everything became the representation of a certain value; even the odours of the city were drawn into the economy of meanings. 'Every rotten smell in the house, in the street, in the town', it was said, 'signifies . . . a loss of fertiliser in the countryside.'[11]

The Delta town of Tanta, which gained a sizeable European colony during Isma`il's reign, was one of several provincial centres outside Cairo to undergo these new methods of 'organisation'. 'Its lanes were narrow and disorganised', explained the Under-Secretary of the new Bureau of Schools, in a textbook he wrote on Egyptian geography. 'They were damp and putrid because the air could not move and the sun could not enter.' What was required was *tanzim*, a word often translated as 'modernisation' for this period, though it means something more like 'organisation' or 'regulation'. In context it could mean simply 'the laying out of streets', and it became the name of the Department of Public Works. Tanta, along with most other large towns of Egypt in this period, received two officials appointed from Cairo, a Planning Engineer and a Medical Officer, under whose orders houses were pulled down to cut open the blind alleys that previously lead into courtyards, and great thoroughfares across the town were opened up.[12]

The 'disorder' of Cairo and other cities had suddenly become visible. The urban space in which Egyptians moved had become a political matter, material to be 'organised' by the construction of great thoroughfares radiating out from the geographical and political centre. At the same moment Egyptians themselves, as they moved through this space, became similarly material, their minds and bodies thought to need discipline and training. The space, the minds, and the bodies all materialised at the same moment, in a common economy of order and discipline.

The connection between urban order and individual discipline was indicated in the unusual location of the new schools. They were placed at the centre of the urban space, from where the new boulevards were to radiate outwards. It was a novel idea for the nineteenth century that places of government instruction should stand in the centre of the city. When the first military school had been set up by Muhammad Ali more than fifty years before, in 1816, it had been housed in the Citadel, which stood on the south-eastern edge of the city. Other places of military training had been established later, in Bulaq, in Qasr al-Aini, at the Nile Barrage, in Giza, in Khanka, on the island of Rawda, and in Abbasiyya. None of them had been built in Cairo itself, but always (like the new barracks) in outlying villages or suburbs. By the time Muhammad Ali's grandson Isma'il came to power in 1863, however, his grandfather's military schools had mostly fallen into disuse and been shut down.[13]

Within a week of assuming power, Isma'il had reestablished a Bureau of Schools. Ibrahim Adham, the government inspector already noted for his fondness for coloured-glass spectacles, who had been responsible from 1839 to 1849 for the administration of the government's schools, factories, arsenals and workshops, was now made responsible for the schools alone. He proceeded to set up government primary and preparatory schools in Cairo and Alexandria.[14] In October 1867, Ali Mubarak was appointed Under-Secretary of the Bureau. His instructions were 'to supervise the existing government and the popular schools in Cairo, in other major towns and in the provinces, to attend to their improvement and their organisation, and to see that they are properly managed'.[15] He then made his trip to visit the Exposition Universelle in Paris, and returned to set up his office and his schools in the palace in the new centre of the city.

The placing of the schools at the centre of the city can mark the moment when a new politics of the modern state appeared. From this centre was to extend the surface of a field that had no previous existence. Education was to be set up as an autonomous practice, spread over 'the entire surface of society', with a distinct purpose. The new schooling introduced earlier in the century under Muhammad Ali had been intended to produce an army and the particular technicians associated with it; schooling was now to produce the individual citizen. To understand what was envisaged in a system of civilian schooling, two important innovations from the 1840s can be picked out as an indication, the 'model school' (*al-maktab al-unmudhaji*) in Cairo and the Egyptian school in Paris. I will begin with the model school, which had been set up by Ibrahim Adham in 1843 in a large room attached to the military primary school.[16] Its purpose had been to introduce into Egypt the so-called Lancaster method of schooling.

Implicit obedience

The Lancaster or 'mutual improvement' schools had been developed for the instruction of the industrial classes in England. A group of twenty Egyptians had been sent to study at Joseph Lancaster's Central School in London in the 1820s, and in 1843 Adham himself had recently returned from England, where he had been sent to study the organisation of factories. The Lancaster school, like the factory, consisted of a single large room, which contained rows of benches with individually numbered places for up to a thousand pupils. Each bench constituted a 'class' of eight or ten pupils, and was under the supervision of a senior pupil who monitored the behaviour and work of the other students. At the command of a whistle or bell each class moved from its bench to one of the boards that were placed on the walls around the room, and stood on a semi-circular line marked on the floor around it. The boards were numbered in a sequence of ascending difficulty, and on each

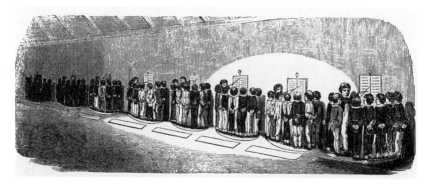

7 Lancaster school: monitors and students at their reading stations.

one there were written letters, numbers, or words, which another student monitor was allocated to teach.

The classes were taught 'silently to measure their steps, when going round the school in close order, to prevent what else would often occur from numbers, treading on each other's heels, or pushing about. In this case, measuring their step commands attention to one object, and prevents disorderly conduct. It is not required that the measure should be exact, or be a *regular step*; but, that each scholar should attempt to walk at nearly a regular distance from the one who precedes him.'[17] The monitor of each class was also responsible for 'the cleanliness, order, and improvement of every boy in it'.[18] All instruction was received standing, which was said to be better for the health, except at certain periods when they returned to their benches and sat down for the writing exercise. The exercise followed numbered instructions (to be memorised by the monitors), with all pupils writing the same words or the same letter, starting the word or letter at the same moment and finishing it at the same moment.

...9: Hands on knees. This command is conveyed by one ring on the bell; 10: hands on table, head up; 11: clean slates: everyone cleans his slate with a little saliva, or better still with a piece of rag; 12: show slates; 13: monitors, inspect. They inspect the slates of their assistants and then those of their own bench. The assistants inspect those of their benches and everyone returns to his own place.[19]

Such instructions were to be few in number and often repeated. This ensured that authority, instead of being concentrated in the personal command of a master, would be 'systematically diffused over the whole school, and capable of delegation, without diminution, to any agent.'[20]

To assist in the diffusion of authority, the commands were issued by means of a semaphore telegraph. 'The telegraph placed at the head of the school, consists of six squares, each square about four inches by three. These squares play on pivots, in the sides of a wooden frame. On each side is a letter as F. *front*, on seeing which, the whole school faces the master; or, S.S. as *show slates*, on which the whole school shows slates. The attention of the school is called to this by means of a very small bell *affixed*, which does not require loud ringing but has a sharp clear sound.' The telegraphic signals trained the pupil in 'implicit obedience', which created a 'system of order'. The visual effect of this order, from the viewpoint of the individual master at the head of the school, was considerable. For example:

It is wished to know that the hands of every boy in school are clean, a command is given 'show fingers', each pupil at once holds up his hands and spreads open his fingers. The monitors pass between the desks of their respective classes, and each inspects his own class. An examination as to cleanliness is thus effected, over the whole school in five minutes, and the practice of inspection, anticipated by the pupil, promotes habitual cleanliness. In a school of three hundred pupils, three thousand fingers and thumbs will be exhibited in a minute, and the effect on the eye is as singular, as the examination is beneficial.[21]

As well as student monitors who instructed and supervised, there were monitors who promoted students up or down in the order of seating, monitors who inspected the slates, monitors who supplied and sharpened pens, monitors who checked on students who were not in their position, and a monitor-general who checked on the monitors.[22]

The school was a system of perfect discipline. Students were kept constantly moving from task to task, with every motion and every space disciplined and put to use. Each segment of time was regulated, so that at every moment a student was either receiving instruction, repeating it, supervising, or checking. It was a technique in which the exact position and precise task of each individual at every moment was coordinated, to perform together as a machine. Authority and obedience were diffused, without diminution, throughout the school, implicating every individual in a system of order. The model school was a model of the perfect society.

In 1847, after four years, the model school in Cairo had fifty-nine pupils. It is not known how faithfully it was modelled on the English original, although the Lancaster school was actively promoted abroad by its English proponents as a model, whose geometric pattern and mathematical functioning could be exactly reproduced abroad, as it was, in almost every part of the world.[23] The Cairo school was under the supervision of Abd al-Rahman Rushdi, who had studied the Lancaster method in England and was to serve later as minister for schools. The experiment, anyhow, was deemed a success, and in 1847 an order was obtained for the establishing of a school on the Lancaster model in each of the eight sections of the city of Cairo.[24] These schools were not for creating soldiers, but for creating disciplined members of the community. They were to be called *makatib al-milla* (national schools) to distinguish them from the military establishments, and it was planned to build them throughout the country.

The school in Paris

In the same period, from 1844 to 1849, the Egyptian government set up a school in Paris, organised and run by the French Ministry of War, which introduced a similar regime of order and obedience. The Egyptian students sent to study there included Isma`il Pasha, the future ruler of the country, Ali Mubarak, his future minister, and a significant proportion of the future educators and administrators who from the 1860s were to attempt to construct a new system of disciplinary power in Egypt.[25] In October 1844 the

Ministry of War had assisted the responsible Egyptian officials in drawing up regulations for the new school. They are as follows.[26]

Regulations of the Egyptian School in Paris, October 1844

1 Students are to respect the Instructors, Assistants, and Staff, obey their orders, and greet them with the military salute.
2 Students will be called to assemble every morning, fifteen minutes after the reveille. A list of names of those absent will be given to the Director. If all are present, this will be noted.
3 The hour of the roll call will depend upon the time of year. Any student who fails to answer at the roll call will be detained in school on one of the days of leave. On the second occasion he will be fined.
4 No book or drawing is to be brought into the school without special permission.
5 The playing of backgammon, cards, or games of chance is forbidden.
6 No student may enter any class except the one he is assigned to.
7 All students are to wear their particular uniform, both inside and outside the school, and are to pay careful attention to their dress.
8 Students may not employ servants to perform errands outside the school, unless permission is obtained.
9 Packages and letters delivered to the school for any student must be inspected by the porter.
10 It is forbidden to bring into the school any chemical substances, foodstuffs, or wine or other alcoholic beverages.
11 Students are allowed out of the school on Sundays and Thursdays, from 10 a.m. on Sundays and from 3.30 p.m. on Thursdays. They must return by 10 p.m., unless they have obtained permission to return later from the Director of the School. No student may go out at any other time or return late without permission. Students are to sign their names in the register at the porter's office, and indicate the time at which they return. Those with special permission to go out must also sign their names when leaving the school.
12 It is forbidden for any student to introduce strangers into school.
13 No student may take rooms in the town, for any purpose whatsoever.
14 The punishment of students will be by detention in school on days of leave, for one or more days, or by fines.
15 The first penalty entails that the student be made to study, from 10 a.m. to 3.30 p.m. on Sunday or from 7 p.m. until 9.15 p.m. on Thursday.
16 Requests to the Director of the School must be handed to the sergeants.
17 Students are to maintain silence in the classrooms. Their place in each classroom will be permanently assigned, by the drawing of lots.
18 A student is not permitted to change his place in any of the classrooms, without permission. This order is to be kept in all classes.
19 During lessons the students are to refrain from play of any kind, are to make no noise, and are to abstain from anything that may cause them to be distracted from their lessons.

20 Students may not leave the classroom to go to their rooms, or to walk in the corridors or the garden.
21 No student may leave the classroom until the lesson has ended and the signal for the break has been given.
22 All written work must be signed by the students, and collected up by the master after they have completed it . . .

As in the Lancaster model school, learning is a process of discipline, inspection and continuous obedience. Like the army, the school offers unprecedented techniques by which students can be 'fixed' in their place and their lives meticulously regulated. Every hour of the day has been marked out, divided into separate activities whose boundaries are given not in the unfolding of the activity but in the abstract dimensions of hours and minutes. The students' life in Paris had the following daily structure:[27]

5.15 :	Reveille
5.15– 6.45 :	Study
6.45– 7.45 :	Breakfast
7.45– 9.45 :	Military Science or Fortification
10.00–10.45 :	Lunch
10.50 :	Roll Call
11.00– 1.00 :	Mathematics, Geography, History
1.15– 3.15 :	French
3.15– 5.15 :	Gunnery
5.15– 6.45 :	Dinner
7.00– 9.00 :	Military Exercises
10.00 :	Lights Out

Between the reveille that opens it and the lights extinguished to mark its end, 'time' is written out upon the exterior surface of the day. The device of the timetable separates out the dimension of time to form a framework, in which the activities of studying, eating, and exercising are to be contained.

By a process which can be considered analogous, individuals are being deliberately distributed among pre-arranged positions, allocated in each classroom to a desk that is 'permanently assigned'. 'A student is not permitted to change his place in any of the classrooms without permission; this order is to be followed in all classes.' Similarly, each student is assigned to a military rank – corporal, sergeant, or sergeant-major.[28] There is a meticulous concern for the discipline of rank and place. It is not the particular place that matters – desks can be assigned by drawing lots – but the act of positioning and remaining in place.

Punishment is a more overt expression of this concern with order. Reprimanding and penalising wrongful behaviour was nothing new, and indeed the penalties here are less violent than those of the earlier military

73

schools mentioned in chapter 2. Students are now deprived of leave or confined to their rooms rather than beaten with the leather whip. In this way punishment is made an aspect of discipline, of that continuous technique of control whose method is to position, to divide, and to set limits.[29]

As with the Lancaster school, an essential aspect of this discipline is the act of inspection. At 5.15 every morning students are woken up to stand and be inspected. Their written work is submitted to a similar inspection, and their work and behaviour is under constant surveillance. In the classroom they are to stay attentive, and any act that distracts attention will be penalised. Even to talk, at any point except when authorised, is forbidden. The effect is a rigorous discipline of movement, sound and gesture. These separate acts of supervision and discipline combine to position and articulate each individual. He is endowed with an individuality that exists only in the act of obedience, or by virtue of position in a sequence. A person's name, which he is constantly required to repeat, becomes something new – a label attached to an object, a liability attached to a piece of written work, or a moment in the sequence of the roll call.

In 1849 both the monitorial schools in Cairo and the school in Paris came to an end, after Abbas Pasha came to power and abolished virtually all government instruction.[30] When Sa`id Pasha succeeded Abbas in 1854, Ibrahim Adham put forward the proposal for 'national schools' organised on the Lancaster model once again, this time in association with Rifa`a al-Tahtawi, another of the European-trained school administrators.[31] The plan was again rejected, but not completely. Permission was given for Adham to organise elementary instruction among the Egyptians now being recruited for the first time, alongside members of the Turkish elite and Europeans, as officers and NCOs of the army. To carry out this project Adham enlisted the services of Ali Mubarak, who had returned from studying at the school in Paris to work as an administrator and military engineer. Mubarak proceeded to teach the soldiers at the barracks and camps, using a procedure modelled on the Lancaster method of instruction. He began with just a few pupils, and then used them as monitors to instruct larger groups. Having no rows of benches or classroom walls, he improvised by marking out the letters or numbers which the monitors were to teach with a stick in the sand, or with charcoal on the paved floor.[32]

A power without external manifestation

The precise methods of inspection, coordination and control of the model school in Cairo and the Egyptian school in Paris indicate the intentions and style of the practices that were to come into being in the 1860s, once Isma`il came to power and Ibrahim Adham, Ali Mubarak and Rifa`a al-Tahtawi

74

were once again given office. The order and discipline of modern schooling were to be the hallmark and the method of a new form of political power; a power required, as I suggested earlier, by the system of private landowner-ship and production for the European market that was becoming established in this period. The requirement, as one of the new class of large landowners expressed it, was to introduce into Egypt 'the European element, the pro-ductive element'. The productive element, it was said, included 'com-mercial companies, incentives, financial facilities', and the introduction among the population of 'new ideas and new processes'. What were required, in other words, were the new methods and social relations of an agricultural life organised to produce for the market. These in turn required a new technique of political power, a method of working upon the popu-lation individually and continuously to make them into efficient parts of the productive process. 'In the introduction of these new ideas and new pro-cesses, authority alone has no power. Power resides in persuasion. One can-not take one-by-one four or five million individuals to convince them that one such thing is better than another.'[33] It was to elaborate a method of power which would work upon an entire population 'one-by-one' that the representatives of this landowning class – whose most powerful member was Isma`il himself – began to advocate and finance the establishing of the new system of schooling.

We, the masters, should seize on our subjects in their early youth. We shall change the tastes and habits of the whole people. We shall build up again from the very foundations and teach the people to live a frugal, innocent, busy life after the pattern of our laws.[34]

The words are from Fénelon's *Télémaque*, which was translated into Arabic by Rifa`a al-Tahtawi, and published in 1867.[35] To change the tastes and habits of an entire people, politics had to seize upon the individual, and by the new means of education make him or her into a modern political subject – frugal, innocent and, above all, busy.

One of the first steps taken was the summoning in 1866 of a Consultative Chamber of Deputies, whose seventy-five members were chosen from among the leading landowners and provincial officials of the country. The Chamber was intended to help extend political power over the rural popu-lation, by agreeing to the imposition of increasingly harsh levels of taxation on a 'frugal' peasantry, for example, and increasing the effectiveness of taxation and military recruitment by approving a census that was to cover 'every hamlet, encampment and village in Egypt'.[36] The Chamber was itself conceived as part of a system of power whose method would be that of discipline and instruction. 'Our parliament', it was explained, 'is a school, by means of which the government, more advanced than the population, instructs and civilises that population.'[37] The education of the population was taken up immediately by the Assembly, not only as a metaphor to convey the idea of the political process, but as its major practical method.

In the first session, a deputy who was close to the government proposed the setting up of primary schools in the provinces.[38] It was announced at the same time that the Khedive Isma'il had endowed to just such a project the entire income of the new agricultural land in Wadi Tumilat, the valley created across the Eastern desert by the construction of the Isma'iliyya Canal, which carried sweet water to the new towns on the Suez Canal. With this incentive, a group of landowners and local officials from the towns and villages of Lower Egypt formed together to raise among themselves and fellow landowners similar donations. There was an enormous and highly publicised response. In the ensuing months over two thousand of the medium and large landowners of the Delta donated funds towards the founding of schools according to the government plan.[39]

At the same time, a comprehensive plan for institutions of elementary instruction throughout the country was drawn up, which became the Law of 10th Rajab 1284 (7th November 1868). The Organic Law, as it was called, determined the subjects to be taught in every school and those who were to teach in them, those who were to administer, the books to be used, the timetable of instruction, the clothes that students were to wear, the plan of buildings, the layout of the classroom and its furniture, the location of each school, the source of its funds, the schedule of its examinations, the registration of students, and the physical handicaps for which they should be excluded.[40] Learning, in every detail, had very suddenly become the state's active and extensive concern, a field of organisation, a major realm in which what is called 'the state' was to exist and build relations of power.

At the beginning of this chapter I marked the birth of this new field of order by mentioning the new Bureau of Schools that was set up in the palace at the centre of the country's reconstructed capital city. With the building of schools there are several other respects in which a new order was inscribed. First, the distribution of the schools themselves was made the deliberate expression of an administrative hierarchy, the hierarchical order of the new nation-state. The Commission on the Organisation of Knowledge (Qumisyun tanzim al-ma'arif) laid down in December 1881 that the elementary schools were to be classed in three ranks according to their required size, corresponding to the size of the village or town. Every village or group of hamlets with a population of 2,000 to 5,000 was to have a third-class elementary school (one teacher and forty pupils), every town or group of villages with a population of 5,000 to 10,000 was to have a second-class elementary school (two teachers and two classes), every large town was to have a first-class elementary school, every provincial capital was to have a secondary school, with one school per 10,000 inhabitants, and in the very centre of Cairo, in the new Bureau, were located the highest schools.[41] The schools were precisely distributed by size and rank, as expressions of the correct ordering of the separate elements – individuals, villages, towns, and provincial and national capitals – in terms of which a nation-state could be conceived as an integrated and bounded totality. Thus it was claimed that the separate schoolrooms distributed all over the country, regulated by the 'Organic Law', would 'form a whole by their coordination'.[42]

Second, schooling was divided into three stages, primary, preparatory, and final. By specifying the separate ranks of people eligible for each successive stage of schooling, a social order was represented in the exact form of a pyramid of social classes. Primary instruction was to be for all children, boys and girls, rich and poor alike. 'They require it as they require bread and water.' The curriculum was to include learning to read and write through the study of the Quran, and the rudiments of arithmetic and grammar.[43] It was also to include training in 'swimming, and horsemanship, and throwing and handling the javelin and sword and other implements of war, to train children in the methods of protecting and fighting for the nation. These things are of the general good, and children must be trained in them while young.'[44] Preparatory or secondary education was of a 'higher rank' than primary, and was to be correspondingly less wide-spread among the people. Unfortunately they had little interest in it, Rifa`a al-Tahtawi wrote, because of the hardship involved. 'It is the duty of organised government to encourage and exhort the people in this kind of schooling, for it civilises the community.' Higher education, on the other hand, was for the political elite (*arbab al-siyasat wa-l-ri'asat*). Each person who sought to study at the higher level had to be someone of wealth and status, so that devoting his time to his studies did no damage to the country. It would be harmful for someone who had an occupation from which he earned a living, and from which others benefitted, to leave that occupation and enter the realm of higher learning.[45]

Third, examinations provided a particular practice in which schooling presented the new hierarchy of the nation-state. They were events of enormous social, and structural, significance. The Law of 1867 laid down that students in the local schools were to be examined, at the end of every month by their teachers, at the end of every term by the superintendent of the school, government inspectors, and other officials, and at the end of every year by the governor of the district, the local judges, and other government advisors and officials. The same structure was laid down at each of the higher levels of schooling, with officials of the appropriate rank brought in to preside at each ascending stage of the examination process. The year-end exams were to be followed with a prize-giving ceremony, according to the law, and a procession of the students in their uniforms. At the schools of the provincial capitals, military music was to be played. At the top of the pyramid, in the government schools on Darb al-Gamamiz, annual examinations were held in the large amphitheatre within the palace, attended by the Khedive and the highest officials and dignitaries of the state.[46]

In the schools themselves a similar sort of order was to be inscribed, as it seemed, as a structure upon the surface, written down in regulations and constructed in desks and benches and classroom walls. In all the schools the layout and furnishing of the classroom was to be identical: rows of benches without backs, a dais and blackboard of the correct size, a chair for the teacher.[47] The separate buildings of a school were to be placed in geometrical relation to one another, to achieve the same 'order'. The government primary school in Cairo was laid out, and described, as follows: around a large courtyard stand four main buildings. The largest, at the rear, is for the classrooms; the one on the right, for kitchens and refectories; the one on the left, for the infirmary and the wash-house; the remaining one, which faces onto the street, contains the dormitories. This geometric pattern was copied in the other primary schools built in the following years at Alexandria, Benha, and Asyut.[48]

The elementary schools, of which about thirty had already been built all over the country by 1875, expressed a similar geometry. The Commission on the Organisation of Knowledge published twelve separate sets of building plans. The correct plan was to be chosen for each school, according to whether it was of the first, second, or third rank, and to whether it was on a site adjoined by other buildings on four sides, on three, on two or one, or on none at all (this to ensure the correct passage of air and light). These plans were used, for example, to construct new schools at Giza (1880), at Zaqaziq, Shibin al-Kum, and Damanhur (1883), at Suez and Madinat Fayyum (1888) and at Isna (1900), all of which were built according to plan number four (an elementary school of the first rank, on a site with no adjoining buildings).[49]

The interior space for eating and sleeping in each building was planned and laid out with the same regularity. 'In the refectory there are seventeen tables, with thirty places to each table. In the dormitories the beds are placed at intervals of one to every 21 cubic metres of respirable air.' The entire establishment, it was said, should have 'a pleasing appearance of order'.[50]

What characterises all these descriptions is a common attempt to construct order, which has come into being as an end in itself. As with the new streets of the city, physical space – even respirable air – has become a surface and volume that can be divided up and marked out into places where individuals are positioned.[51] Such acts create order in the abstract, not only by marking divisions and determining where things are to be put, but by distributing according to intervals that are identically spaced and geometrically aligned. The regularity of the interval (every 21 cubic metres) and the precision of the angle (the four sides of a square) create a framework which appears prior to, and therefore separate from, the objects actually distributed.

As with the architecture of the model village or the layout and timetable of the model school, this is the essence of what is now going to be seen as 'structure': that it is separate from the 'content' distributed within it. Creating the impression of a structure separate from its contents – constituting reality in terms of this separation – is precisely the effect of acts of regulated distribution. The act of distributing and fixing in place, repeated again and again in a sequence of exact and equal intervals, creates the impression that the intervals themselves are what exist, rather than the practices of distribution. The repetitive ordering creates the impression that the gaps between things are an abstraction, something that would exist whether or not the particular things were put there. This structural effect of something pre-existent, non-particular and non-material is what is experienced as 'order', or, the same thing (since it seems to exist apart from the material realisation), as the 'conceptual'.

The gaps are further made to stand forward by causing the objects they are to 'separate' to appear as similar to one another as possible – by clothing them, for example, in identical dress ('the shirt has a single row of buttons, and is dark blue; the trousers are of bright red; the badges, in gilded leather, are attached to the front of the collar; on the head is worn the tarbush; the different schools are distinguished only by the colour of the collar or the lapel, and by the colour of the trouser stripe').[52] In the uniformity of appearance, the equidistant interval, and the geometric angle, the acts of distribution, if practised quietly, unceasingly, and uniformly, almost disappear from view. As the techniques of distribution create an appearance of structure, the techniques themselves are to become increasingly invisible.

The Inspector-General of Schools, appointed in March 1873 to organise a national system of school inspection, compared these techniques of order and surveillance to the uniform and invisible force of a magnetic fluid. 'The pedagogic influence of the master on the pupil', he wrote, 'is like a magnetic fluid which transmits itself in a manner that is slow, hidden, and permanent . . . without external manifestation. At the moment when you attempt to surprise it, it may be absent, because it does not like to be under surveillance. Remove yourself and it will return, reactivated once more; the current will be reestablished.'[53] The appearance of order means the disappearance of power. Power is to operate more and more in a manner that is slow, uninterrupted and without external manifestation.

As the process of control becomes a question of achieving the continuous appearance of structure or order, there suddenly appears an equally continuous threat: the problem of 'disorder'. Disorder now emerges as a natural and inevitable liability, requiring a constant vigilance. Disorder though, like order, is a notion produced in the distributive practices themselves. It is only now that it appears as an ever present threat.

Disorder

Disorder seems about to break out, or already to prevail, whenever the old uncoordinated, undistributed style of learning was now described, especially in descriptions of the famous teaching-mosque of al-Azhar. 'What is astonishing at al-Azhar is the crowd that throngs in its halls', we are told by the Inspector-General. 'A thousand students of every age, of every colour . . . scattered into groups, the diversity of costumes.'[54] One writer complains of the 'chaos' and the absence of *nizam* (order, discipline), noting that the teachers do nothing but sit at the pillars of the mosque giving lessons, without bothering to record the presence or absence of students or their progress through different lessons.[55] Another writer describes 'the brouhaha' as 'the students, lacking all direction, move haphazardly from professor to professor, passing from one text to another, understanding nothing of passages

8 The interior of a corridor and view of the courtyard of the al-Azhar mosque, from F. Bonfils & Cie, *Catalogue des vues photographiques de l'Orient*. The Bonfils catalogue was exhibited at the Exposition Universelle, Paris, 1889.

on which the masters comment in a language about which they have no clue, and ending with everything confounded and confused'.[56] 'What is lacking more than all is height, and space. One suffocates beneath the endless ceiling.' But worse than this is 'the noise and the perpetual movement'.[57] Some are sleeping on their mats, we are told, some eat, some study, some engage in argument, vendors move haphazardly among them selling water, bread, and fruit. Organisation is absent, and anarchy hovers at the gate. A bout of horseplay breaks suddenly into a fight, and a master must step in swiftly. He separates the combatants and administers two or three blows with the whip, 'to reestablish order'.[58]

Just as the model schools offered the model of a modern system of power, this image of the old style of teaching was also the image of existing Egyptian society. Movement is haphazard and undisciplined, space is cramped, communication is uncertain, the presence of authority is intermittent, individuals are all unalike and uncoordinated, disorder threatens to break in at any point, and order can be reestablished only by the swift and physical demonstration of power.

For the Europeans involved in introducing into Egypt an organised system of education, and some of the Egyptians, this evident disorder of traditional learning presents a paradox. There must have been some method at work that enabled people to cope with the absence of any organisational framework. The Inspector-General of Schools offered an explanation. 'The apparent noise and the disorder', he wrote, ' . . . result from the pedagogical method.' This he characterised as a technique of individual instruction employed even in the teaching of large groups. The instructor, he explained, 'proceeds always by individual instruction, that is to say he never teaches to an entire class, but always to a single pupil. Each child in turn goes up to the master, sits down beside him, recites what he has learnt, shows what he has written, receives a new task and returns to take his place among his fellow students.'[59]

Despite the problem of disorder, the weakness of authority, the absence of regulation and system, and the confusion of noises, of colours, of ages, of clothing and of activities, nevertheless the pedagogical style manages, it is said, to maintain some sort of order. Its form is the individual exchange between master and student. This relation is seen as both the limitation and the strength of the social order. It is the limit, because every instruction, correction, encouragement and admonition must be given separately and repeated for every pupil. Compared with the systematic pedagogy that will replace it, where the master can instruct, correct, encourage and admonish all individuals simultaneously and continuously, this is enormously inefficient.[60] Yet given this limitation, the individual relation is also its strength, because somehow it keeps an otherwise inevitable disorder at bay.

Chaos is kept out, and the European observers attribute this, in the absence of a system of discipline, to the operation of a series of discrete, one-to-one relations, in which the master confronts, instructs, and disciplines each student individually. This kind of order must be continually reestablished, and so appears precarious, negotiated, and continually in flux. Such order was, of course, precarious; but our image of it is required and given value by the wider set of assumptions in which it stands, that of order versus disorder. It is an image that fails to break with, to historicise, our contemporary notion of order. Its notion of disorder is a condition created conceptually only in the mirror of order. It is visible and thinkable only as the absence of the geometric lines, the equal intervals, the regulated movements of a system of order, of *nizam*. And this order was a recent innovation. 'Disorder' is not a condition that precedes thought, a threat fundamental to the human condition, against which thought itself is ever busy organising the conceptual order. Disorder goes with order, as the polarity and boundary of a particular sort of world. Disorder, moreover, though it appears to stand as a pair with order, as the equal and opposite condition, is not of the same value. It is the unequal end of the polarity, the negative element. It is the void that places order as the centre, existing only to allow 'order' its conceptual possibility.

Life within the teaching mosque of al-Azhar required no walls to divide classrooms, no desks, no ordered ranks, no uniforms, no timetable, and no posted curriculum. In short, as with the city, there was no order in the sense we expect, as a framework, code or structure that stands apart. To see, once again, the peculiar historical strangeness of the new kind of order, I want to look briefly at the ways in which an institution like the teaching mosque of al-Azhar may have worked.

The order of the text

The great teaching mosques of Cairo and of other large towns in Egypt, like those elsewhere in the Islamic world, were centres not of education, or even learning *per se*, but of the art and authority of writing. They had been established in earlier centuries by those who held political power, as endeavours to secure and extend through those learned in law, language and philosophy the authoritative support of its word. The study and interpretation of this writing was a *sina`a*, a profession or craft. To stress the professional, political and economic aspects of this craft, I will refer to it as 'the law', though the word should be understood to include a large body of linguistic, philosophical and theological scholarship.[61] Al-Azhar, the name of a particular mosque but also the general name for a group of mosques and lodgings gathered in the older part of Cairo, was not a school for law, but the oldest and most important centre in the Islamic world of law as a profession. As with other crafts and professions, one of the continuous and pervasive activities of those involved was the learning and teaching of its skills. Learning was a part of the practice of law, and it was from this practice, rather than from any set of codes or structures, that it took its sequence and its form.

The process of learning always began with the study of the Quran, the original text of the law (indeed the only original text, the only text which could not be read in some sense as the interpretation or modification of an earlier writing). The student then moved on to the *hadith*, the collections of sayings attributed to the Prophet Muhammad which interpret and extend Quranic doctrine, and then on again to the major commentaries upon the Quran and to the other subjects dealing with its interpretation, such as the art of its recitation and the study of variant readings. From there one moved on to the studies related to the reading of the *hadith*, such as the biographies of the transmitters, then to the principles of theology (*usul al-din*), then to the principles of legal interpretation (*usul al-fiqh*), then to the divergent interpretations among the different schools of law, and so on according to a sequence given in the reading and interpretation of the law, which was the nature of the art being studied. Though the choice of secondary texts might vary, there was no need of a syllabus or curriculum. The order of learning disclosed itself, by the logic of interpretation, in the order of the texts.

In the same way there was no need for a daily timetable. The ordinary sequence of the day's lessons mirrored on a smaller scale the same textual order. The first lessons would be given immediately after dawn prayers, by those teaching the Quran. These were followed by lessons in *hadith*, followed by Quranic interpretation, and so on, working outwards eventually to the study of mysticism, left to the period after evening prayer. The order of teaching, in other words, even the order of the day, was inseparable from the necessary relation between texts and commentaries that constituted legal practice. Practice was not something organised within the indifferent order of the timetable; it unfolded in its meaningful sequence.

The sequence of learning was also the sequence of scholarship. A scholar at al-Azhar, we are told, would prepare a legal opinion, a lesson, or a disputation, by placing all the books which discussed the question he wanted to elucidate on a low table in front of him, arranging them in sequences radiating from the middle: 'at the centre is the original text (*matn*), then the commentary (*sharh*) on this text, then the gloss on the commentary (*hashiya*) and finally the explication of the gloss (*takrir*)'.[62] The books often repeated this arrangement themselves, as the picture on p. 147 illustrates: a text might be accompanied by a commentary written between the lines, or even inserted between the words themselves, with a further gloss upon the commentary written in the margin, surrounding the text on all sides, just as the circles of commentaries on the table surrounded the central text.

There were other respects in which the patterns of learning were repeated in the forms of legal practice. The lessons in which the works of law were read took place with the participants seated in a circle, each participant's place in relation to the teacher determined by his or her command of the text being studied. Again, the process of mastering the art was what gave learning its order. The circle of participants, in fact, was the common form of all the aspects of the legal profession carried on within the mosque. It was variously used to hear cases and issue opinions, to dispute questions of law, to deliver addresses, and to dictate and discuss the texts.[63] The activity of learning, in other words, was simply one aspect within the daily practice of the law. It took its form from those practices, and was not set apart by a separate code, location, time, or body of instructors.

On one hand, this style of learning was remarkably flexible and free of coercion, when compared to the modern disciplinary schooling typified by the Lancaster system. Learning occurred as a relationship that, as in every craft, might be found between any individuals at almost any point. Beginners learned from one another, according to their differing aptitudes, as much as from those who were masters; and even masters continued to learn from those who possessed other skills, who had mastered other texts. The method was one of argumentation and dispute, not lecturing. The individual was to be deferent where appropriate, but never passive. Whatever punishments may have been inflicted on unruly students, no system of discipline ever kept individuals under continuous supervision or surveillance, or obliged them to study with one particular teacher, or to remain in place, or to continue at a certain task for a certain period.[64] Whatever their weaknesses, these methods made the teaching mosque of al-Azhar the oldest continuing centre of scholarship and law anywhere in the world.

On the other hand, it would be a mistake to overstate the neatness or effectiveness of the kind of order I have just described. It shared the limitations and the weaknesses that I mentioned earlier, as endemic to the kind of political authority of which it was a part. In the nineteenth century it was breaking down in the same way. Law was the profession in which important Egyptian families, from every region of the country, acquired and protected positions of rural and urban authority. After a number of years at al-Azhar or one of its sister institutions, the sons of the leading families might return to their districts and take up positions of local authority, serving as leaders of the community, preachers, interpreters and judges. Ali Pasha Mubarak, for example, the educator and urban planner with whose work I introduced this chapter, was the son of such an official. His father's family had held the office of local judge and prayer leader in the village of Birnbal al-Jadida for at least three generations. By the mid nineteenth century this system of political authority was under enormous stress, as the misfortunes of Ali Mubarak's own family indicated. The important posts in provincial Egypt were still reserved for the increasingly unpopular Turkish-speaking elite (a situation that was about to change in the provinces, just as Ali Mubarak's career marked the emergence of a native, Arabic-speaking bureaucracy in Cairo), oppressive levels of taxation had forced men like Ali Mubarak's father to flee from their villages, the income of the teaching mosques had been drastically cut by the government's appropriation of their endowments, and the precincts of al-Azhar had become an overcrowded sanctuary for those escaping the military draft. The techniques of order and authority exemplified in the learning of al-Azhar could not cope with the political and economic transformations taking place.[65]

Village learning

In the account I have just given of the way learning in al-Azhar acquired its order, an order without recourse to regulation or structure, certain features of learning in general have emerged. These can be summarised as follows. First, learning occurred within the practice of the particular profession or craft to be learnt, and was not separated out as 'schooling'. The law was one such profession, centred upon the mosque; other professions and crafts were studied in their own locations, in similar ways. Second, within the profession, learning was not a relationship that separated practitioners into two distinct groups, students and teachers. The relation of teacher and student could be found between almost any two or more members of the occupation group (though of course the more senior practitioners might distinguish themselves from the rest in several ways, including the way in which they gave instruction). Third, present at almost every point in the practices of a craft, learning did not require overt acts of organisation, but found its sequence in the logic of the practices themselves.

Education, as an isolated process in which children acquire a set of instructions and self-discipline, was born in Egypt in the nineteenth century. Before that, there was no distinct location or institution where such a process was carried on, no body of adults for whom it was a profession, and no word for it in the language. To refer to centres of scholarship such as al-Azhar as places of 'traditional education' is a misnomer, a misapprehending of the kinds of practice in which the life of the community, up until the last third of the nineteenth century, was lived. It is to take a dominant practice of the late nineteenth and twentieth century, and project it back onto a world in which it did not exist, resulting in unhelpful observations about the limited nature of its 'curriculum' and the absence there of order and discipline. The introduction of classrooms, desks and discipline was not the reform of so-called traditional schooling. The innovations appeared suddenly, when the new techniques of order made suddenly obvious the need for such 'structure'. Thus the setting up of learning as a process separate from life itself corresponded, for reasons I will examine further at the end of this chapter, to the apparent separation of the world into things in themselves on the one hand, and on the other their meaning or structure.

The view I have just offered of traditional learning requires a re-explanation not only of the teaching mosque in the city but also, finally, of the so-called Quran school, or *kuttab*, of the village. Like the teaching mosque, the *kuttab* was ordered around the meaning and the power of words, in their need to be interpreted and properly handled. Not just mosques and *kuttabs*, in fact, but a good part of the communal life of town, village, and city, of marketplace and courtyard, of family and of work, was dependent upon differing practices in relation to the authority of writing. The *kuttab* in the village and the teaching mosque in the city represent two places of such practice. Their differing treatment of the same text and words, furthermore, was an aspect of the political relation between the authority of the city and the popular life of the village.

For the life of ordinary Egyptians, the correctly written or articulated word (the word of the Quran, in most cases) was a critical resource. Life, as I have suggested, was negotiated against, or in terms of, those not always knowable forces which if correctly attended to were propitious and sustaining, but if mishandled were the source of barrenness and misfortune. The most common idiom for conceiving of the person's vulnerability to such forces was the idiom of exposure. The risks of exposure were expressed in particular in terms of the power of the human gaze, the eye. (Europeans understood this, in their own terms, as the 'evil eye', though in Arabic it was just *al-ayn*, the eye.) The proper respect for the risks and potential associated with the human gaze established a set of practices for dealing with vulnerability towards strangers and those more powerful, and with the vulnerability of the weak and the very young. The risks of the gaze also established particular procedures and explanations in cases of death, childbirth and ill health.[66] To deal with these latent forces and the threat of exposure demanded various strategies of propitiation, protection and concealment. A particular resource on which ordinary people could call for such purposes was the power of the word. Michael Gilsenan's anthropological study of religion in the modern Arab world describes how 'the conception and communal experience of the Word in prayer, in study, in talismans, in chanting of the sacred verses, in *zikr* (Sufi rituals of remembrance), in the telling of beads, in curing, in social etiquette, and in a hundred other ways are at the root of being a Muslim. The directness of the relationship with Allah through the Word and its intensely abstract, intensely concrete force is extremely difficult to evoke, let alone analyze, for members of societies dominated by print and the notion of words standing for things.'[67]

The employment of the word in these and other ways was the particular craft and occupation of the *fiqi*, the local healer, Quran reciter and holyman.[68] One thing the *fiqi* did was to teach children in the village the art that was the source of his craft, the correct recitation and writing of the words of the Quran. For this reason he is often described as the village school teacher. His role in the village was not to 'educate' however, but to provide at proper moments the written and spoken word of the Quran. He was required to write charms or cures, and to recite the correct words in the correct manner at marriages and funerals, in homes, and at the tomb of the local saint, in the seeking of a husband and on the conclusion of a business deal.[69]

Like the practitioners of other crafts he would give instruction in his art, an art that had a common prominence and value because of the critical importance of the sacred word in communal life. This instruction would take place in a mosque or a room, at the tomb of a local saint or in larger towns in a building erected at the public fountain, the *sabil* (there was an important connection between the power of words and the propitious use of water). Such a place might be referred to as the *kuttab*, though the word conveys not only the sense of a place but of a practice, the practices associated with writing and in particular with the Quran. To explain the *fiqi* as a school teacher is clearly inappropriate, and leads inevitably once again to observations of the sort that the curriculum of the 'school' was restricted to the memorising of a single text, the Quran. Schooling did not exist before the last third of the nineteenth century, and it was not the purpose of any distinct individual or institution to give organised instruction. The *fiqi*'s role was formed within an idiom of the power of words and the problems of vulnerability and powerlessness. It was this very idiom of powerlessness that the system of education was to oppose, offering instead, as we have seen, an idiom of indiscipline and disorder.

Instructions for use

Learning was now to be separated from the practices in which it was entwined, assigning it a distinct place, the school, and a distinct period of life, that of youth. 'L'instruction publique' (*al-tarbiya al-umumiyya* in Arabic) was the novel phrase for this practice. It referred, it was said, to 'that which is studied by boys and girls in schools and colleges and in all establishments where a specific number of people are brought together for instruction'.[70] Schooling was to be an autonomous field, defined not by its subject or method, but as an activity that took place in a specialised location, among a specific group of people of a particular age. The organisation (*tartib*) of instruction, wrote Rifa'a al-Tahtawi, required that a room be taken in the market or the main street of the town and set aside for the purpose of teaching. Children were not to be taught in places that served other functions, particularly not in the mosque.[71] This coincided with the administrative separation, in April 1868, of what were to be called the 'civil schools' from the military.[72] The new civilian education was to be entirely separate from the military project, just as it was to be separate from the life and the learning of the mosque; its purpose was the discipline and improvement of every individual.

The word education (*tarbiya*) in this sense was itself a new usage. In Rifa'a al-Tahtawi's well-known work *Takhlis al-ibriz*, published in 1834, the first modern Arabic account of Europe, the term *tarbiya* does not occur, except once or twice in the word's general sense of 'to breed' or 'to produce', as in a description of the Ecole Polytechnique in Paris: 'In the Polytechnique mathematics and physics are taught, to produce engineers (*li-tarbiyat muhandisin*).' Nor is there any single word in its place, referring to the distinctive social practice of education.[73] The themes of the book's description of learning, like its description of Europe in general, are order and organisation. Its opening pages are addressed to those who criticised Muhammad Ali for building a military order using experts from Europe: 'Look at the workshops,' he wrote, 'the factories, the schools and the like, and look at the discipline (*tartib*) of the soldiers of the army . . . the order.'[74] The subject of the book is this same discipline and order as it was found in France, in all its aspects.

The section of the work which discusses learning in Paris in some detail begins with the title 'The progress in fields of knowledge, skills, and manufacture among the Parisians, and their organisation'. The editor of the 1973 edition of Tahtawi's works entitled the same section 'Knowledge, skills, and education among the French', substituting the word education (*tarbiya*) for the similar-sounding word organisation (*tartib*) and omitting the word manufacture which no longer fits.[75] In making the substitution the editor had repeated a transformation in vocabulary and in thinking that actually occurred in nineteenth-century Egypt. The word *tartib*, meaning such things as 'arrangement (into ranks)', 'organisation', 'discipline', 'rule', 'regulation' (hence even 'government'), was replaced in the field of learning where it had come to be universally used by the like-sounding word *tarbiya*. Until perhaps the last third of the nineteenth century *tarbiya* had meant simply 'to breed' or 'to cultivate', referring, as in English, to anything that should be helped to grow – the cotton crop, cattle or the morals of children. It came to mean 'education', the new field of practices developed in the last third of the century.[76]

As schooling was introduced to achieve this discipline, those who were responsible for its organisation and inspection wrote books and manuals in which the new practices were discussed. In 1872, for example, Tahtawi published his principal work on education, *al-Murshid al-amin li-l-banat wa-l-banin*, a guidebook for boys and girls, in which he explained the need for the new educational practices in terms of human nature. 'Man emerges from the mother's stomach knowing nothing and capable of nothing, except by education (*al-tarbiya wa-l-ta`lim*).' Upon the process of instruction depended his ability to sustain himself, to use language, and to think. For these, Tahtawi explained, 'he needs to be equipped by endless drilling and practice and exercise over a length of time'.[77] The language suggests immediately an extension of the techniques originally introduced in the military. And it was towards the very possibility of the country's military and political strength that the language led back. The abilities formed by the endless drilling and exercise of education enabled people to harmonise and associate with one another, in order to create a community. By developing this capacity to the fullest extent, the community gained its strength and acquired the ability to dominate others.[78]

Thus Tahtawi now distinguished between two senses of the term education (*tarbiya*). The first was what he called 'the *tarbiya* of the human species', using the word in its older sense as the cultivation, breeding or production of some particular thing. In this case it referred to 'the *tarbiya* of the human being as such, that is, making the body and the mental faculties grow'. The second sense was 'the *tarbiya* of individual human beings, which means the *tarbiya* of communities and nations'. It was the second meaning that was new and that came to count. The official government textbook on education published in 1903 began with the clear statement that 'the *tarbiya* of things does not mean making them increase in size'. Rather, *tarbiya* referred to the discipline and exercise of individuals, which would coordinate them to perform as a unit. 'It means putting them in readiness and strengthening them to perform their function as required, in the most efficient manner. There is no way to educate and strengthen something, except by training and drilling it in the performance of its function, until it can accomplish it with smoothness, speed, and precision.' The author of this textbook was Abd al-Aziz Jawish, who had spent three years training at the Borough Road School in London, the school set up by Joseph Lancaster to train teachers for his monitorial schools. He went on to become Inspector-General at the Ministry of Education, and was later a founder of the National Party and the editor of its newspaper *al-Liwa'*.[79]

The case of Jarwish can remind us that the new discipline of education was to be implemented not only through organised schooling. Schooling was only a part of the wider political process of discipline and instruction.

Husayn al-Marsafi, the senior professor at the new government teacher training college, set up in the same period to produce instructors for the village schools, explained that there were three parts to the meaning of education – three institutions in which this new hold upon the individual would be developed: the school, the political assembly, and the press.[80] Marsafi's more famous colleague at the training college, the great reformist thinker Muhammad Abduh, developed a similar view of *tarbiya*. Education, for him, expressed the necessary political role of the intellectual, who would use as his particular 'school' the new organs of the press.[81] Having discussed already both the government schools and the political assembly, I want to look briefly at the importance of the new printing presses.

In 1868 an organisation called the Society of Knowledge for the Publication of Useful Books (Jam`iyyat al-ma`arif li-nashr al-kutub al-nafi`a) was founded in Cairo by Muhammad Arif Pasha, one of the graduates of the Egyptian school in Paris. It was perhaps modelled on Lord Brougham's Society for the Diffusion of Useful Knowledge, the organisation set up to teach the values of self-discipline and industriousness to the working class of England. Muhammad Arif was a high-ranking government official, as were many of the other men involved in its founding. It was established by general subscription, and 660 people participated as shareholders, most of them landowners or government officials.[82] As part of the same process of 'education', the government also began the publication of journals, newspapers and books.

Since the year 1828 the government had produced an official gazette, *al-Waqa'i` al-Misriyya*, for the announcing of decisions, decrees, appointments, public works, and other domestic events, up until the 1850s, during the reign of Sa`id, when it had ceased to appear.[83] In December 1865 it was decided to produce the gazette again, but in a new form, with a new and more careful purpose. 'Rather than announce its affairs to the world through its own officials,' an internal order stated, 'the government has decided to give the right of producing the gazette to an editor, who will publish without the government's intervention.' This decision marked an alteration in technique, not a relinquishing of control. Two government servants, Ahmad Rasikh Efendi of the Office of Foreign Affairs and Mustafa Rasmi Efendi from the retinue of the Khedive, were appointed to the new Office of the Gazette, and instructions were issued to the Minister of Finance that 'they are to continue to be considered government servants and be given the salary and benefits of government employees, and are to receive pay from no other source.'[84]

The change in technique corresponded to a change in the nature of what was published. The gazette was no longer to be simply a written announcement of the government's orders and instructions, precisely as government itself was no longer conceived as the mere issuing and enforcement of orders. Information and instructions were to become the method of politics, something 'useful' which the political process was to publish and make public. There was an entire realm of thought, of meaning to be made public (while the authors of this public knowledge were to become more hidden, to disguise themselves).

9 The *ex libris* of King Farouk.

Following the reestablishment of the gazette, the government became more and more involved in the publishing of journals. In 1867 a weekly journal named *Wadi al-Nil*, the first Egyptian journal that was not an official organ, was published under the editorship of Abdullah Efendi Abu Sa'ud. Abu Sa'ud, however, was an official of the Bureau of Schools, and the journal was actually established and funded by the government.[85] Three years later, in April 1870, another journal appeared, this time issued publicly by the Bureau of Schools, entitled *Rawdat al-madaris*. This monthly journal was devoted to the spread of modern subjects of knowledge, and was printed and distributed free to all students in the new government schools. It was under the supervision of Rifa'a al-Tahtawi, all of whose subsequent writings were first published in its pages.

Working from the inside out

I will be returning in a later chapter to this question of the transformation in the organisation, nature and distribution of writing, a transformation whose beginnings I have just tried to sketch. Like schooling, the written was now to appear as something apart from life itself, a separate realm of instruction, representation and truth. In the scholarly world of al-Azhar, whatever the importance attached to the written word, writing had never formed its own realm of representation, meaning, or culture; there had been no fundamental division between 'text' and 'real world'. It is in this context, as we will see, that the continued rejection of the technology of printing by al-Azhar scholars of the nineteenth century is to be understood. For the time being, however, I want simply to conclude this chapter by suggesting a connection between the new realm of instruction – of knowledge as a code of instructions to be taught – and the new methods of creating order as a structure. I am going to argue that the new methods of enframing, containing and disciplining which I have been examining in this and the previous chapter not only made possible the modern process of schooling; they created the very need for it. To illustrate this, I will return to the structured world of the model village.

Model villages continued to be built in Egypt throughout the nineteenth century, especially on the new kind of large private estate known as the *izba* and on the 'company estates' under the control of European commercial interests.[86]. In the first part of the twentieth century, Henry Ayrout, a Jesuit working in rural Egypt, noted that those who were obliged to live in these organised villages generally considered them a 'geometric jail'. He explained this by saying that the peasant,

being of a child-like disposition, cannot be presented a model house without being taught, in a kindly way, the 'directions' which go with it, the way of using the new device, and how it is better than his old house. This pedagogy is more important than the material realization.

The model village, it seems, introduced a distinction between the materiality of the buildings and the set of 'directions for use' required to live in them. This was something new; such a distinction was unthinkable in the Kabyle village described by Bourdieu, which I suggested could be taken to typify the ways of building, dwelling and thinking that the colonial order sought to replace. As we saw, there was nothing in the building or the life of the Kabyle village that could be artificially distinguished as the mere 'material realization', as we say, of a separate set of directions, meanings or plans. The very building of the house was not the realisation of a plan but the re-enactment, in such processes as the joining of a 'female' pillar to the 'male' roofbeam, of the union that formed the household.[87] The house was never a mere device, and did not present its inhabitants, like a modern device, with separate instructions for use. Nothing was set apart in distinction to its mere materiality as the realm of the symbolic, of the cultural code as anthropologists sometimes say, or the directions to be learnt.

The new order of the model village introduced this notion of the code or plan, and this notion of materiality. Like the classrooms examined in this chapter, its geometric construction presented the world as something simply two-fold: a world of what we call 'things', which exist by appearing as the material realisation of a separate realm of intentions or instructions. This mysterious technique, the new order, was the origin of the sudden possibility and need for organised education. Suddenly, apart from such 'things', it appeared as though there was a cultural code, a set of instructions, which every child, and every 'peasant, being of child-like disposition' as it now seemed, needed to be taught. 'No model village', Father Ayrout continued, 'can be realized or kept presentable unless the architectural enterprise is linked with teaching, education and instruction; in short one should work with the fellahin. The reconstruction of the Egyptian village demands the re-education of its inhabitants, and first of all of women. We must work from the inside out.'[88]

I began this chapter with the story of Ali Mubarak returning from Paris and proceeding to build a new capital city and a new system of education. In the intervening pages I have been exploring this connection between the street and the school, between new kinds of spatial framework and the means of coordinating and controlling those who move within them. These means of coordination were something particular and physical, offering what Michel Foucault has called a microphysical power; a power that worked by reordering material space in exact dimensions and acquiring a continuous bodily hold upon its subjects. Yet at the same time, I have tried to show, this power was something meta-physical. It worked by creating an appearance of order, an appearance of structure as some sort of separate, non-material realm. The creation of this metaphysical realm was what made the education of the individual suddenly imperative – just as the micro-physical methods were what made such education possible. Power now sought to work not only upon the exterior of the body but also 'from the inside out' – by shaping the individual mind.

Chapter 4

After we have captured their bodies

In his book *Recognizing Islam*, Michael Gilsenan cites from the report of a French military officer in Algeria, on an insurrection put down by his troops in 1845–46. To establish political authority over a population, wrote the officer, there are two modes, one of suppression and one of tutoring. The latter is long-term and works upon the mind, the former works upon the body and must come first.

In effect the essential thing is to gather into groups this people which is everywhere and nowhere; the essential thing is to make them something we can seize hold of. When we have them in our hands, we will then be able to do many things which are quite impossible for us today and which will perhaps allow us to capture their minds after we have captured their bodies.[1]

In the previous two chapters I have been examining new methods of military control, architectural order and schooling, which made it possible for the first time to speak of 'capturing the bodies' of a population. Drawing on the work of Michel Foucault, I have tried to show the emergence in Egypt of a political power that sought not only to capture the individual body but to colonise it and maintain a continuous presence. The words of the French officer indicate something further about this colonising power. As I suggested at the end of the previous chapter, it was a power that seemed to construct its object as something divided into two separate concerns, body and mind. In the following pages I am going to argue that this very division was something new, that it was produced by the new methods of power, and that the essence of these methods was in fact to effect such a separation. Analysing the duality of mind and body will connect the study of disciplinary power to the larger theme of the world-as-exhibition.

I will begin, like the French officer, with the control of the body. The system of surveillance was to start not in the school or the army, but from birth. Following the British military occupation of Egypt in 1882, a central office was set up to organise the official registration of births in every Egyptian village. This required what Lord Cromer, the local agent of the British government, liked to call 'systematic English inspection', the everyday method of power that colonialism sought to consolidate. 'In connection with registration and the value of systematic English inspection', he reported to the Foreign Office in London, 'there cannot be a better example than a recent case in the Province of Benisouef. The English Inspecting Officer had reason to believe that there must be a large number of adults and children who had not been registered on a certain "esbeh" [estate] belonging to a wealthy Egyptian. The Sheikh who was responsible had certified that there was no one in the village on the [estate] liable to conscription or non-registered . . . The Inspecting Officer, with a force of police and watchmen, surrounded the village at night; in the morning over 400 were found unregistered, and the Sheikh will be tried by court-martial.' The immediate purpose of registering the country's births was to organise recruitment into the army, whose own methods of surveillance and control I have discussed earlier. But such 'English inspection' had a wider value, as Cromer himself explained in the report to the Foreign Office. Inspection 'enabled a systematic supervision to be exercised over the military and medical work of Recruiting Commissions, and, indirectly, over much of the civil work of the Mudirieh [provincial government] authorities'.[2]

Similar methods of supervision and control were required at a local level for the new methods of capitalist production, in particular the cultivation and processing of cotton. Private ownership of large estates and the investment of European capital were creating a class of landless workers, whose bodies needed to be taught the disciplined habits of wage-labour. Two Englishmen who owned a cotton-ginning factory in the new town of Zagazig employed an English youth to oversee 'Mansoor', their Egyptian overseer. Mansoor's job, in turn, according to the English youth, was 'watching the natives whilst at work and keeping them in order, for most of them were naturally of indolent disposition . . . As moral persuasion was of very little use, he carried with him a sort of kourbash or long whip, with which he encouraged industry among the men and boys; when, however, any man had been found stealing or committing a more serious crime, he was sent round to the police headquarters for punishment, and it fell to me to accompany him, explain the crime to the chief officer, and see that he was properly flogged.'[3]

Capitalist production also required the creation and management of large bodies of migrant workers, to build and maintain the new structures being laid in place across the Egyptian countryside – roads, railways, canals, dams, bridges, telegraphs and ports. Larger projects such as the digging of the Suez Canal required the movement and supervision of tens of thousands of men. Smaller gangs of labourers were brought from southern Egypt for seasonal employment in constructing and maintaining the new network of perennial irrigation canals in the north, on which the cultivation of cotton depended. The British placed such gangs under continuous police control.

They also introduced a system of 'tickets', which were handed out to the workers in their villages before they travelled north, but only to those men whom the local police deemed not to be troublemakers.[4]

Perhaps the practice of issuing 'tickets' was borrowed from the country's rapidly expanding system of railways, another locus of unprecedented mechanisms of discipline. By the end of the century the number of miles of railway in Egypt, per capita and per inhabited area, was among the highest in the world. The railways carried 4.7 million passengers in 1890 and almost 30 million in 1906, and they employed the largest permanent workforce in the country. Besides supervising and controlling this workforce, the railway authorities had to organise the issuing and collecting of tickets for every one of the millions of passengers, and run their own army of guards, policemen and inspectors 'for the maintenance of discipline upon them'.[5]

Rural Egypt was to become, like the classroom and the city, a place wherever possible of continuous supervision and control, of tickets and registration papers, of policing and inspection. Besides the particular supervision of fields, factories, railways and work gangs, the government wished to establish a general system of policing that would be 'intelligent, active, and ubiquitous'.[6] At first, following the breakdown of government authority in 1882, this required a system that was, as Cromer admitted, 'tantamount to the introduction of martial law'. The so-called 'Brigandage Commissions' with which the government attempted to crush local armed groups in the countryside employed all the now-familiar techniques for overcoming peasant resistance to the new power of a modern state: military raids, secret police, informants, massive imprisonment (the country's jails were filled to four times their capacity), and the systematic use of torture. Examples of torture used to extract confessions from suspects included hanging people from iron collars, and, in the case for instance of Mahmud Ali Sa`idi, arrested at a café in Tanta by two secret policemen in April 1887, burning the body with red-hot iron nails.[7]

A decade after they were introduced, the Brigandage Commissions were replaced with a more disciplined, widespread and continuous system of policing. Colonel Herbert Kitchener, one of the British officers of the Egyptian army, was appointed Inspector-General of the Egyptian police. Kitchener exemplified the new style of late nineteenth-century soldier-administrator, like Lyautey in Morocco, who transformed modern military methods of inspection, communication and discipline into an uninterrupted process of political power, succeeding where the earlier attempts I have discussed had failed. 'A first-rate military administrator, every detail of the machine with which he had to work received adequate attention', wrote Lord Cromer of him. 'Each portion of the machine was adapted, so far as human foresight could provide, to perform its allotted task.'[8] Besides the organisation of a police force, a comprehensive system of English inspection was established, set up within the Ministry of the Interior (as this new bureaucracy was called); the 'interior' of Egyptian village life was thus to be brought under continuous supervision. To assist in this the local village watchmen, 50,000 in number, were placed on government salaries, and later brought to provincial centres for military training and provided with arms. The watchmen were to collaborate in 'the surveillance by the police of criminals and suspected persons' and indeed of all 'noted bad characters'. Finally, a series of government regulations were introduced aimed at the repression of further rural 'disorder', including a prohibition on the carrying of guns by all except 'government or local officials, or substantial landowners and traders'. The new methods of control were enormously successful. The groups of rural resistance were broken up, their leaders were shot or captured, the attacks on the new private property were brought to an end, and the power of 'substantial landowners and traders' made secure.[9]

Sanitary and other reasons

The new methods of power sought to police, supervise and instruct the population individually. It was a power that wanted to work with 'known individuals' and 'noted characters', who were to be registered, counted, inspected and reported upon. The first census of the population was carried out in 1882. As with the registration of births and the procedures for medical inspection, the concern with the individual body of the political subject was both military and economic. The new medico-statistical practices, moreover, adopted from the armed forces, provided a language of the body – its number, its condition, its improvement, its protection – in terms of which political power might operate.[10] Such language could be used to control and restrict any large movements or gatherings that might be difficult to penetrate and police. It was used in this way, for example, to suppress the popular fairs that marked out the calendar of social and economic life all over Egypt.

The biggest of the country's annual fairs – indeed one of the great popular gatherings of the whole Mediterranean world – was the feast of al-Sayyid Badawi, which took place in the Delta town of Tanta. The feast was an enormous occasion, and had grown particularly following Tanta's connection to the railway system in 1856. Its visitors in the 1860s and 1870s were said to number more than half a million every year.[11] Already in this period the festival began to receive criticism: that religious practices which occurred there contravened the law, and that it was harmful to the country because it kept people from their work. Such criticisms were answered at the time by pointing out that the festival was an enormous annual market, like the great markets found in every part of the world, at which business and commerce thrived.[12] These views, however, did not prevail, and in the last three decades of the century the entire festival was suppressed, an act carried out in the name of hygiene. There was concern in the 1870s about 'the profusion of diseases and bad air' each year following the event. The problem was blamed at the time on the town's physical structure and resulted in the destruction of buildings to create open streets, discussed at the beginning of the last chapter. These measures were evidently insufficient for the purpose however, because by the turn of the century the government had suppressed the festival more or less completely, 'for sanitary and other reasons'.[13]

The language of health and physical hygiene was also used in the government schools, as part of the new discipline of the body. The teaching of personal hygiene, and the accompanying school books, were intended of course to promote individual cleanliness and tidiness. But their language and method aimed to eliminate an entire way of understanding personal vulnerability among ordinary Egyptians, particularly in the village, and to replace it with a nineteenth-century notion of the body. The body was to be treated as a physical machine, and disease as a mechanical process of cause and effect.[14] The customs of the village were persisting in Egypt 'because they have not been sufficiently combatted' argued one of the authors of these school textbooks, and the hope was to see them, in the phrase of the Orientalist who translated part of his work into English, 'relegated to the archives of human error'.[15] The author was a man in his mid-twenties from a village in the Delta, who had trained as a doctor at the government medical school in Cairo, and was commissioned by the Ministry of Education to write two textbooks for the government schools, the first on hygiene, which appeared under the title *Health Measures Against the Habits of Egyptians* and the second, published in 1896, on manners and morals more generally.[16]

The method of these books was not simply to discredit the local practitioners of healing among the poor – though all of them were roundly condemned as 'impostors', 'charlatans', and 'public robbers' – but to impose an alternative idiom of explanation and an alternative medical practice. The author admitted, in fact, that many of the remedies of folk medicine were successful, but explained that they succeeded 'not from any therapeutic peculiarities in them, but from the play of the imagination and nervous volitional influence, which according to biologists in most recent times, has a very dangerous action upon the constitution'.[17] In other cases he admitted that the local remedy was scientifically correct, but attacked the local understanding of how it worked upon the body, replacing this with 'the true explanation' which accounted for its working in an alternative idiom drawn from late nineteenth-century medical science. The power of the evil eye, for example, he explained in terms of 'electric magnetism'. 'The evil magnetic electricity, which we name *envy*, directs itself by way of man's senses.' He cited as an illustration the case of a healer in a certain village who was 'envying' children and other objects by staring at them. 'Whenever the envier directed his gaze upon the envied one, in the moment of excitement his poison affected that current and weakened the life movement in animals and plants, and they were wasted and lost. And in proportion to the power of the envier in overcoming the power of the envied, so is the strength or weakness of the danger, and there results a slight or severe illness, or death, or the snapping of trees, or the destruction of lofty palaces.' He even admitted, finally, that some of the imported European pills and elixirs were chemically identical to the folk medicines they were displacing, although this did not prevent him from condemning the use of such local medication. He simply added: 'How marvellous it is of Science to abolish it at first in its capacity as a natural product, and then find it (or something counterfeiting it) by way of industry!'[18]

Curative practices were continually isolated as harmful, mistaken, and mischievous in the literature of the period. A well-known work in Arabic on *The Present State of the Egyptians and the Causes of their Retrogression*, by Muhammad Umar, attributed much of the cause of the country's backwardness to the ignorant practices of the poor, including such manifestations of 'ignorance' as the popular trance-inducing practices of the *dhikr* and the *zar*. There were also several critical and more extensive diagnoses put into print, such as Muhammad Hilmi Zayn al-Din's *Madar al-zar* (The harmfulness of the zar), published in 1903, which criticised such practices in particular for the dangerous power they enabled women to acquire over their husbands.

Political science

The attempt to introduce new methods of working upon the body was only one aspect of the changes that were taking place. In treating the body as a machine, requiring continuous supervision and control, politics constituted the person as a thing of two parts, just as it constituted the world as something twofold. The mechanical body was to be distinguished in political practice from the individual's mind or mentality, just as the material world was to be made something distinct from the conceptual order – or what in nineteenth-century France was often called 'the moral order'. Nubar Pasha, a member of the new landowning elite who served as Prime Minister of Egypt three times after the British occupation, understood the political process in terms of this distinction. Referring in a memorandum to what had been achieved 'in the army, the railways, . . . bridges and roads, the health and sanitation services', he argued that 'what has been done in *l'ordre matériel* must be done in *l'ordre moral*'.[19] Nubar's memo was concerned with the introduction of a European legal system, which would consolidate the power of private property. Thus the phrase 'the moral order' referred to law in the modern sense, meaning a community's code of rules (a sense very different from existing Islamic law, which was never understood as an abstract code setting limits within which 'behaviour' was to be confined, but rather as a series of commentaries on particular practices, and of commentaries upon those commentaries). The phrase referred more broadly, however, to a community's general moral code. In this broader sense, the moral order was a nineteenth-century term for speaking of the realm of 'meaning', as we might say today. It was a name for the abstract code or structure which is thought to exist, in the world-as-exhibition, as something separate from the world's materiality. By the end of the nineteenth century the moral order had given way to new names for this abstraction, such as 'society' or 'culture'.

To consider the political nature of these abstractions, I want to reach them via a further discussion of the person; for the new notion of the person, as composed of two separate entities, body and mind, can be connected to such abstractions as 'the moral order'. At the same time as it denoted the social realm, morality was something to be possessed by individuals. Upbringing and schooling were intended not only to discipline the body, but to form the morals – the mind – of the child. The new notion of culture had the same double sense. It referred both to the moral order of the community and to the set of rules or values to be acquired by the individual. Thus the moral or cultural dimension was both a dimension of the world (its conceptual order, as distinct from its materiality) and a space or process within the person (the individual's mind or mentality, as distinct from his or her body). The political methods of the world-as-exhibition lay in producing this coincidence between an apparent duality of the person and an apparent duality of the world.

Schooling was a process that treated the person in this dual manner. Its powers of monitoring and instructing were designed to keep the mental as well as the material under observation. The paragraph of a government report of 1880 discussing 'the nature of inspection' explained that the task of school inspectors, as 'the eyes of the Minister of Education', was to examine the condition of each school 'both materially and morally'.[20] Correspondingly, the purpose of schooling was to form both the body and the mind of the child. The two objects were clearly distinguished in the standard work on Egyptian educational practice, written for the Schools Administration in 1902 by Abd al-Aziz Jawish, the future nationalist leader who had been trained in the Lancaster method. Education, Jawish wrote, was intended both to train the physical body of the child, and to form the mind and character. The latter process was the more vital, because character alone guaranteed the existence of society (*mujtama`*) and secured the order of its affairs. The formation of the person's mind or character in school was the means to social order, Jawish explained, because the students 'are taught obedience and submission to the school's discipline and regulations, thereby becoming accustomed to respecting the regulation, discipline, and laws of the state'. The school, he concluded, renders in this respect an enormous assistance to the government. Unlike the home, moreover, the school 'is a place of competitive activity; this instils in the student's spirit a liking for diligence and industry in his work'.[21]

The power of working upon the individual offered by modern schooling, as I suggested in the previous chapter, was to be the hallmark and the method of politics itself. Politics was a process to be conceived according to the same processes as schooling, and was to work in the same way upon both body and mind. This new notion of 'politics' appears in Egyptian writings from the 1860s, first of all as something to be taught and practised in the new schools, where it would provide what Rifa`a al-Tahtawi called 'a general governing power'.

The custom of the civilised world has been to teach children the Holy Quran, in the case of the countries of Islam, and in other countries their own books of religion, and then to teach them an occupation. This in itself is unobjectionable. The Islamic countries, however, have neglected to teach the rudiments of the science of sovereign government and its applications, which are a general governing power, particularly as regards the inhabitants of the villages.[22]

Politics in this sense was not, of course, a field of study previously neglected or overlooked. It was a new notion, brought into being by the introduction of schooling and other practices, including the writing of those who organised and directed the new schools. 'The principles and precepts by which the country is governed', Tahtawi explained,

are known as the Art of Sovereign Government (*fann al-siyasa al-malakiyya*), and as the Art of Administration (*fann al-idara*), and also as the Science of Statecraft (*ilm tadbir al-mamlaka*), and the like. The study of this science, the general discussion of it, debate and discourse upon it in councils and assemblies, and its examination in the newspapers, all this is known as 'Politics' (*bulitiqiyya*), that is, government (*siyasa*), from which is derived the adjective 'political', meaning pertaining to government. Politics is everything connected with the state (*dawla*) and its laws, treaties and alliances.[23]

The modern notion of politics was to be defined by taking an Arabic term, *siyasa*, and associating it with the European word 'politics'. *Siyasa* before now meant, among other things, the exercise of authority or power, 'government' in the sense of the activity of governing rather than of the body that governs. Lending the word an association with the European term 'politics', its meaning is altered from being one of several words for governing, to stand for a definite field of knowledge, debate, and practice. It was by no means the influence of a European word alone, however, that accomplished this change. Particular practices had developed for which *siyasa* was already an expression. The term had been used in such nineteenth-century phrases as 'siyasat sihhat al-abdan', a phrase translated into French at the time with the single word *hygiène*, and 'arif bi-umur al-siyasa' (literally 'one learned in matters of *siyasa*'), which in 1864 an Arab scholar rendered into French as *criminaliste*; *siyasa* could also mean simply 'to police'.[24] Similarly the word *tadbir*, meaning arrangement, administration, or management, which occurred twice in the passage above defining the meaning of politics, was used to mean 'treatment (of an illness)'.[25] In other words, the appearance of the notion of 'politics', *siyasa*, was neither simply the adoption of a word from Europe nor a concept creating its own space out of nothing. Politics was a field of practice, formed out of the supervision of people's health, the policing of urban neighbourhoods, the reorganisation of streets, and, above all, the schooling of the people, all of which was taken up – on the whole from the 1860s onward – as the responsibility and nature of government.

These activities required the elaboration of a new concept denoting an entire field of practice, of thought. Using the long-established word *siyasa*, however, caused an apparent continuity with the past, so that the knowledge and practices it referred to appeared not as the introduction of something previously unthought, but simply the reintroduction of something 'neglected'. In earlier periods, as I suggested in chapter 2, the government of the country had been practised as the aggregating of certain goods – bodies, crops, monies – required by ruling households for their treasury and their armed forces. The political process was intermittent, irregular, obliged generally to expand as the only means of increasing its revenues, and concerned always with aggregates. As Foucault argues, modern politics was born with the concern not for aggregates but individuals – individuals who could be separately cared for, schooled, disciplined, and kept clean in an economy of individual order and well-being.

Politics, wrote Tahtawi as he introduced the concept, 'is the pivot on which the organisation of the world turns' (*fa-madar intizam al-alam ala al-siyasa*).[26] The organisation of the world, its order and well-being, was now to be taken up as the political programme. Politics, according to Tahtawi, was divided into five parts. The first two, *al-siyasa al-nabawiyya* (prophetic) and *al-siyasa al-mulukiyya* (monarchic), conveyed the common and older sense of *siyasa* as leadership or rule. In the third and fourth categories, *al-siyasa al-amma* (public) and *al-siyasa al-khassa* (private), the new meaning of political practice appears. 'Public *siyasa*' is defined as 'the leading of groups (such as the leadership of princes over countries or

103

armies), the organisation of matters as necessary for the improvement of people's condition, proper administration (*tadbir*), and the supervision of law and order and finances.[27] The narrower concept of leadership is broadened to include the regulation, management, and supervision of a nation's affairs.

The definition was extended further in 'private *siyasa*', also known as the *siyasa* of the house, and the fifth kind, *al-siyasa al-dhatiyya*, the *siyasa* of the self, in which politics was expressed in terms of hygiene, education, and discipline. The '*siyasa* of the self' is 'an individual's inspection of his actions, circumstances, words, character, and desires, and his control of them with the reins of his reason'. 'Man', Tahtawi added, 'is in fact his own doctor – some refer to this as *al-siyasa al-badaniyya* (the *siyasa* of the body).'[28] These statements extend the meaning of *siyasa* from leadership or government to embrace the practices of 'political policy' – the policing and inspection (the word used has a military connotation, *tafaqqud*) of the body, mind, and character of the individual subject.

Ethnography and indolence

Modelled on the processes of schooling, the new politics was to acquire an individual hold upon both the body and the mind. The need for a hold upon the mind was explained by Lord Cromer in terms of the very process of constructing a colonial authority. The problem for the British colonial regime in Egypt, he explained, was that the traditional communal bonds between a ruler and those who were ruled – the 'community of race, religion, language and habits of thought' – did not exist. It was therefore necessary for the government to forge what he called 'artificial bonds' in their place. These artificial bonds were to consist above all in the government's information about and understanding of those whom they ruled, a kind of understanding that Cromer called 'reasonable and disciplined sympathy'. He insisted on 'the exhibition of reasonable and disciplined sympathy for the Egyptians, not merely by the British Government, but by every individual Englishman engaged in Egyptian administration'. How was this artificial bond of understanding to be forged, in a manner that would keep it something 'reasonable and disciplined'? It was to be 'based on accurate information and on a careful study of Egyptian facts and the Egyptian character'.[29] The Egyptian character – a notion later to be replaced with terms such as culture – was to be carefully examined, for a disciplinary politics was predicated upon this object. Such examination was itself part of the disciplinary mechanism of power – the mechanism that places under surveillance and continuously watches.

As with the registration, counting and inspection of bodies, the politics of the mind would have to begin with the process of description, in order to constitute its object as something separate. The first task of government was 'to make an account of all the defects of the popular character', wrote one of the inspector-generals of Egyptian schools, 'to look for their origin, and to bring about their cure by means contrary to those which have caused them'.[30] In 1872, therefore, he produced a book on schooling in Egypt whose first fifty pages were devoted to 'the Egyptian character'. 'To describe public instruction', he explained on page one, 'is to paint at the same moment a picture of the manners and the character of a people.' This he did, in clear, political terms: the Egyptian is timid and yet defiant; he is susceptible to enthusiasm yet lacking in all initiative; his character is one of indifference and immobility, engendered by a lack of security about the future and an instability of property, which has killed the spirit of industry and the need to acquire.[31]

The Egyptian 'mind' or 'character' is formed in such ethnographic decription as a solid object, the object upon which the educational practices in which the writer was engaged could work. 'Ethnology shows us the effect, history gives us the cause. But it also indicates to those who would profit from its lessons, the remedies to those ills that the neglect or the harmful influences of preceding ages have created.' The descriptive process of 'ethnology' and the disciplinary practice of the school worked together in this way to create the new subject of colonial politics, the individual character or mentality. Like the more sophisticated ethnographic concepts that would replace it – first 'race' and later 'culture' – the concept of character was to acquire explanatory force by representing the historically moulded 'nature' of both the individuals and the society studied. 'The national character', wrote the Inspector-General, drawing analogies from biology and geology, the major sciences of the day, 'is the slow but constant product of the historical events that the nation has had to traverse. Resembling those alluvial plains to which each passing flood has added another layer, this character forms, condenses little by little, and, just as each different geological layer indicates to us a new natural phenomenon, so each physiological peculiarity leads us to a new phase of formation.'[32] Modern, educative politics is an ethnological process, predicated upon the formation and maintenance of this mind or character.

Politics was to produce and to remedy the individual character. The true nature of this character, moreover, was to be a producer. Ethnography emerged in the early nineteenth century, not just to describe the nature of man, but as part of a larger process of describing man as, by nature, productive. The first serious ethnography of the Middle East, Edward Lane's *Manners and Customs of the Modern Egyptians*, was subsidised and published in England by the Society for the Diffusion of Useful Knowledge, the organisation set up by Lord Brougham, as I mentioned earlier, to introduce books and schooling to the new industrial working class in order to teach them the virtues of industriousness and self-discipline. Lane's book included successive chapters on 'Character', 'Industry' and 'Use of tobacco, coffee, hemp, opium, etc.'. These pages described how 'indolence pervades all classes of the Egyptians, except those who are obliged to earn their livelihood by severe manual labour' and how 'even the mechanics [manual labourers], who are extremely greedy of gain, will generally spend two days in a work which they might easily accomplish in one'; how Egyptians 'are extremely obstinate and difficult to govern' and 'have been notorious from ancient times . . . for refusing to pay their taxes until they have been severely beaten'; how 'it is seldom that an Egyptian worker can be induced to make a thing exactly to order: he will generally follow his own opinion in preference to that of his employer; and will scarcely ever finish his work by the time he has promised'; how 'in sensuality, as far as it relates to the indulgence of libidinous passions, the Egyptians, as well as other natives of hot climates, certainly exceed more northern nations'; and finally, how the immoderate addiction of Egyptians to tobacco, coffee, hashish and opium had made them still 'more inactive than they were in earlier times, leading them to waste . . . many hours which might be profitably employed'.[33]

There was nothing unusual about the theme of indolence as the essential characteristic of the non-European mentality. Earlier in the nineteenth century Georg Bernhard Depping, a French scholar, argued for the seriousness of studying empirically the manners and customs of other peoples – referring to it as the 'moral part' of geography and history, for which he proposed a new name 'ethnography' – by stressing what it could reveal about the effects of indolence versus industry. 'When you compare the nations of Asia and Africa with those of Europe,' he wrote, 'you cannot fail to discover a striking difference between them. The former seem to be almost plunged into such a state of indolence as prevents them performing any thing great.' Indolence, in fact, was the major theme of Depping's work. It was the character of less civilised peoples and the cause of their condition. Such arguments were uncompromisingly empirical. 'The savages of America are so indolent that they choose rather to endure hunger than to cultivate the earth', he noted, while others were reduced by laziness to eating the broiled flesh of their own kind or even, in the case of one South American tribe, to a diet of mud and clay (kneaded, baked before a slow fire, and sometimes seasoned with a small fish or lizard). Depping drew a clear lesson from studying the manners and morals of the less civilised. 'Shun idleness . . . You must not imagine that in countries where idleness and thoughtlessness become habitual, men can be as happy as in others.' The decline of a people was due to the indolence of those who work in the fields, 'to produce what is necessary for the subsistence of the inhabitants'. They were to be taught from their youth 'not to waste in doing nothing a single moment that can be usefully employed'.[34]

The Egyptian students who were brought by the French to study in Paris in the 1820s were given Depping's work to read. Its theme that productive labour formed the true nature of man was at the heart of French plans for the political and economic transformation of Egypt. Rifa`a al-Tahtawi, the most outstanding of the Egyptian scholars, was asked by the French director of the mission to produce an Arabic translation of Depping's most recent book, *Aperçu historique sur les moeurs et coutumes des nations*.[35] When Tahtawi returned to Egypt in 1831 carrying in manuscript the numerous translations he had made of French works, the book by Depping was the first that he revised and had printed.[36] At the same time he tried to obtain permission to establish a school in Cairo to teach the 'moral part' of geography and history. Although the attempt failed, Tahtawi was later allowed to set up a School of Translation, where amid the demands for translating works of military instruction he was able to teach these subjects.[37]

Tahtawi wrote that he wished to spend the rest of his life translating into Arabic the entire corpus of French writing on geography and history. Government duties prevented this, however, until after a change of regime in 1850 when he was sent to open a school in Sudan, which he considered a form of exile. In Khartoum he produced his translation of Fénelon's *Aventures de Télémaque*, which expressed the same themes of the need for diligence and industry among the population, in the earlier form of a moral tale. Wherever Télémaque went in his travels outside Greece, to Thebes, Tyre, and Crete, he found people 'industrious, patient, hard-working, neat, sober and thrifty', and enjoying '*une exacte police*'. He found 'not a single field where the hand of the diligent labourer had not made its mark; everywhere the plough had left its deep furrows: brambles, thorns and all the plants that occupy the earth without profit were unknown'.[38]

It is in terms of the problem of 'industriousness' that one can interpret Tahtawi's book *Manahij al-albab al-misriyya*, one of the first major works in modern Arab political writing. The book's importance is in introducing the concept of production, in the form of an extended interpretation of the phrase 'the general good' (*al-manafi` al-umumiyya*). After elucidating the meaning of the phrase, the work considers its three parts, agriculture, manufacture, and commerce, and then examines their development in Egypt from the earliest times to the present. The 'general good' refers to the common wealth that is produced in the material production of agriculture, manufacture and commerce, but it also refers to production as the habitual process that creates society. At one point in the work, Tahtawi states that the phrase 'general good' corresponds to the French term '*industrie*'. The cause of Egypt's condition is diagnosed as the absence of this habit of industry, the characteristic of the productive individual and the civilised society. Its absence makes Egyptians indolent, and indolence is fundamental to their 'character'. Using European sources, Tahtawi traces the trait of indolence all the way back to the ancient Egyptians.[39] The theme of industry reappears at the end of the work, where Tahtawi argues that there should be a government teacher in every village, 'to teach the principles of government and the general good'.[40] The new government schools were needed to form the proper mentality in the individual, to make every citizen industrious.

Self-help

All those writers involved in the organisation of schooling developed the theme of indolence and industry in discussing the mentality of the Egyptian – including the Inspector-General quoted above, and Ali Mubarak. They were assisted by a continuing translation of books from Europe on the same theme. Probably the most influential of these translations was by the editor of the Cairene journal *al-Muqtataf*, Ya`qub Sarruf. In 1880 when he was a teacher in Beirut, Sarruf translated into Arabic the famous book by Samuel Smiles, *Self-Help, with Illustrations of Conduct and Perseverance*.[41]

The theme of *Self-Help* coincided exactly with practices taking shape in Egypt. 'The worth and strength of a state', wrote Smiles, 'depend far less on the form of its institutions than on the character of its men. For the nation is only an aggregate of individual conditions, and civilisation is but a question of . . . [their] personal improvement.'[42] The book was about 'character' (*akhlaq* in the Arabic translation), and about the 'moral discipline' (*tarbiya*) by which those of an idle character are made 'industrious' (*mujtahid*). The habit of industry (*al-ijtihad*) is the moral quality upon which the state and its progress depend. 'National progress is the sum of individual industry, energy, and uprightness, as national decay is of individual idleness, selfishness, and vice.'[43]

The book made 'character' the object of its study in order to make three arguments, each of which was to contribute to its enormous usefulness in Egypt: (1) that the political task of those who govern is to mould individual habits and morals; (2) that government should not concern itself therefore with further legislation or greater rights, all of which lead to 'overgovernment' while failing to make the idle industrious; and (3) that to make the idle industrious requires the discipline and training of an education – the aim of which is not to supply knowledge as a 'marketable commodity' whose acquisition makes men 'better off', but to train those who must do society's daily work in the mentality of perseverence and industry.[44]

The translation was used as a reader at the Syrian Protestant College (later the American University) in Beirut, where Sarruf taught, and its vocabulary and ideas influenced a generation of students there.[45] Several of these students, together with Sarruf, were driven out of Beirut in the 1880s by their American employers, for espousing the theories of Darwin. They moved to Egypt, to work and to write under the patronage of the British. No more devout believers in the ideas of self-help could have been found in this period than the British administrators in Egypt. The British considered their task to be to relieve Egypt of the evil of overgovernment, so that the productive capacity of the Egyptian peasant could be realised to the full.[46]

Several events indicate the impact of Smiles' book in Egypt. In 1886 a Self-Help Society was founded in Alexandria.[47] In 1898 Mustafa Kamil, the young leader of the nationalist opposition to the British occupation, founded a private school – an act which he declared to be his own practical application of the doctrine of self-help.[48] The phrase 'self-help' was inscribed on the wall of the school, together with several other mottoes from Smiles' book.[49] Mustafa Kamil's patron, the Khedive, is said to have gone even further and had the words of Samuel Smiles written up on the walls of his own palace.[50] Two years after founding his school as an act of self-help, Mustafa Kamil became the first person to call publicly for the founding of a university in Egypt, criticising as he did so the habit among Egyptians of relying upon the government rather than themselves in their affairs.[51] At the same time he established the newspaper *al-Liwa'*, which was to become the political mouthpiece of the National Party. Its early issues referred frequently to the subject of education, and argued that schools should be founded not primarily for the instruction of children, but for the forming of their character.[52] The newspaper saw its own role in the same way. It devoted an entire column every day to the 'character and habits' of Egyptians.

With the translation of works like *Self-Help*, then, the Egyptian character or mentality could be treated as a distinct and problematic object, the object upon which society and its strength were said to depend. The very occupation of the country by the British could be blamed upon defects in the Egyptian character, defects whose remedy was Egypt's political task.[53] Nationalist writers in the first years of the twentieth century frequently compared the colonial occupation of their country with the situation of Japan, as the Japanese defeated first the Chinese and then the Russians at war. The major difference accounting for the success of the Japanese in defeating the largest country in Asia and the largest country in Europe was the difference between the Japanese and Egyptian mentality. The Japanese, it was explained at length, had organised education and instruction, and concentrated on 'the formation of character'.[54] Egyptians were light-hearted, lazy, and fond of idling their time, while the Japanese were 'serious and industrious'.[55] Earlier, in 1881, the journal *al-Muqtataf* had compared the industry and seriousness of the Japanese with the light-heartedness of

Egyptians, mentioning among other things the industry of the Japanese in translating European books and giving a list of works they had translated, at the head of which was the book *Character*, by Samuel Smiles. A similar comparison between the mentality of the Japanese and the Egyptian was made in the journal in 1889 – by comparing the Japanese and the Egyptian exhibits seen in Paris that year at the world exhibition.[56]

After the translation into Arabic of *Self-Help*, perhaps the next work to have a similar impact in Egypt and the Arab world was a translation of the book by Edmond Demolins, *A quoi tient la supériorité des Anglo-Saxons*, a book which understood the political process again in terms of the problem of individual character.[57] The work attempted to explain how Britain had become the greatest and most successful colonial power, supplanting the French in North America, India, and Egypt, and dominating the rest of the world in commerce, industry, and politics.[58] It attributed the success of the Anglo-Saxon to his distinctive moral character, created and transmitted by the unique style of English education. France and other nations, in contrast, had failed to find a means of transmitting a modern character and way of life from one generation to the next, and the result one saw in these countries was a condition of 'universal social crisis'.[59]

As the means of forming a modern character and thereby producing order in a world where everything was 'in a state of disarray', the book was written to advocate not just English methods of schooling but the teaching of a new and particular kind of knowledge: social science. Demolins, who was editor in Paris of the journal *La science sociale*, described social science as 'at this moment, the single thing not scandalised by a similar disarray'. Social-scientific knowledge, he explained, was something correct and conclusive, and its very method of classification and comparison gave an order to the world. The particular form this order took was a division of the world into two. Social science, he continued, 'by all the things that it analyses, that it compares, that it classes, knows that at this moment the world is passing, necessarily – and for its own good – to a new condition, which is not transitory, which is durable, and which separates, as though into two, the time preceding and the time to come'.[60]

This division of the world 'as though into two', moreover, was a division not only between epochs, but between mentalities. As much as there was a difference between savage people and ourselves, Demolins wrote, a moral or mental gulf had opened between those whose minds were formed by the social sciences and the rest.[61] The resulting condition, he concluded at the end of the book, was 'a moral inferiority; of the Red-Skin in relation to the Oriental; of the Oriental in relation to the Westerner; and of the Latin and German peoples of the West, in relation to the Anglo-Saxons'.[62]

It was to these levels of mental inferiority that Ahmad Fathi Zaghlul, the author of the Arabic translation, drew attention in the introduction he wrote to the Arabic edition. His aim in translating the book, he said, was to make people consider the causes of this inferiority, by comparing the Egyptian 'character' to the character of the English who had occupied their country.[63] He enumerated what he considered the areas of weakness in the Egyptian character. They included weakness in affection and friendship, in determination, in dignity, and in the willingness to do charitable works. Above all there was the habit of relying for everything upon the government, whose real function was only to provide order and security, and to carry out justice. Weakness had been added to weakness he said, and the country's wealth and affairs were now in the hands of foreigners. The foreigners could not be blamed for this, because they had benefitted by their own efforts, and by their social-scientific knowledge.[64]

The translation of Demolins' work had a wide impact in Egypt, among a certain social class. It aroused immediately a great deal of discussion in the press.[65] Several years later it was recalled by a leading Egyptian intellectual as one of the few works that 'spread among the masses a scientific basis for development, so that people could apply its principles to their situation'.[66] The book became widely known among educated men, even in provincial Egypt. The governor of a province of upper Egypt told a French traveller that he had read Demolins' book, soon after it had been published. He had decided to send his son, who was a student at the government preparatory school in Cairo to complete his studies at the new school established by Demolins near Paris.[67] The famous Ecole des Roches was set up by Demolins following the success of his book on Anglo-Saxon superiority. He described the principles of its organisation in another work, *L'Education nouvelle* (1898) – which Hasan Tawfiq al-Dijwi, a lawyer employed under Fathi Zaghlul as a clerk to the native courts, translated almost immediately into Arabic.[68]

A generation of mothers

A particular theme that could be drawn from these political discussions of the Egyptian mentality was a link between the country's 'moral inferiority' and the status of its women. The retarded development of the nation corresponded, it could now be argued, to the retarded development of the Egyptian woman. This was a favourite theme of the British colonial administrators. 'The position of women in Egypt', wrote Lord Cromer, is 'a fatal obstacle to the attainment of that elevation of thought and character which should accompany the introduction of European civilisation.' This civilisation would not succeed, he argued, if 'the position which women occupy in Europe is abstracted from the general plan'.[69] The 'position' the British had in mind was that of modern motherhood; for the political and economic transformation of Egypt required a transformation of the household.[70] If modern political authority was to work through the forming and disciplining of 'character', the individual household, it followed, had to be transformed into a site of this discipline. To this end it was necessary to break down existing patterns of association and segregation, mystified and romanticised under such labels as 'the harem'. 'The unwholesome – and frequently degrading – associations of the old harem life', wrote Cromer's Oriental Secretary Harry Boyle, should 'give place to the healthy and elevating influence of a generation of mothers, keenly alive to their responsibilities as regards the moral training and welfare of their children.'[71] In such ways political power would hope to penetrate that 'inaccessible' space invisible to 'the observation of the police' and thus commence, recalling a phrase from a previous chapter, to 'work from the inside out'.

The need to open up the inaccessible world of women and thereby produce 'a generation of mothers' was a theme taken up among Egyptian writers, in particular by Qasim Amin, a member of a large landowning family and one of the young government prosecutors employed, like Zaghlul, in the new, Europeanised legal system. If men were to study the situation of women in Egypt, he wrote, as men had already done in Europe, they would find that women are 'the source of their decline and the cause of their ruin'.[72] Around the turn of the century he published three widely discussed books on this general theme. The first of them, *Les égyptiens*, published while he was still in his twenties, was written in French as a response to a work by the Duc d'Harcourt that had attacked Britain's claim to be civilising the Egyptians.[73] The backwardness of the Egyptians, Harcourt had said, was due to certain mental traits that no administrative reforms by the British could ever noticeably alter. These included a submissive character, an insensibility to pain, a habit of dishonesty, and above all an intellectual lethargy that had rendered all Oriental societies immobile, unable to undergo any real historical or political transformation. The ideas, customs, and laws of the Arabs today were just as they had been one thousand years before. This sterility, said Harcourt, was due partly to the stifling effects of climate, but more to the element most uniform throughout the region, Islam. Islamic teachings created a profoundly altered moral sense, which destroyed all intellectual curiosity. So deep and longstanding were these traits that the people with whom one rubbed shoulders in the streets of Cairo differed from the people of France, Harcourt concluded, not only in the dazzling colour of their flowing robes, but in the very nature of the men.[74]

It was not unusual that an Egyptian writer should reply to these views. What is interesting is the form of the response. Qasim Amin did not question Harcourt's essential distinction between vitality as the characteristic of the

West and the thousand-year immobility of his own country, or the ascription of its causes to certain mental traits. In fact he went further and said that their consequence in present-day Egypt was a condition not just of relative decline, but of 'désorganisation absolue'. He differed with Harcourt by attributing this disorder, as he saw it, and the mental traits that caused it, not to Islam but to the abandoning of Islam. Religion had provided the principles of an order that was now lost. Egypt as a result faced a choice, between attempting to reestablish order by a return to the principles of Islam, and seeking a new basis altogether for social organisation – in the laws and principles of social science. In fact by starting to adopt over the last few decades ideas from contemporary Europe, Egypt seemed already to have chosen the second course. Whatever its merits, the choice had been something inevitable and impossible to resist, he felt, for the movement of European civilisation 'prend partout un caractère envahissant'. Europe's civilisation, he said, was 'la dernière dans l'ordre des civilisations' and possessed 'un caractère de longevité, j'allais dire d'irrévocabilité'.[75]

The end was to overcome the state of 'absolute disorganisation', which was to be done by making social science the new organising principle of society. This gave a new extent to the country's need for scientific knowledge. How in practice could this political need be met? The old method, sending a cadre of students to Europe to acquire and bring back science, would not be sufficient. One solution was to be the building in Egypt of a national university to produce an educated elite at home. But Qasim Amin began by proposing the formation of something far larger than an intelligentsia: an educated Egyptian motherhood. 'Je suis partisan absolue', he announced in *Les égyptiens*, 'd'une instruction relative pour les femmes.' Dismissing Harcourt's fanciful accounts of harems and eunuchs, Qasim Amin explained that within the Egyptian home it was women and not men who held power. It was this power that was to be engaged, in order to establish science as society's principle of order. Education must be given to girls, he said, to enable them as mothers to offer scientific answers to the eternal questioning of their children.[76] As he argued repeatedly in his subsequent writings, the process of creating a modern political order was to begin on the mother's knee.

Writings of this kind sought to isolate women as the locus of the country's backwardness. They were the holders of a power that was to be broken up by the new policies of the state, transformed into a means of social and political discipline. The family was to be organised as this house of discipline, which would then be able to produce, alongside the schools, the military and the other practices I have mentioned, the proper 'mentality' of the Egyptian – upon which the very possibility of a social order was understood to depend.

I now want to return to this question of the social order. Like the notion of mind or mentality, the social order was an abstraction. Like the mind, it indicated a mental or conceptual realm existing apart from the visible world of 'mere things' – the realm of order or structure. Discussing the army, model housing and the school in chapters 2 and 3, I suggested that the new methods of discipline and distribution in each case produced this sort of effect of a non-physical structure existing apart from things in themselves. Thus in the military, for instance, the coordination and control of men made an army seem like a machine, something more than the sum of its parts. The appearance of the military as a machine made the absence of such a structure in old armies suddenly visible; old armies now seemed like 'a crowd in a place of diversion'. Similarly, as we saw, the methods of discipline in the modern school made it suddenly possible to talk of the 'chaos' and the 'brouhaha' of the teaching mosque. Once the same methods of coordination and control were envisaged for the civilian and the city, existing cities in the same way suddenly appeared filled with the crowd. In terms of the new perception of the crowd one encounters the same sudden discovery of the problem of a social order.

The problem of society

The question of the crowd has already been mentioned in Egyptian accounts of journeys to Europe. What was remarkable about Paris or Marseilles was not only the layout of the buildings and the shops but the disciplined, industrious manner of the individual in the busy streets. 'Each person was occupied with his own business, proceeding on his way, taking care not to harm or interfere with anyone else.' Such descriptions are reminiscent of Edgar Allan Poe's 'Man in the crowd', who observed from his café window how 'by far the greater number of those who went by had a satisfied, businesslike demeanour, and seemed to be thinking only of making their way through the press. Their brows were knit and their eyes rolled quickly; when pushed against by fellow-wayfarers they evinced no symptom of impatience, but adjusted their clothes and hurried on.'[77] The crowd in the street, in fact, became a common topos in both Western and Egyptian writing. 'No subject', observed Benjamin, 'was more entitled to the attentions of nineteenth-century writers.'[78]

The crowd in the city's streets was the theme in a work of fiction that appeared in Egypt at the end of the nineteenth century. Like the works I examined in earlier chapters, the story was written in the form of a journey. But although its protagonists eventually find themselves in Paris (travelling there, I should add, to see the Exposition Universelle of 1900), for the first time in a work of modern Egyptian fiction the major events are set not in

Europe but in Cairo. The two protagonists, a young writer named Isa ibn Hisham and his elderly and respectable companion, the Pasha, are jostled by crowds from the very start of their journey. They meet in one of the cemeteries outside Cairo, where the Pasha, who lived in Cairo fifty years before, has returned from the dead to discover with shock and confusion what has happened to the city since. As they set off into the city, a donkey driver tries to cheat the Pasha over the payment of a fare and an argument breaks out. The Pasha calls the donkey driver an 'insolent peasant'. He in turn warns the Pasha 'we are in an age of liberty, and there is no distinction between the donkey driver and the prince'. Around them, we are told, a crowd has already formed. A policeman arrives, more interested in a bribe than in 'preserving order,' and marches the Pasha off to the police station. They are accompanied, the author adds, by the enormous crowd.[79]

In subsequent chapters the two characters journey through the modern streets of Cairo and the new spaces of its public life. They find themselves in the court house and the gaol, the hotel and the restaurant, theatres and dance halls, bars, cafés and brothels, accompanied throughout by the restless, noisy crowd. 'What is this enormous commotion?' asks the Pasha on one occasion, as they walk during the evening in the centre of the city, ' . . . this cleaving multitude, this crowd?' He supposes there must be some fantastic feast or funeral. 'No,' answers Isa ibn Hisham, 'just people congregating in public – companions spending an evening together and drinkers getting drunk.'[80]

This combination of the unruly commotion of life and the absence of all moral and political discipline repeats itself in almost every episode of the novel. The crowd is encountered not only in the brothel and the café but even at the final place they visit on their journey, the theatre. The theatre in Europe (a companion explains to the Pasha) is a place where people's morals are refined, by the portrayal of their history and other themes in dramatic form. Here it was very different. The actors danced, shouted, and caroused on stage, and the audience, composed of people from every class, did not sit silently like Europeans, as spectators, but joined in, laughing and applauding as a raucous crowd.[81]

The Tale of Isa ibn Hisham, as the book was called, was described by later writers as the most important work of imaginative literature of its generation.[82] It was very widely read. An expurgated version was later used by the Ministry of Education, as a text in all government secondary schools.[83] It has been interpreted as a work of social criticism that expresses the liberalism which emerged in the political thought of the period. The term liberalism tends to be misleading. The donkey driver's statement about an age of liberty has been cited to illustrate a major theme of the book, that Egyptians must be taught the principle of equality before the law.[84] But these words

115

come from the mouth of an insolent peasant. The concern of the book is not with equality of rights but with social chaos, a chaos suddenly visible in the indiscipline of the city's streets where the peasant behaves as an equal of the Pasha. Indiscipline is not usually considered a central concern of liberal thought, but rather than abandoning the label of liberalism I would prefer to use these writings from Egypt to understand liberalism in its colonial context. Egyptian liberalism spoke about justice and legal rights; but these concerns were contained within a wider problematic. Rights could only be enjoyed within a society of obedient and industrious individuals, and it was these characteristics, as we have seen, that Egyptians now suddenly seemed to lack. Liberalism was the language of a new social class, threatened by the absence of the mental habits of industry and obedience which would make possible a social order. *The Tale of Isa ibn Hisham* articulated the political fears of this class.

The novel was written by the thirty-year-old Muhammad al-Muwailihi and published between 1898 and 1902 in *Misbah al-Sharq*, a paper founded and edited by his father. The father was a member of a leading merchant household of Cairo, the Egyptian branch of a wealthy textile-trading family from the Hejaz (the Red Sea coast of Arabia). The history of the family is worth mentioning, for it illustrates the fortunes of this mercantile class. The Muwailihi's had grown prosperous in the eighteenth century with the prosperity of Egypt's Red Sea trade, and in the nineteenth century had become close political allies of the Egyptian ruling family. Such alliances, however, were unable to secure the country's large merchant families against the expansion of European commerce. In the 1870s, after being rescued from commercial ruin by the Khedive, the Muwailihi's were among those who led the nationalist opposition to Egypt's commercial and financial control by the European powers.[85] By the 1890s the son was employed as a government official under the British, who had responded to the nationalist uprising in 1882 by placing the country under military occupation.

Muhammad al-Muwailihi wrote *Isa ibn Hisham* at the same time as two influential friends of his own age, Qasim Amin and Ahmad Fathi Zaghlul, were writing the similar works of social criticism I have already mentioned, one describing the country's condition as a state of absolute disorganisation, the other as part of a universal social crisis.[86] The three men were all members of the same social and literary salon, where they mixed with fellow government servants, magistrates, and prosecuters, with members of some of the country's important Turkish families, with British officials, and with visiting Orientalist scholars.[87] The concern among those who gathered in such salons towards the end of the nineteenth century was not so much the colonial occupation, from which as landowners, merchants and government officials their families were beginning to benefit even as they resented the fact of European control, but the crowd that threatened in the streets and cafés outside.

Noise and confusion

The number of cafés, bars, and gaming rooms in Cairo increased more than threefold, from 2,316 to 7,475, in the last decade of the nineteenth century.[88] Descriptions of café life are found frequently in the literature of the period, particularly that concerned with describing the country's state of disorder. They enabled the writer to follow the existence of the crowd into confined, interior spaces.

> The café in Cairo is a place where the rabble gathers . . . in a space so confined that its occupants are almost overcome by the fumes that rise from the stoves and the smoke of the pipes and nargilehs; so that a person who walks in feels he has entered a burning fire, or the cramped confines of a prison. It is the source of numerous infections and diseases, and a refuge for the unemployed and the indolent, particularly in those places known for the consumption of hashish. The only thing one hears once inside are words repugnant to the ear and offensive to one's nature. The place is a scene of continual arguments and fights.[89]

In the café, as in the bar and the brothel, the particular 'disorders' of the crowd could be diagnosed – the first and most prevalent of which was always indolence and unemployment. In 1902 the work in Arabic on *The Present State of the Egyptians, or, The Causes of Their Retrogression* by Muhammad Umar discussed at length some of the further consequences of this indolence and these new forms of social life, including alcoholism, drug addiction, promiscuity, disease and insanity.[90] All of these were spreading alarmingly, the book said, especially among the poor.

Schooling among the poor was still insufficient, and if anyone should learn to read, the books available to them contained more illustrations than text, full of unwholesome stories such as 'The Fellah and the Three Women'. One such book had recently gone through six reprints in less than a month.[91] Family life was neglected. Men had taken to spending their days or their entire evenings in the more disreputable cafés, where women entertained and men told the stories of Don Juan.

Lunacy was another symptom that could now be diagnosed. Umar's book warned that the hospital for the insane in Abbasiyya, a new institution only recently set up by the British, was already so overcrowded with members of the lower classes that it was discharging into the streets hundreds who were still diseased, to make room for others even worse afflicted. A list of known causes of insanity for those admitted in 1899 was quoted, from the annual report of Mr Warnock, Director in Lunacy for the Egyptian government.

117

The careful classification of causes offered at least some sense of order:

Hashish	205	Loss of blood	7	Sexual incontinence	13
Alcohol	16	Typhoid fever	3	Food deficiency	13
Senility	10	Epilepsy	39	Idiocy and imbecility	10
Syphilis	27	Tuberculosis	2	Grief, poverty and distress	34
Heredity	29	Weakmindedness	24		

Addiction to alcohol and drugs, the author summarised, was part of a general weakness of will, which was causing more damage to social life among the poor than poverty itself.[92]

The author's own class – those who worked for the prosperity of the community in commerce, agriculture, and manufacturing (to be distinguished from the old aristocracy, he explained, who lived off income from property, emoluments, or inheritance), together with those who worked as scholars and writers – were set apart from all this by their sense of 'order'. They were not afflicted with the indolence found among the poor and even the very rich. This, the book emphasised, was thanks to the order introduced by the British, which had given them self-confidence and initiative in their affairs. The order stood in contrast to the chaos caused by the Urabi revolution that had preceded the British occupation of the country.[93]

'Noise and confusion' were the sort of terms in which men of this class described the situation around them. These were the words used by the writer Abd al-Hamid al-Zahrawi to describe the country's general condition. Zahrawi, a Syrian who lived in Egypt in this period, was later to serve in Paris as President of the First Arab Congress and was one of several dozen prominent Arab nationalists hanged for 'treason' by the Turkish government during the First World War. The noise and confusion was a social disease, he wrote, that had broken out over the community. The intelligent men one found among the scholarly community and those trained in modern science, among the old respectable families, and among those involved in large-scale agriculture and commerce, were in danger of being silenced and destroyed by this disorder, he wrote, this noise and confusion.[94]

Another threat to 'order' singled out in the writings of this class was Cairo's youth. They were under-educated, under-employed, and under-amused, and formed a distinct and potentially disruptive social problem. They lacked the discipline of an education, it was said, for schooling had done nothing to keep pace with the increase in population, and except among the country's Christian population had actually declined.[95] The youths took to the streets of the city every evening and roamed about in groups. Their latest fad (*bid`a*), we are told, was practical joking. The author of *The Present State of the Egyptians* mentioned that he himself had been a victim, accosted at his club by three strangers two of whom were dressed as women. They turned out to be young men from the government office where he worked, the sons of well-to-do families and probably drunk at the time.[96] During the daytime, instead of being occupied with school or work, young men idled their time, like the poor, in cafés, particularly in the late afternoon when the daily newspapers appeared, and argued without point or end over the latest Reuters reports. They should be made to understand, wrote Umar, that in civilised countries politics was a science, just like the other social sciences, and not a subject of idle debate in cafés.[97]

The social order

The nationalism that emerged during the later nineteenth century in Cairo, in its cafés and in the newspapers young men read there, in the salons of the new landowning families and government officials, in officers' quarters and in the open street, has often been understood as an 'awakening'. The image depicts a community that suddenly became self-aware, usually because prompted by Europeans. This awareness, it is said, was then gradually articulated, until it grew by the end of the First World War into anti-colonial revolt. The image of national awakening is problematic – not only because it has always implied that people were previously unawake and unaware (yet Cairo never lacked an active and resistant political life), but because there seems to follow from this the implication that nationalism always exists, as a singular truth about 'the nation' waiting to be realised. It is something discovered, not invented.[98]

Nationalism was not a singular truth, but a different thing among these different social groups. My concern here is with those who secured new wealth and political power under the British, and maintained it as the British withdrew. Their political writings were concerned with the threatening presence of the mass of working and unemployed Egyptians. This threatening presence took most often the form of the crowd. Somehow this crowd was to be ordered and made obedient and industrious. Its individuals were to be formed into an organised and disciplined whole. It was this obedient and regulated whole that was to be imagined under the name of the 'nation', that was to be constructed as Egyptian 'society'. And the word for this political process of discipline and formation was education.[99]

It was in terms of education that the notion of 'society' or 'social form' had first been introduced in the writings of the 1870s. 'The proper state of the education of individuals (both male and female), and its spread among them, Tahtawi had written, 'organises the proper state of the education of the collective form, that is, the community in its entirety.'[100] The formation of individuals was to be the means to the formation of a 'collective form'. Several such attempts were made to find a particular phrase or word for this collectivity that was to be organised by the discipline and instruction of individuals. Phrases such as *al-intizam al-umrani* (social organisation)[101] and *al-jam`iyya al-muntazima* (organised association)[102] were used, but the sort of phrase that became common was *al-hay'a al-mujtama`iyya* – *hay'a*, meaning 'form' itself, in the sense of visible shape or condition, qualified with the adjective from the word *mujtama`*, collective. Tahtawi in this case glossed the unusual and awkward expression *al-hay'a al-mujtama`iyya* (the collective form, society) by explaining that it stands for 'the community in its entirety'.

The Pasha in *The Tale of Isa ibn Hisham* had encountered this new expression in the midst of his encounter with the crowd. After his argument with the donkey driver and his night in gaol, he had found himself before the state prosecutor, amid 'a crowd of litigants'. 'Who is this servant-boy', he asked, 'and what is this crowd?' His companion explained that the young man, from a peasant family, was the prosecutor. According to the new order he was responsible for prosecuting criminals, 'on behalf of society (*al-hay'a al-ijtima`iyya*)'. What, asked the Pasha, is 'society'? It is the whole community (*majmu`at al-umma*), he was told.[103]

The neologism was explained but the Pasha's confusion concerning the new order remained – 'that people should be ruled over by a peasant, the community represented by a ploughboy!'[104] His confusion reflects the difficulty of imagining this new object called society. It was new in several respects. Its order was not a hierarchy of personal status, for peasants now appeared as equal members with gentlemen. Its membership was not a pattern of kinship extending outward, however distantly, from one's own connections. 'Society' was something encountered above all in the form of crowds. Somehow the strangers crowded together in the courtroom were to be conceived as parts of a social whole to which one belonged, even though nothing seemed to connect the Pasha to the crowd except their occupying the same space at the same moment. To conceive of these connections, and to construct them into a social whole was not necessarily a matter of extending one's horizons or enlarging one's imagination. It was more a matter of adopting new political and social practices, which brought a new set of assumptions. Certain practices involving self and space, order and time, body and mentality were to be adopted, of the kind I have been describing in this book, so that the dimensions of space and time and mentality appeared to stand apart as a conceptual structure, a whole; and it was to be forgotten that they were mere appearances.

In Europe in this period one finds the same attempt underway to envision 'society' as both a political and conceptual structure existing apart from people themselves, the same connection with the process of schooling and the same fears of the crowd. In order to bring out the peculiar nature of the connections between the crowd, the school and the conception of an object called society, it may help to recall the writings of a major European social theorist from this period. The work of Emile Durkheim, who trained as a school teacher in Paris in the 1880s and later lectured there on education and social theory, laid the base on which was built much of the twentieth century's scientific study of this new object, society. Durkheim's importance to social science was that he established society as something with an 'objective' existence, as a mental order independent of the individual mentality, and showed how this imaginary object might be studied.

Durkheim demonstrated that the social realm had an existence independent of particular individual minds by referring, in the first place, to the behaviour of the individual who joins a crowd. 'The great movements of enthusiasm, indignation, and pity in a crowd do not originate in any one of the particular individual consciousnesses', he wrote in *The Rules of Sociological Method*, published in 1895. 'They come to each one of us from without and can carry us away in spite of ourselves . . . Thus, a group of individuals, most of whom are perfectly inoffensive, may, when gathered in a crowd, be drawn into acts of atrocity.'[105] The tone of this passage already indicates what was to be politically at stake in establishing the object of social science. The problem of the potentially unbounded violence of the crowd is associated with an unbounded individual nature. Modern liberalism's originary fear of what any one of us might do 'in spite of ourselves' is a fear at the heart of liberal social science.[106] From the fear of the unbounded and undisciplined subject arises the need to know and to strengthen the objective existence of society.

The counterpart to the objective nature of society, in Durkheim's work as in all liberal social theory, was the necessity and the universal nature of education. Education, Durkheim wrote, is 'the means by which society perpetually recreates the conditions of its very existence'.[107] If society was an object existing apart from the individual, as a *conscience collective*, it required a mechanism for recreating its collective morality in the individual. This morality was a system of discipline, based on 'regularity and authority', and it was such discipline that schooling in the modern state was to inculcate. 'The child must learn to coordinate his acts and regulate them . . . He must acquire self-mastery, self-restraint, self-domination, self-determination, the taste for discipline and order in behaviour.' The coordination of individuals to form a nation-state depended upon this common discipline. In his lecture courses on 'The teaching of morality in the primary school', Durkheim explained that the purpose of universal secular state education was to make the child 'understand his country and times, to make him aware of its needs, to initiate him into its life, and in this way to prepare him for the collective tasks which await him'.[108]

A number of Egyptians attended Durkheim's lectures on education and social theory at the Sorbonne, including the writer and future education minister Taha Husayn. But the works on education and social theory that Taha Husayn and others chose to translate into Arabic were not those of Durkheim. They chose instead the writings of a better known contemporary, who in 1895, the same year as *The Rules of Sociological Method* appeared, published a famous work on *The Crowd*.

An elite of superior men

'I used to feel a resentment towards Egypt that I felt towards no other human society', wrote a columnist in the Egyptian paper *al-Mu'ayyad* in 1910. 'I would almost believe that its character and condition made it a strange exception – until I read this book.' The book was *Ruh al-ijtima`*, a translation of Gustave Le Bon's scientific study of the crowd, *Psychologie des foules*, and had been published in Cairo the previous year. 'It explains the nature of societies in general, eastern and western,' continued the columnist, 'and determines a single law that applies to all of them, without variants or exceptions. I have learnt that there is no difference between Egypt's people and the people of other countries.'[109] The book establishing this law was translated into Arabic by Ahmad Fathi Zaghlul, the translator of Demolins – and the estranged brother of the future nationalist leader Sa`d Zaghlul. Fathi Zaghlul was known among ordinary Egyptians as one of the members of the government tribunal set up in the Delta village of Dinshawai, following a fight there in which a British officer of the army of occupation had been killed. The tribunal had responded to this threat of popular violence against the colonial regime by ordering six of the villagers to be hanged. Zaghlul was now Under-Secretary in the Egyptian Ministry of Justice.[110] The book he translated seems to have been widely read, at least among those with similar fears concerning the threat of popular disorder. Scarcely two years later the future rector of the Egyptian University was writing that its ideas 'have been completely assimilated by Egyptian minds, as shown in the very vocabulary used by writers in the press'. The assimilation of the results of research by such social scientists (*ulama' al-ijtima`*) was helping to rectify Egyptian ideas about society. The laws it revealed, he said, were to be applied to guide the country forward.[111]

As part of this effort, several other works by Gustave Le Bon were translated into Arabic. Ahmad Fathi Zaghlul produced an Arabic version of *Les lois psychologiques de l'évolution des peuples*, while a translation of Le Bon's scientific study of schooling, *Psychologie de l'éducation*, was produced by the future rector's protégé Taha Husayn – the writer who was to become a dean of the University and later Minister of Education and Culture.[112] Le Bon's work as an Orientalist was equally important, as we will see, and two of his books were translated into Arabic: *La civilisation des Arabes*, and the third

part of *Les premières civilisations*.[113] These works profoundly influenced the
new nationalist historiography that writers of this class were starting to produce. Le Bon, in sum, was probably the strongest individual European
influence in turn-of-the-century Cairo on the political thought of Egypt's
emergent bourgeoisie.

There was nothing unusual about the influence of Le Bon's social
theories. His book on the crowd has been described as 'possibly the most
influential book ever written in social psychology'.[114] His work also influenced political leaders, including Mussolini (who is said to have frequently
consulted the work on the crowd) and Theodore Roosevelt. When the
former American president visited Cairo in 1910 and announced contro-
versially in an address at the new National University that Egyptians were
not sufficiently evolved to deserve self-government, he was carrying with
him, along with the Bible, a copy of Le Bon's book on the psychological laws
of the evolution of peoples.[115]

Le Bon's work as a popular social scientist and Orientalist addressed two
major issues: how to account for the difference between advanced and backward societies, and how to account for the difference within a society
between the mass of its people and the elite. He had contributed in his early
work to the new literature on intelligence, as the variable most closely
correlated to the level of advancement of a race. Intelligence was measured
by the volume and diameter of the skull, which were shown to increase as the
brain itself evolved in size and complexity. (These findings of Le Bon were
used by Durkheim, in his early work on *The Division of Labour in Society*.)[116]
Le Bon claimed to be the inventor of the pocket cephalometer, a caliper
device with which a traveller could record the size of a people's heads, and
thereby calibrate the degree of their advancement.[117] By this criterion, the
black, yellow, and Caucasian races were clearly distinguishable as three
separate stages on the ladder of evolution.

Anatomical variables were unsuccessful, however, in explaining one
major difference in cultural and political development, namely the gap
between the two branches of the Caucasian race, the Europeans of the north
and the Semites of the Middle East. Le Bon rejected language or institutions
as an alternative variable, and in writing about the Arabs introduced instead
the idea of a people's psyche or soul, the collective mind of the group or race.
Every nation had a 'mental constitution' – no doubt corresponding to
anatomical variables in the brain, but variables which science was not yet
precise enough to detect – that was composed of its sentiments, ideas, and
beliefs, and was created by a process of slow, hereditary accumulation.[118] It
was this idea of a collective mind or mental constitution that Durkheim,
originally influenced by Le Bon, developed into the modern concept of
society.[119]

The national mind was 'the synthesis of a people's entire past', Le Bon explained, and took many generations to evolve. It followed from this that Europe would be unable to introduce modern civilisation, as was being frequently proposed, to other parts of the world simply by education. 'A negro or a Japanese may easily take a university degree or become a lawyer', wrote Le Bon in one of his works translated into Arabic. 'The sort of varnish he thus acquires is however quite superficial, and has no influence on his mental constitution.' Europe would have to alter not just the level of intelligence of a nation it hoped to modernise, as was then commonly thought, but its psyche. 'To enable it to bequeath its civilisation to another people, it would be necessary that it should be able to bequeath its soul.'[120]

Le Bon also made the point that the ideas and culture of a nation were developed not among the mass of a nation but largely among its elite. Between the masses in a country such as Egypt therefore, and those in parts of Europe, the difference in the level of development might not be very great. 'What most differentiates Europeans from Orientals is that only the former possess an *élite* of superior men', he explained. This small phalanx of eminent men found among a highly civilised people 'constitutes the true incarnation of the forces of a race. To it is due the progress realised in the sciences, the arts, in industry, in a word in all the branches of civilisation.' As so much of the ethnographic writing of this period was demonstrating, individuals in less civilised communities displayed a great degree of equality among themselves. From this there followed an important conclusion, which helps explain the popularity of Le Bon among writers of a certain class in Egypt. Modern progress must be understood as a movement towards increasing inequality.[121]

Progress involved the steady growth of an elite and its achievement of civilisation by long hereditary accumulation. Yet this accumulation, warned Le Bon, although inherited in the very cells of the brain, could be quickly and easily lost. These cells were subject to physiological laws just like those of any other organ, and when no longer employed to fulfil its function the brain atrophied very quickly. Those qualities of character accumulated over centuries by an avanced people, namely 'courage, initiative, energy, the spirit of enterprise', could very quickly disappear.[122]

The collective mind

Le Bon developed these ideas in his work on the history of Arab civilisation, which was translated into Arabic in Beirut and widely read in Egypt among the country's political elite.[123] (Among those who admired the book was Muhammad Abduh, the Egyptian scholar and educationalist whose re-interpretation of Islamic history and doctrine was to have a wide influ-

124

ence. Abduh's view of a reformed Islam, as a system of social discipline and instruction with which an intellectual and political elite would organise the country's 'political education' and thus assure its stability and its evolution, was indebted to his reading of Le Bon and other French social scientists; and indeed when he visited France he paid a call on Le Bon.)[124] In *Les lois psychologiques de l'évolution des peuples*, the second of Le Bon's works translated into Arabic by Fathi Zaghlul, the same theories were presented more comprehensively. The progress of a nation was conditional upon the growth in power of its elite.

In the work on the crowd which he wrote soon afterwards, the same principles were applied to a problem found not between societies but within them. How was it, Le Bon asked, that when individuals joined a social group they seemed to undergo a mental change, to lose something of their intelligence and moral restraint? To this pressing political question he introduced a novel answer. The group was an organism whose individual cells merged to form a living body, Le Bon wrote, a 'provisional being' that possessed an unconscious collective mind. In this merger individual psychological differences – the source as he had shown of all excellence – were lost, leaving only what was common, the residue of psychological or racial unconscious. Crowds therefore were like less intelligent beings, like children or lunatics or women, said Le Bon, evoking as metaphors the fears of his generation and class.[125] They were impulsive, irritable, alternately generous and cruel, credulous, respectful of force, and wishing always to be dominated and ruled. They were like not only lunatics, children, or women, but also that other less intelligent form, the backward nation or race. This comparison with more primitive states was presented not just as a metaphor but as a factual description of the psychological change that took place when the individual joined the crowd. 'By the mere fact that he joins an organised group,'Le Bon explained in the phrase that for Freud expressed his major contribution, 'a man descends several rungs on the ladder of civilisation.'[126] The difference between the individual and the crowd was identical to that between the advanced nation and the backward. The two inferior social conditions represented the same retarding in the state of psychological evolution caused by the absence of the individual excellence of the elite.

The fear of the crowd, then, was linked to the problematic need to create society, which required on the one hand the formation of an elite, and on the other – as Le Bon himself explained in his other writings – the disciplinary system of modern schooling. Le Bon's ideas were to fall out of fashion, largely because of the weakness of their biological foundation. Durkheim's efforts to address the same issues have lasted much better. A major reason for this is that Durkheim explained the existence of the social order in terms of what I would call the representational nature of social phenomena. His social theory, therefore, coincided with the more and more 'exhibitional' nature of the modern state. To conclude this chapter, I want to point out the role of representation in Durkheim's theory of society.

The behaviour of the crowd, Durkheim explained, was an indication that society was a thing; something with an 'objective' existence. The object consisted of shared ideas or beliefs. In phenomena such as the crowd, he wrote, these collective beliefs 'acquire a body, a tangible form'; their acquisition of a bodily form demonstrated that shared beliefs 'constitute a reality in their own right'. The independent reality or objectness of the social, in other words, was a reality constituted by the ability of this ideal object always to present itself in a non-ideal, material body. Another example of such embodiment was the representation of shared ideas in statistics: 'currents of opinion', Durkheim wrote, '. . . are, in fact, represented with considerable exactness' in such figures, whose average provides a material representation of 'a certain state of the group mind'. Besides this example, what gave an objective character to any aspect of the shared social order – legal, moral or cognitive – was its embodiment in a material representation. The entire social realm was known to exist only through representations: 'Law is embodied in codes; the currents of daily life are recorded in statistical figures and historical monuments; fashions are preserved in costumes; and taste in works of art. By their very nature', Durkheim concluded, social facts '. . . tend toward an independent existence.'[127] The reality or objectivity of the social resided in its representational nature.

Society, thus, was a thing – that is, something that occurs representationally. To the extent that what we call 'material' objects were arranged to represent a non-material realm of ideas – whether in the modern machinery of fashion and the accompanying consumer industry, in works of art arranged in exhibitions (and in the objects displayed in museums, no doubt, and in zoos), in the organisation of historical monuments and the rest of the modern tourist industry, in the codification of law and the general codification of behaviour, or in compilations of statistics and the whole machinery of social science – they indicate or exhibit the existence of a shared conceptual order. In the world-as-exhibition, as I suggested in chapter 1, these processes of representation were taken to be the process of order itself. In the modern state, they were the method by which the apparent existence of a conceptual realm, the separate realm of meaning or order, was to be achieved.

Colonising Egypt, in the broad sense of the penetration of a new principle of order and technique of power, was never merely a question of introducing a new physical discipline or a new material order. In the first place, disciplinary powers were themselves to work by constructing their object as something twofold. They were to operate in terms of a distinction between the physical body that could be counted, policed, supervised and made industrious, and an inner mental space within which the corresponding habits of obedience and industry were to be instilled. But more importantly, this new divided personhood – whose novelty I will be returning to in chapter 6 – was to correspond to a divided world. The world was something to be constructed and ordered according to an equivalent distinction between physical 'things' and their non-material structure. Politically, the most important such structure was to be 'society' itself, a social order now conceived in absolute distinction to the mere individuals and practices composing it.

In the colonial age, as Durkheim's writings indicate, this effect of an abstract social realm is more and more to be built into things. The monuments, buildings, commodities, fashions and experiences of the world-as-exhibition are all to be understood as mechanisms presenting themselves as mere 'things', always thereby claiming to re-present a further realm – the realm of meaning, which is to become synonymous with the social. Such a machinery of the social order and of truth is to become the political principle inhabiting not only colonial urban architecture, methods of instruction, or commercial practice. In the colonisation of Egypt it can be found transforming even the most local mechanisms of meaning, the very process of writing.

Chapter 5

The machinery of truth

The bombardment of Alexandria, we are told by an Englishman who witnessed from a ship at sea the event that had initiated the colonial occupation of Egypt,

commenced on Tuesday, July 11, 1882 at seven o'clock in the morning. From where the *Tanjore* was anchored we could see the whole thing quite clearly through our glasses. To a civilian who had never seen warfare the spectacle was magnificent.[1]

Within two days most of Alexandria was turned to rubble and ash. How far its destruction was due to the British bombardment and how far to the local inhabitants who responded by setting fire to European property was never determined. It scarcely seemed to matter that Britain caused such loss to the Europeans for whom it claimed to be acting in self-defence. 'The patience . . . of the British public was exhausted', we are told, and 'something effectual' had to be done.[2] Following the bombardment the marines were sent ashore, accompanied by a new kind of armament invented in the 1860s, the Gatling machine gun. With the help of this rapid-fire weapon, after a week of street fighting they took possession of the town.

Machine guns then accompanied the British as they proceeded with their larger purpose, to overthrow the new nationalist government. Junior officers in the Egyptian army had assumed power a year before – promising, if not a revolution, at least an end to the absolute power of the Turkish elite and their European creditors, and to the crippling indebtedness of the peasants. They were defeated by the British forces within the space of eight weeks. In the final battle at Tell al-Kabir the new machine guns 'gave most effective support, firing with great judgment upon the enemy whenever exposed to them'.[3] The mechanical efficiency of the invasion was then turned into a demonstration of Britain's military power. 'On the 30th September a grand parade before the Khedive of all the [British] troops took place. The army had for the purpose gradually been concentrated on Cairo. It was no mere question of show and no mere holiday spectacle. It is hardly possible to imagine a sight more calculated to impress an Eastern population than the display of the various arms of the little force which had in so short a time disposed of the fate of Egypt.'[4] More than a mere spectacle, the display of arms demonstrated to an 'Eastern population' the effectiveness and authority of Britain's military occupation. The speed and efficiency epitomised in the new machine guns on show was made the mark of Britain's colonial authority.

Reading the official history of the invasion published by the War Office in London, one senses the remarkable self-certainty with which the British prepared and carried out the occupation. This self-certainty was made possible by the enormous resources of the British Empire, including its new weaponry. It was a certainty that seemed to be generated in particular out of the coordination of these resources, by the modern means of transport and communication. 'The following statement', says the official history in its own self-certain style, describing the days before the shelling of Alexandria, 'will give some idea of the questions that at this time had to be settled.'

Arrangements were made to provide tents, wood as fuel for 20,000 men for sixty days from Cyprus, and to be ready to purchase mules. The formation of a railway-construction company of engineers, the organisation of a corps of military police, regulations as to newspaper correspondents, were determined on. The establishment of hospitals at Gozo (Malta) and Cyprus, water supply, revolvers, carts, the extension of service of men then serving with regiments from six years to seven years,

10 Alexandria after the British bombardment, 1882.

had to be considered . . . The formation of a Postal Corps was determined on and a scheme for it devised. It was decided to arrange with the Indian Government the dispatch of troops from thence. All these points had been settled, and the details departmentally worked out, by the 10th July.[5]

The control of communication brought together all the military resources of the Empire and concentrated them at the scene of the battle. Railways were constructed to carry the forces from one engagement to the next. The telegraph wire and postal service advanced at the same pace, carrying the daily reports of newspaper correspondents – as well as the private letters of soldiers – back to the impatient 'British public' on whose behalf the war was fought.

The coordinated movement of commands, of soldiers and supplies, of news reports, even of private correspondence, all contributed to Britain's military effectiveness; it all provided a further instance, in other words, of the effectiveness of the methods of order and discipline I have been examining in the preceding chapters. But such coordination also contributed, no doubt, to the effect of self-certainty. The sudden breakthroughs in developing the technology of communication during the last third of the nineteenth century, which were to culminate in 1895 in Marconi's successful demonstration of the wireless telegraph, made possible both the continuing penetration of the colonial order and also what might be called its truth. They gave global political power not just its detailed practicality but its facticity. From the tourist spectacles of bombardment and the displays of weaponry to the telegraphed news report and the postcard home, global colonialism came into being not only as a local method of order, seeking to work with individual minds and bodies, but as a process that was continuously reporting, picturing and representing itself. The great exhibitions that I discussed in chapter 1 were only particular highlights of this continuous representational process. Within such a world of representations the general public – that curious body – could be formed and entertained, and a modern political certainty produced. It is this question of certainty, raised in chapters 1 and 2, to which I now want to return.

One could study such global certainty as simply the end result of various long historical developments. In this view the steadily increasing range, speed and certainty of means of communication coupled with the increasing range, speed and certainty of means of destruction would correspond, and contribute, to the increasing range, speed and certainty, so to speak, of the truth and authority of modern political power. Such an approach, however, would take the nature of this kind of power and authority for granted, and examine its growth rather than its peculiar quality. It would not explore, in other words, the representational dimension of this power, a power which worked more and more by the methods I have referred to as the world-as-exhibition. What I want to describe here is the distinctiveness of this kind of power and truth. It is a truth of the age of telegraphs and machine guns, of representations and exhibitions, and is an authority imagined and produced in the image of such mechanisms. Our thinking about this authority, however, is itself something that lives within the language of machinery and communication – the language of representation. Contained in this manner, we are generally constrained from considering the very peculiar way in which the truth of such political authority is produced.

To see the peculiarity of this authority I propose rather than examining its origins to compare it with the modes of achieving authority and truth which colonial power, in the case of Egypt, was to replace. I am going to do so by looking in particular at the question of writing. I have two reasons for examining political authority in the use of words. First, as we saw earlier when looking at the teaching mosque of al-Azhar, the authoritative interpretation of legal and scholarly texts was a significant aspect of the way in which an older political authority used to work. Second, what happened to writing in later nineteenth-century Egypt provides a parallel with wider political changes. A transformation that occurred in the nature of writing corresponded to the transformation in the nature of political authority. Both writing and politics, I am going to argue, came to be considered something essentially mechanical. Their essence in both cases would be considered a process of communication. Communication and machinery might appear to be neutral and matter-of-fact notions. But it was these seemingly innocent processes, the mechanisms of the world-as-exhibition, that served to introduce a modern and mysterious political metaphysics.

Eight words

In October 1881, a month after the nationalist leader Ahmad Urabi had lined up his troops in front of the Khedival Palace and forced the regime to accept his popular demands, thereby precipitating the British invasion to restore Khedival power, a book had been published in Cairo entitled *The Essay on Eight Words (Risalat al-kalim al-thaman)*. The book discussed the meaning of eight words 'current on the tongues of the younger generation today', nation, homeland, government, justice, oppression, politics, liberty and education. It was written by Husayn al-Marsafi, the senior professor at Dar al-Ulum, the *école normale* set up in Cairo ten years earlier to produce teachers for the new government schools, who was among the most prominent of the established scholars and teachers of his time. Significantly, he was also the mentor of Mahmud Sami Pasha al-Barudi, the officer and poet

131

who was to become Prime Minister the following year of the short-lived nationalist government.[6]

The vocabulary and thinking of the nationalist leadership was reflected in *Eight Words*. Addressing the political crisis as a crisis found in the misuse and misunderstanding of words, the book's major theme was the need for the authority and discipline of a national system of education. Colonel Urabi's own ideas concerning 'political matters' had first been formed from reading about the military training of the French and the manner in which they were 'drilled and organised', and in their manifesto of 1881 the nationalist leaders declared that the aim of the Egyptian people was 'to complete their national education'. This they sought to achieve by means of a parliament, the press, and the spread of schooling, adding in the manifesto that 'none of these means of education can be secured except by the firm attitude of national leaders'.[7] Thus the nationalists seized power in October 1881 not so much in the name of revolution as in the name of Egypt's 'national education'. Urabi brought his regiment out of the barracks and took them by train from Cairo to the Delta town of Zaqaziq, near the village of his birth. There he gave a speech asserting 'the usefulness and necessity of a good education', and as his first act of national leadership laid the foundation stone of a new school.[8]

Eight Words was sympathetic to the grievances of the nationalist officers, while warning them against mistaking factionalism for patriotism. The eight words it discussed were the new vocabulary of modern nationalism, whose proper use required, in turn, the school-centred authority of the nation-state. Marsafi supported the general spread of schooling, so that teachers would be able to use words like 'patriotism' repeatedly in the classroom and explain their proper meaning. The book criticised traditional scholars for having lost their moral and political authority, and advocated in their place the new authority of teachers over students in the government schools. And yet, the book was still caught up in other, older notions of authority. Unlike the nationalist leadership, Marsafi was opposed to the uncontrolled spread of printing in Egypt. He argued the need for a body of properly educated scholars who would be responsible for the books and journals to be printed, in order to control the misuse of writing. Indeed, he understood the political crisis as a whole in terms of the breakdown of a textual authority, evident in the proliferation of words 'on the tongues of the younger generation today'.

Although as a scholar of enormous talent Marsafi had been drawn into the educational politics of the new state, in many ways he still belonged to a different tradition of scholarship and authority. He was a man from a small village in the Nile Delta, trained at al-Azhar, and blind from birth. He had grown up within an intellectual and political tradition in which the city depended upon the countryside rather than dominating it, allowing particular villages to provide generations of Cairene scholars. This was a tradition which rejected the use of the printing press and accepted blindness (there was an entire college for the blind at al-Azhar) for the same reason. Namely, that the only way to read a text and retain its uncertain authority was to hear it read aloud, phrase by phrase, by one who had already mastered it, and to repeat and discuss it with such a master.

This sort of tradition in respect of words and their transmission stands in marked contrast to the proliferation of telegraphs, news reports, and even private correspondence among the British. Marsafi was a remarkable scholar. Unlike many Azhar scholars, he was open to the innovations of European methods of schooling and had even acquired, despite his blindness, the ability to read French. It seems strange, that at a moment of profound political crisis he should be as preoccupied as he was with questions of proper linguistic usage and the threat of an uncontrolled spread of new vocabularies. Marsafi's response to the crisis echoes that of an earlier Egyptian scholar, the historian al-Jabarti, writing on the previous occasion when the country faced the threat of occupation by a European army. The French forces that invaded Egypt in 1798, like the British in 1882, had employed innovative methods of communication. Jabarti's account noted, as I mentioned in chapter 2, how the French 'make signs and signals among themselves that they follow and never deviate from'. Still more indicative of the unusual nature of European power was that the French arrived to conquer Egypt with a printing press.

Landing at Alexandria and advancing upon Cairo, Napoleon's first act had been to issue a printed proclamation to the Egyptian people, prepared in Arabic by French Orientalists. Jabarti's response to this strange innovation, in a chronicle written in the midst of the crisis, was an interesting one. He began his account by copying the text of the proclamation, and followed it for several pages with a detailed list of its grammatical errors. Phrase by phrase he pointed out the colloquialisms, misspellings, ellipses, inconsistencies, morphological inaccuracies and errors of syntax of the French Orientalists, drawing from these incorrect usages a picture of the corruptions, deceptions, misunderstandings and ignorance of the French authorities.[9]

The contrast between the critical and sometimes hostile response among Muslim scholars to the introduction of an Arabic printing press and the efficient and advanced techniques of the French military scholars is sometimes taken to exemplify the history of Egypt's relationship with the modern West. It took the Napoleonic occupation to introduce to the Middle East the first Arabic press, and the absence of printing over the preceding centuries has often been cited as evidence of the backwardness and isolation of the Arab world that the French occupation was to shatter. After the departure of the French soldiers the Egyptian government did manage to set up its own press. But this was essentially a part of the country's new military equipment; the bulk of what was printed in the first half of the century was for purposes of military instruction.[10] The few individuals who tried to extend the use of the press outside the military project subsequently found themselves removed from office and in some cases exiled. By the 1850s, when Egypt had been forced to abandon its military ambitions, the press had fallen into disrepair, and in 1861 it was formally shut down.[11] Printing was started up again by the government under Isma`il, and by the time of the nationalist uprising there was an active periodical press. But the government attempted to suppress whatever publication it did not control, and establishment scholars like Marsafi spoke out against the press, blaming the political crisis in part on the wanton spread of printing.[12] Thus the story of printing in Egypt seems to confirm the backwardness of the Arab world, its continuing resistance to change, and the irrational hostility of Muslim scholars towards modern learning. However, rather than evidence of others' backwardness, resistance and irrationality, I think these attitudes towards the technology of printing can point us towards an understanding of some of our own strange ideas about the nature of writing, and the political assumptions to which they correspond. To understand these ideas, I am going to examine Marsafi's own purposes in writing *Eight Words*.

Ibn Khaldun

The first clue to an understanding of Marsafi's purpose is the book's title. 'Eight words' refers to the eight political terms discussed, but it also refers, I think, to politics itself. The reference is to the so-called 'ring of eight words' found in popular wisdom literature and political writings, in which the nature of the political was always expressed. Rifa`a al-Tahtawi's major work *Manahij al-albab al-misriyya*, for example, which had appeared a decade before Marsafi's text, began its interpretation of the meaning of politics by citing the circle of eight words.[13] The eight words denoted the eight parts of the political world, with the meaning of each one interpreted in terms of the next: ' . . . the sovereign is an order supported by soldiers, the soldiers are assistants sustained by means of wealth, wealth is nourishment gathered by the subjects' and so on, so that 'each term is tied to the next and the last returns to the first, joining them in a circle whose end is not marked'.[14] The circle derives from the same origins as Aristotle's golden octagon, but the source for Arab scholars of the nineteenth century was the work of the great fourteenth-century North African writer, Ibn Khaldun. Ibn Khaldun's seven-volume study of the conditions and history of human social life, *Kitab al-ibar*, had been one of the first works published on the new presses set up in Cairo in the 1860s, in the first printed edition of the complete text.[15] The work was being read among students and intellectuals, in particular at the new teachers' training college, where both Marsafi and Muhammad Abduh are known to have lectured on Ibn Khaldun.[16]

Book one of Ibn Khaldun's work, known as *The Muqaddima*, presented his theory of human society, a theory addressed to the political crisis of his own age. The entire theory of the governing of human communities, he wrote, if studied with due attention, could be understood as a commentary upon the ring of eight words.[17] Marsafi, taking his title perhaps from this passage, was also writing in a period of political crisis. In many ways, of course, the crisis of Marsafi's age was unique, for the penetration of European capital had caused an unprecedented weakening of the kind of local authority whose nature I want to describe. Yet the weaknesses of this authority were something generic, and were described better than anywhere in the work of Ibn Khaldun. It was an authority, in the first place, as I suggested in an earlier chapter, that seemed by nature to be unstable. Its tendency was to expand continuously, until its strength began to degenerate and it proceeded to fragment itself and become dispersed. Its effectiveness always decreased towards its edges, being weaker in the countryside than in the city and weakest of all where the countryside met the desert. Its strength lay in the strength of those who ruled, and the strength of the bonds between them. In the second place, it was an authority that made particular use of the authoritative interpretation of texts. Texts too carried their own authority, an authority which mirrored that of politics in its tendency to degenerate over time and become corrupt. The proper preservation and interpretation of the authority of writing was in this sense an essential resource of political power. The crisis and collapse of political power, in turn, was addressed by Ibn Khaldun in terms of the degeneration and collapse of scholarship.

Marsafi's own intellectual career was part of an attempt, on the part of himself and other Azhar-trained scholars drawn into the educational politics, to extend and make secure political authority in Egypt by means of the revival of learning. He wished to draw on Ibn Khaldun's discussion of scholarship, in an effort to revive on the basis of existing notions of authorship and the power of writing a political authority that worked through literature. The attempt failed, but the failure can throw light on the change in the nature of writing and politics that was to take place.

The subject of Marsafi's lectures was the art of proper writing in Arabic, taught through the study of its literature. Marsafi had revived through his lectures the study of an enormous range of Arabic literature, both poetry and prose, which most al-Azhar scholars, entrenching themselves intellectually during the upheavals of the previous fifty years or more, had neglected.[18] The purpose of this learning was more political than the term 'literature' might suggest. The body of literature being taught was known as *adab*, a word meaning manners, politeness, or propriety. 'Polite letters' was a literature that embodied the manners of a threatened social order and the values of an imperilled social class. There was an *adab* appropriate to every social position, establishing in life the patterns of proper conduct.[19] The study of polite letters would establish among people the boundaries and the patterns of social action. 'The real meaning of *adab*', Marsafi explained, 'is that each should know the limits of his position, and not overstep them.'[20]

The manner in which a proper learning would serve a political authority was made clear in *Eight Words*. The book was introduced as a *sharh*, a work of textual criticism, which would interpret the real meanings of important words.[21] The book was full of references to written sources whose texts were grafted into its own, including the Quran, the Traditions of the Prophet, an enormous range of works in Arabic literature, and even a number of works in French.[22] But these were not its only sources. Political activity itself was a sort of reading, that is, an interpretation of words which required criticism.

Marsafi understood the political crisis within which he wrote as the attempt by particular groups to give particular meanings to words, such as liberty and injustice.[23] The liability of these words was to be misused and misinterpreted. Like all words, they carried the risk of being placed out of context, or spoken in the wrong sense. This verbal liability was not the result of the prevailing political disorder, but the symptom and nature of the crisis. There was no analytic separation in this approach between writing and politics, or between theory and practice. Every political act was an interpretation of words, and thus a textual act, a reading. Marsafi's own purpose was to interpret the 'real meaning' (*haqiqa*) of every word he treated, and from there to see that meaning 'realised' (*haqqaqa, tahaqqaqa*) in political life. The political world was not a posited object, independent of written language. Words were not labels that simply named and represented political ideas or objects, but interpretations whose force was to be made real.[24] The scholar responded, therefore, to a socio-political crisis such as the events of 1881–82 with attempts to provide the proper interpretation of words.

Employing and reworking the writing of Ibn Khaldun, Marsafi said that besides the specialised knowledge required in every occupation there was a general body of understandings (*umum al-ma`arif*) that all individuals must acquire. The survival and well-being of the community depended on the acquisition of such shared understandings, for it was these that enabled the separate social groups to think of their work, in its variety and diversity, as the labour of a single person. Without this conception of a single body that a shared understanding produces, the 'realisation of the community' (*tahaqquq al-umma*) was not possible. It was through its common learning, shared among its members, that the community itself is distinguished from other groups. The danger for a community that failed to realise these shared meanings was that the community would split into separate factions and fall into the hands of foreigners.[25] It was to counter such a crisis that Marsafi wrote.

Marsafi concluded *Eight Words* by stating that intelligent men in the community were to pay particular attention, within these understandings, to what concerned the habits and character of the people, and distinguish between the good and the bad; and that those who taught in the new schools were to make patriotism (*al-wataniyya*) the basis of their instruction. Every trade and occupation was to be taught in a way which brought out that the work is in the service of the community. By using the word 'patriotism' frequently in class, teachers could help to realise its meaning, so that the community would deserve its name and become one in reality.[26]

To sum up so far then, Marsafi's book was suspicious of printing and suggestive of Ibn Khaldun. Printing was part of the general problem of the 'spreading of words' that seemed somehow the nature of the political crisis. Political authority, in turn, was associated with the authority of writing. Extending the authority of writing, through schools and proper learning, was the means to restore and make secure political authority. The importance of Ibn Khaldun was that he addressed the general question of authority in terms of the question of authorship, thus directly linking the political crisis to the issue of writing. To understand the nature of this link, I want to compare what writing was, for Ibn Khaldun and for Husayn al-Marsafi, with our own understanding of how words work. I will begin with certain strange assumptions of our own.

This ideal existence

In the events of 1880–82, Ahmad Urabi and his fellow political leaders called themselves *al-hizb al-watani*. A *hizb* is a party or faction, and the phrase meant the patriotic or nationalist faction, those who were opposed to the control of Egypt by foreigners, whether Turkish or European. In *Eight Words* Husayn al-Marsafi warned the nationalists against dividing the country into hostile ethnic groups, invoking for the purpose some further associations of the word *hizb*. Compared to the unity implied by the word *umma*, which means community or nation, Marsafi argued, the word *hizb* implied self-interest and factionalism (*tahazzub*). The word's associations were brought out to discredit the politics of those who used it. Political argument always worked through this power of language, seeking out the contradictions in words or their ability to evoke alternative meanings. Urabi

137

in turn tried to bring out different associations of the word. When he was put on trial after the defeat of the nationalist movement by the British, his interrogators asked him why he had allowed himself to be called 'the leader of *al-hizb al-watani*'. Urabi replied by associating the word *hizb* with the fractures running through the whole country, and its domination by foreigners. The inhabitants of Egypt, he pointed out, are divided into separate races each of which could be considered a *hizb*. 'The native people of the country (*ahl al-bilad*) are a *hizb* in themselves', he argued before the judges, adding that 'they are called "the peasants" in order to humiliate them'.[27]

Urabi's statements in court are quoted in the article on the modern term 'Hizb' in the *Encyclopaedia of Islam*, with a very different approach to language. The article's purpose is to show how the word *hizb*, 'albeit slowly, unconsciously and hesitatingly . . . has come to be stabilized in meaning and to signify unambiguously a political party'. Urabi's powerful claim that both the nationalist leadership and the Egyptian people could be called a *hizb* is cited to illustrate what is called the originally 'ambiguous and fluctuating' meaning of the term. The word 'stands in Urabi's mind for two different meanings', says the *Encyclopaedia*, 'which he cannot clearly distinguish'. Since Urabi's time, it can then be shown, the word has evolved, 'albeit slowly', from this state of confusion to one of clarity – a movement, in other words, from hesitation to certainty, from ambiguity to unambiguousness, from instability to stability, and from unconsciousness, it is implied, to political awareness. The movement traced by the *Encyclopaedia*, moreover, is not just the history of a word. The word stands in people's minds for a meaning, and its development is taken to represent the gradual development of this meaning, this political mind.[28]

There are two assumptions that govern this approach to language, neither of them fully shared by Urabi or his contemporaries. The first is that the proper nature of words is to be clear, stable and univocal, and that a word acquires more power the closer it comes to this ideal. The second is that the study of words is the study of some larger abstraction for which they stand – the political mind or culture or meaning of a certain community.

Telegraph signals

At the time of Urabi's trial, as the countries to the north were embarking on a global expansion of their colonial power, European theories of language were dominated by the work of those who had come to be known as 'Orientalists'. Oriental scholarship, as Edward Said has shown, grew in importance in the nineteenth century with the growth of European commercial and colonial interest in the Orient. If the expansion of Orientalism was due to the position of the Orient within Europe's expanding power, the strength of Oriental studies was also due to the position of this Orient within the patterns of nineteenth-century European knowledge. Since the end of the preceding century, to know a thing had come to involve knowing the stages of its internal development, its 'history' in the new sense of that word. This was true of the two pioneering nineteenth-century sciences, geology, which had unfolded the life-history of the earth, and biology, which had unfolded the life-history of the physical organism.[29] It was equally true for the life-history of the human mind, whose unfolding was Orientalism. 'Whether in the petrified strata of ancient literature or in the countless variety of living languages and dialects,' claimed Professor Max Müller of Oxford, invoking the parallels of geology and biology in a single phrase, ' . . . we collect, arrange, and classify all the facts of language that are within our reach.'[30]

Analogously with his physical body and his planet, man himself was now to be understood not in the psychology of his power of reason, but in the development of this relatively new and peculiar object, the human mind. Orientalism was 'the experimental science', in the words of the great French Orientalist Ernest Renan, which would uncover 'an embryogeny of the human mind'.[31] The raw material of this empirical science of 'the mind' was provided by Oriental languages. Just as geology had given a meaning to be read in the strata of the rock, and biology a meaning in the fossil, Orientalism had given to ancient words, uncovered in Oriental texts, the means of providing 'a comprehension, in no other way obtainable, of the gradually advancing condition of mind and state of knowledge' of the human race.[32]

Language was to be thought of as an organism, evolving in accordance with natural historical laws. Its cells were formed of individual words, each of which was an entity with a plenitude of meaning whose development could be traced back to an etymological origin. In the birth of individual words and the stages of their growth could be discovered the stages of evolution of the human mind. 'Every new word', it was claimed at the inauguration of the Ninth International Congress of Orientalists, 'represents really a most momentous event in the development of our race.'[33]

The study of languages was of particular political usefulness because Orientalism shared a further feature of nineteenth-century science. It introduced from its sister disciplines the fundamental idea of the 'survival'. Like fossils to the biologist, contemporary non-European languages were survivals, remnants from the past of the human (that is, the European) mind, preserved at various stages of 'backwardness'. As Renan explained: 'la marche de l'humanité n'est pas simultanée dans toutes ses parties . . . Telle est l'inégalité de son mouvement que l'on peut, à chaque moment, retrouver dans les differentes contrées habitées par l'homme les âges divers que nous voyons échelonnés dans son histoire.'[34] Orientalism was not merely some

139

esoteric study of alien languages, which the political requirements of European geographical expansion had turned into a thriving institution of colonial power. It was the proper study of mankind. Man was to be studied in terms of the history of the human mind; the stages in the development of this new mental object, lost in the vertical depth of the past, were made available by Orientalism, captured in time, distributed across geographical and colonial space.

Orientalism, however, like all nineteenth-century science of man, had its limitations. It enabled colonial administrators to talk of the 'Oriental mind' and to conceive of its 'backwardness'. But because its theory of language considered individual words to be plenitudes of meaning in themselves, Oriental Studies tended to remain caught up in the detailed analysis of texts. What was needed was a way of moving quickly from these empirical particulars to the abstraction of an Oriental mentality. What was needed was for words themselves to be considered insubstantial objects, mere tokens, and for the Oriental mind to become a fuller, more substantial structure – to give way to some new abstraction, such as Oriental (or Middle Eastern) 'culture' or 'society'.

The breakthrough was made by suddenly considering a language to be in essence not an organism but a means of communication. It was a breakthrough that came with the coming of modern communication. In 1895 Marconi demonstrated for the first time his system of wireless telegraphy; such events made it possible to explain the nature of language in a new way. 'Words are signs', it was now declared. 'They have no other existence than the signals of the wireless telegraph.' This claim was made in 1897 by Michel Bréal, professor of comparative grammar at the Collège de France.[35] The significance of arguing that words were mere signs, as empty in themselves as telegraph signals, was that a language could now be thought of as something more, existing apart from words themselves. The meaning of a language existed not in the plenitude of words, which were arbitrary marks meaningless in themselves, but outside them, as a semantic 'structure'. Bréal illustrated the separate existence of this structure by comparing the effect of words to 'the illusion' that occurs when looking at paintings in an exhibition. Standing before a picture, he wrote,

our eyes think they perceive contrasts of light and shade, on a canvas lit all over by the same light. They see depths, where everything is on the same plane. If we approach a few steps, the lines we thought we recognised break up and disappear, and in place of differently illuminated objects we find only layers of colour congealed on the canvas and trails of brightly coloured dots, adjacent to one another but not joined up. But as soon as we step back again our sight, yielding to long habit, blends the colours, distributes the light, puts the features together again and recomposes the work of the artist.[36]

Words were not a living organism but the parts of a representation. Placed together they formed an image of something, a coded message, a telegraph. They were made of marks that were meaningless in themselves; inspected closely, they dissolved into dots. In forming a representation, moreover, they presupposed a subject, who stands apart like the viewer of a painting or the visitor to an exhibition: 'everything proceeds from him and addresses itself to him'.[37] The purpose of linguistic representation was this communication between speaking subjects.

Linguistic meaning was to be found, then, neither within the material of the words themselves nor simply within the mind of the individual. It lay outside both, as a 'structure' with an 'ideal existence'. (Bréal's discovery of linguistic 'structure' occurred in the same years as Durkheim's discovery of social structure, which rested as we saw on making the same separation between the material realm of representations and an ideal realm they represented.)[38] 'It does not diminish the importance of language', Bréal wrote, 'to grant it only this ideal existence; on the contrary, it means placing it with the things that occupy the first rank and exert the greatest influence in the world, for these ideal existences – religions, laws, customs – are what gives a form to human life.'[39]

Language was to be considered part of an ideal realm, like law and custom (and later culture or social structure), the realm that gives 'form' to people's ordinary life. This form was something unique to a particular people. Such forms or structures had not been visible to nineteenth-century Orientalists, who had mistakenly argued that a people's conceptual world was limited to the words one found in their vocabulary. For Bréal there was something more. 'By not admitting a people to have ideas other than those that are formally represented, we run the risk of neglecting perhaps what is most vital and original in its intelligence . . . It does not suffice at all, in order to give an account of the structure of a language, to analyze its grammar and to trace the words back to their etymological values. One must enter into the people's way of thinking and feeling.'[40] Once words were conceived as mere instruments of communication, mere representations of something, it became possible to move from the words themselves to this something, this larger abstraction – a people's mentality, its way of thinking and feeling, its culture.

To sum up again, in Europe the words of a language had come to be considered not meanings in themselves but the physical clues to some sort of metaphysical abstraction – a mind or mentality. Since the end of the nineteenth century, this mentality has been formulated into an entity in its own right, existing apart from mere individuals and mere words, as an abstract realm of meaning that gives order to ordinary life. This view of language did not emerge in isolation. As we saw with Durkheim's arguments for the metaphysical existence of 'society', in the world-as-exhibition everything one encountered was coming to be ordered and grasped as though it were the mere physical representation of something abstract. Politics itself in its colonial age, as I suggested at the start of this chapter, was beginning to proceed more and more by continuously ordering up the representations that would produce this apparent realm of meaning. Husayn al-Marsafi on the other hand, opposed to the spread even of printing, shared a belief in no such metaphysical realm. His ways of using words, it followed, did not carry the same assumptions about the nature of meaning. It is to these ways and assumptions I will now turn.

Ordinary language

Perhaps the first thing that one notices about a work like *Eight Words* is that it is not 'organised', in the way we expect of a text and especially of a text addressing an urgent political crisis. The book has no table of contents – no structure that might seem to stand outside the text itself – and offers no straightforward authoritative definitions of the words it treats, but seems to wander through all the associations each word evokes, in a way that seems disorganised and even badly written. 'The statements of ideas are illustrated', according to one analysis of the text, 'in what seems a wilful disorder, with amusing anecdotes, with comparisons of human habits with those of animals, with verses of the Quran and hadiths, and with stories drawn from the personal experience of the author.' The analysis seeks the necessary remedy to this problem, explaining that it 'will not follow the whimsical arrangement of the work, but will put in order the main themes'.[41]

The problem of understanding what seems like a 'whimsical arrangement' and even 'wilful disorder' appears throughout the scholarship of Middle Eastern studies. It is encountered not only in the study of texts, but also as we saw in the way cities are built or in the absence of political institutions. Again I want to explore this apparent absence of order more closely. By examining a line or two from Marsafi's text in some detail, I propose to show that the supposed disorder is a consequence of reading it according to our own strange assumptions about how words work.

The first of the eight words examined in the book is *umma*, a term that can be translated into English as community or nation. The word is interpreted first of all as *jumlatun min an-nas tajma`uhum jami`a*, which could be translated as 'a group of people united by some common factor', the common factor, it is added, being tongue, place, or religion.[42] But this idiomatic English translation misses the force of the phrase. First of all, *jumlatun* can mean not only a group or gathering, but also a combination of words, a clause or sentence. And *j–m–ʾ*, the verb, means not only to gather or unite but also to compose, to compile a text, to write. The community is something that coheres, according to this semantic echo, in the way a gathering of words compose a text.

But there is much more than this. The force of the phrase gathers not simply from the various references of the separate words, but from the reverberation of senses set up between the parts of the phrase by their differing sounds. The initial sound *j–m–l* indicating sum, totality, is echoed at the other end of the phrase in the sound *j–m–ʾ* indicating a union, gathering, assemblage. An almost identical sound, *m–n*, fills the middle of the phrase, *min an-naas*. These sounds in turn recall other potential sounds, such as *j–mm*, to gather, be numerous, *j–m–d*, to congeal, *j–mh–r*, multitude mass, *j–l–s/m–jl–s*, to sit together/assembly, perhaps *m–l–ʾ*, to be full, crowd, assembly, and so on. All these further sounds are implicated in the meaning, the force, of the phrase. Each combination of sounds connects with and evokes a further sound, so that from one combination to the next a potentially endless chain of meaning can be made to reverberate, however distantly, in the movement of a single phrase.

This writing does not seek to discover and realise the power of words in a unique, univocal meaning, but in allowing the sounds and suggestions of a word to mix with those around it and proliferate. In English we would call this proliferation poetic or literary. 'Literary' language has been defined as a kind of writing where 'words stand out as words (even as sounds) rather than being, at once, assimilable meanings' and where their 'quality of reference may be complex, disturbed, unclear'.[43] In explanations of this kind, the literary or poetic is defined in opposition to something normal, to the plain or ordinary use of language. For the author of *Eight Words*, there was no such plain language. All writing worked by making words 'stand out as words', that is by evoking the echoes and resemblances in which one word/sound differs from the next.

In so-called plain language, as we have seen from Bréal, we understand words to work as signs. Bréal's successor in linguistics was Saussure, who formulated our modern theory of language, accepting that its essence was communication. According to Saussure, the word or linguistic sign is a two-sided entity consisting of a sound-image ('signifier') and a meaning (the 'signified'). Just as the physical dots on the canvas, in Bréal's example, represent a picture, the sound-image represents, or signifies, a meaning. The word is thus composed of a 'material' image, as Saussure says, and a non-material thought. Its two sides, as inseparable as the two sides of a sheet of paper, are the material and the conceptual.[44]

The two sides of the sign, though inseparable, are not equal to one another. The material element in the word is merely the representative of the meaning. The sound-image stands for the idea, which originates elsewhere, in the mind of the speaker or author. Thus the material element is secondary, in both rank and sequence. It merely represents a meaning in material form, in order to communicate it. The conceptual element is prior, closer to the original thought being communicated, to the author, to the origin. As Jacques Derrida has pointed out, this hierarchy is found, at another remove, in our understanding of the relationship of speech to writing. The written word, it is said, is a representation of the spoken word. Writing is a substitute for direct speech, and can make an author's words present for a reader in the author's physical absence. Just as the material element in spoken language is secondary to the conceptual, writing is secondary to speech. It is still further separated from its author's mind, from the original intention being communicated. It is further removed from the meaning itself.[45]

It is this hierarchy of original meaning and secondary representation that is at work, and at stake, in the distinction we make between normal language, whose purpose is to communicate, and the literary or poetic. Words that 'stand out as words (even as sounds)' are words that do not know their proper place in the hierarchy. In so-called literary writing, words are not the dutiful representatives of their authors. They do not mechanically make present a simple, original meaning from their absent author's mind. As we saw from the line in Marsafi's text, such words usurp larger powers, gathering their force from their associations with other words and setting loose an almost endless play of semantic/verbal echoes.

To label this usurpation a poetic or literary effect, and therefore oppose it to what is 'normal', protects the hierarchy. Poetic language is treated as an exception, which proves the validity of the normal process of communication. The essential opposition of material sound and immaterial meaning is preserved, preserving the hierarchical relationship between the two elements. More than just a linguistic theory is at stake here. On this hierarchical opposition rests an entire metaphysics of meaning, of the broadest political importance.

Just the same only different

What exactly is this strange two-sided sheet, the sign? Suppose, as Derrida suggests, we refuse to take for granted the opposition of ideal versus material (and hence of text versus world) of which it is said to consist, and their hierarchical relationship. What kind of a thing then is the sign, what sort of event? Derrida's answer would be that the sign is never exactly a thing or an event, in the sense of a unique and isolated empirical particular. Words do not work in that manner. In the first place, as Saussure himself elsewhere explains, a particular word always exists in relation to other similar sounding words. Its particularity is simply an effect of the way it differs from like-sounding words, as we saw just now with certain Arabic words. The English word 'bit', for instance, acquires its uniqueness only by differentiating itself from words like 'bet' and 'big'. 'Big' in turn establishes itself as different from 'dig' and from 'pig', and so on. The same is true of what we call the word's meaning. The meanings of 'pig', for example, are determined by other words, such as the existence in English of the word 'pork' to refer to pigs when served as food. The very bond between a word and its meaning, which was said to be the essence of the sign, can be shown to be just an instance of this process of difference. To find the meaning of a word (to borrow an example from Terry Eagleton) we look up its definition in a dictionary. The definition we are given is made up of other words. These words in turn are defined by more words, and so on. Words acquire their meaning from other words, not from the accuracy with which they 'represent'. A word and its meaning turn out to be not a unique, two-sided object, but the product of interwoven relations of differences, one 'element' of which exists only in terms of others, in a weave that has no edge or exterior.[46]

If meaning is not simply that abstract realm we gain access to in dictionaries, how is it that words nevertheless do mean? It can be argued, Derrida shows, that what is most essential about words, for them to work as words, is that they are repeatable. A sign that was unique even in this sense, that happened only once, would not be a sign. So even when we insist on something's identity as 'the same word', it is in fact something reiterated on different occasions, in different contexts. The simplest identity of a word, its self-sameness in this sense, is formed out of differences, the difference of reiteration. This reiteration has something paradoxical about it. On the one hand, each occurrence of a word is different. The word may differ in time or place, and may be modified in a diversity of empirical characteristics – being written, for example, instead of spoken. Language depends on the possibility of such diverse and different repetitions of the word, just as it depends upon the differences between words; it occurs only as such differing repetition. On the other hand, what is reiterated must remain the same word. In the midst of different repetitions, through every modification, there must remain a trace of something recognisably the same. It is this trace of sameness that we experience as the word's 'meaning'.

Meaning arises, then, because the word is always a repetition, in a double sense. It is a repetition in the sense of something non-original, something that occurs by modifying or differing from an other; and a repetition in the sense of the-same-again. Meaning is an effect of this paradoxical quality of sameness and difference, whereby a word always happens to be just the same only different.[47]

The paradox of repetition is not something to be resolved, Derrida would argue, as a strange consequence of language. On the contrary, language is something made possible by the movement of repetition and differing. The paradoxical effect of an inseparable sameness within difference is not acknowledged, however, but avoided. It is avoided by supposing, with Saussure, that the word is an object made up of two opposing aspects, the material and the conceptual. These belong to two distinct realms, one physical and the other, somehow, meta-physical, which are assumed mysteriously to be conjoined in the unity of the word. It is this mystical distinction between two realms that Derrida shows to be no longer fundamental, but a 'theological' effect. 'It depends entirely on the possibility of acts of repetition. It is constituted by this possibility.'[48] I now want to return to Arabic, and argue that this theological effect of a distinct 'realm' of meaning was not produced; or at least, to the extent that it was produced it was acknowledged to be something theological, and treated as such.

The absence of the vowel

In examining earlier a phrase from Husayn al-Marsafi's *Eight Words*, I have already suggested that the so-called literary use of language, in which 'words stand out as words, even as sounds' was not an exception to ordinary writing but the only kind of writing there could be. There was no 'white mythology', as Derrida calls it, according to which the play of differences between words would be something additional to the ordinary way in which words evoke a meaning. Or rather, so as not simply to invert the white man's mythology and make Arabic the example of its absence, the questions of meaning and the play of difference remained problematised in the writing of a work such as *Eight Words*. Rather than representing an author's univocal meaning, the words produced their force from the play of differences between them, differences which cannot be resolved into a distinction between the conceptual and the material. But this argument about the nature of Arabic writing can be made from several other features.

First of all there were its inscriptional features. Saussure argued that the material form of words was something arbitrary, attached to their meaning only by phonetic convention. Derrida points out that this separation between material form and meaning ignores all the non-phonetic aspects of writing, which are 'material' and yet create effects of meaning – such as punctuation, spacing and the juxtaposition of different texts. In Arabic, writing proceeded generally without recourse to punctuation or even spaces between words, often juxtaposed several texts on a single page in various significant relations to one another, made careful and meaningful distinc-

11 Page from a *Commentary on the hundred grammatical regents of al-Jurjani* by Sa'd Allah, known as al-Saghir, copied in 1808 by Ahmad Abd-Rabbih, with marginal and interlinear notes and glosses; Naskhi script.

tions between different styles of script, and in general extended the art of inscription into the most elaborate and deliberate forms.

A second set of features problematised by Derrida are those that make a book or other piece of writing seem an 'interior', an internal place of meaning separated from the 'real world' outside. The title page, the preface, and the table of contents are examples of such features, which seem to stand apart from the text and, like the map of a city, provide it with a form and exterior frame. Arabic writing, again, in general did not employ these devices, and instead began every work with a lengthy invocation (*khitab*) and indeed made the method of transition from the *khitab* into the rest of the text (*fasl al-khitab*) a subject of important theoretical debate. There are many other features one might mention: the significance of the verb 'to be', which in Arabic occurs only in the 'past' (Derrida, following Heidegger, has to use the present tense of the verb 'to be' 'under erasure', writing it and crossing it out at the same time, because the empty device of the verb 'to be' makes us forget how problematic is the notion of 'being'); the conception of language as a code, existing apart from the words themselves as a grammatical structure (the Arab grammarians did not study the rules of a code, but the modes of sameness (*nahw*) and difference (*sarf*) in language, terms that are now translated as 'syntax' and 'morphology'); and finally, what Orientalists have called 'the absence of the vowel' in Arabic. I will look briefly at this last idea.

In the Arabic script, it is said, the vowels are not normally marked. An English transcription of an Arabic phrase, such as mine of Marsafi's earlier in this chapter, has to insert the missing vowels. But this way of putting it is misleading. The vowel is a peculiar European invention, and is not something 'missing' from Arabic. Arabic words are formed by what Arab grammarians call the 'movement' of a sequence of letters. Each letter is pronounced with a particular movement (of the mouth and vocal cords), referred to as 'opening', 'fracturing' and 'contracting', and different movements of the same letters produce differences in meaning. The letters *k–t–b*, for example, can mean 'he wrote', 'it was written', 'books', and so on, according to the different ways in which each letter is moved. It is the different kinds of movement that the Orientalists translate into vowels.

The movement, however, is not the equivalent of a vowel. As the Tunisian linguist Monçef Chelli has pointed out, the movement cannot be produced independently of the letter and a letter cannot be produced without a movement, whereas vowels and consonants seem to exist independently of each other.[49] This independence, Chelli suggests, gives words in European languages a peculiar appearance of fixedness, as opposed to the movement of Arabic words. In treating words as moving combinations of letters, Arabic writing remains closer to the play of differences that produces meaning. Seen in this way, the vowel is not something missing in Arabic. It is a strange artifice, whose presence in European writing masks the relations of difference between words, giving the individual word the apparent independence of a sign. Chelli goes on to argue that this apparent independence endows words with an object-quality. As sign-objects they seem to exist independently of their being said. Their existence appears as something apart from the material repetition of the word, and seems to precede such repetition. The realm of this prior and separate existence is labelled the 'conceptual', the independent realm of meaning.

The purpose of this discussion of Arabic writing has been to suggest that in diverse ways Arabic is much closer than European languages to the play of difference that produces meaning, and correspondingly much further than European languages from producing the metaphysical effect of a conceptual realm, a realm of 'meaning' that is believed to exist quite apart from words themselves under the theological name of 'language' or 'truth' or 'mind' or 'culture'. Derrida's work is usually employed to demonstrate, in the reading of a particular text, how this effect of meaning can be made to collapse. That is not my interest. Despite the ease with which such feats of deconstruction seem to be accomplished, what needs explaining is not why meaning collapses but why it does not. Politically, what seems important is not just to show that outside the text, or outside the exhibition, there is only a further text or a further exhibition, but to consider why, in that case, we have come to live more and more as though the world were a real exhibition, an exhibition of reality. My study of nineteenth-century Egypt is intended as a study of how a world comes to be ordered and experienced as though it were an exhibition, divided in this way into two realms, the realm of things and the separate realm of their meaning or truth.

In earlier chapters of this book I have described some of the ways in which Egypt was organised in the nineteenth century to produce the effect of a conceptual realm. One example was the rebuilding of cities, with a regular plan to the streets and exterior façades; another was the geographical hierarchy of schools, arranged to represent the structure of a nation-state. More generally, the technique of order I called enframing, in military manoeuvres, in timetables, in the layout of classrooms and hospitals, in the rebuilding of villages as well as cities, in each case tended to produce the effect of a structure, which seemed to stand apart as something conceptual and prior.

Meaning is an effect not only of conceptuality, however, but also of intention. 'To mean' implies at the same time both to signify and to have intention or purpose. If a piece of writing or other process of representation produces meaning, in doing so it produces the impression of an authorial intention or will. The more effectively this meaning is made to stand apart as its own realm, the more effective will be the impression of such intentionality. In order to return to the questions about modern political certainty that I raised at the beginning of this chapter, I want to show how the methods of effecting the existence of a separate conceptual realm were at the same time a new method of effecting intention, certainty, authorial will, or more generally authority itself.

Author and authority

We understand writing to be a means of communication, a vehicle which can carry the words, and within them the ideas, of an author across the distance of time and space. Thanks to the mechanical efficiency of linguistic signification, an author's intention or meaning can be made present to an audience despite his or her physical absence. In writing, the author's absence is overcome. According to this understanding, printing, for example, is simply a more efficient means of overcoming absence. It provides a wider and more lasting representation of an author's meaning.[50]

In this ordinary understanding of writing the mechanical nature of words is never in doubt. If writing can represent an absent author's mind or meaning, if it can make an absent author present to a reader, this is because it is the nature of words to operate as the representatives of singular meanings. Such a mechanism of meaning appears normal and unproblematic. If words do have the potential to multiply in meaning, to work ambiguously, to slip beyond their author's original intention, to be misread, this liability, as we saw just now, is considered an exception, rather than something essential to the way in which writing works. Ambiguity is declared to be simply a question of minor error, or else a poetic effect. The liability then remains within the control of the intention of the author, who can decide whether or not to be poetic, to allow the words a little licence.

It seems to me that before the introduction of printing no Arab writer found these assumptions similarly unproblematic. Writing was not the mechanical representation of an author's meaning, and in this sense there was no simple 'presence' of an author in a text. Authorship, and authority, were far more problematic concerns. Because writing could never unambiguously represent an author's unambiguous meaning, it follows, no proper Arab scholar would have been interested in the power of the printing press. The problem of the author's presence in writing, furthermore, corresponded to a problem in the presence of political authority in society. As evidence for these assertions I will return to the work of Ibn Khaldun, in which the crucial issue was precisely this absence of author and authority.

Ibn Khaldun shares the assumption that writing attempts to extend the presence of an author. The art of writing, he says, 'enables the innermost thoughts of the soul to reach those who are far and absent. It perpetuates in books the results of thinking and scholarship.'[51] But here the similarity with our own assumptions about writing ends, for Ibn Khaldun does not understand this overcoming of absence in terms of any mechanical practice of written representation, but rather as a problem at the centre of human social life.

To write, according to Ibn Khaldun, is to risk being misread or misunderstood.[52] Words that survive beyond their author's presence are cut loose. Their tendency is to drift, to become altered, to be read without regard for context, and to germinate new meanings. And there is always their ordinary ambiguity.[53] It follows that words do not mechanically signify a singular meaning. The reading of a text is always a work of interpretation. 'The student of ideas', he says, 'must extract them from the words (sounds) that express them.'[54] The meaning arises, as we have seen, only from the differing movement of the letters. The letters are moved, hence differed and made to mean, only when recited by the reader. For this reason, the scholar in his work 'does not copy comments directly from books but reads them aloud'.[55] A text is never to be read mutely, it must be recited aloud in order to mean.

To read a text, then, one must recite it, for the bare letters on the page are ambiguous. Properly, one must read it aloud three times, following a teacher. On the first reading the teacher gives only brief comments outlining the principal issues, on the second he gives a full interpretation of every phrase, including the differences in interpretation among the different schools, and on the third he explores even the most vague and ambiguous terms.[56] The teacher, moreover, must be the one who wrote the text, or failing that, one of those to whom the author read the text, or one who read it under one of them, and so on in an unbroken chain of recitation leading back to the original author.

In the Iranian town of Nishapur, to give an example, those who wished to study and teach the *Sahih* of Bukhari, one of the most authoritative collections of the sayings of the Prophet, 'travelled some two hundred miles to the town of Kushmaihan near Marv where there was a man who recited the text from a copy made from a copy made from Bukhari's own dictation'. The scholar Abu Sahl Muhammad al-Hafsi, we are told in another example, 'studied the *Sahih* of Bukhari under al-Kushmaihani who studied it under Muhammad b. Yusuf al-Farbi who studied it under Bukhari himself. Seventy-five years after the death of his master al-Kushmaihani, Abu Sahl Muhammad al-Hafsi found himself . . . to be the only man alive who had studied under him.' He was therefore brought over two hundred miles to Nishapur, and honoured personally by the ruler. 'Then in the Nizamiya madrasa he gave a class, in which he dictated the *Sahih* to a great crowd.'[57]

These kinds of practices should not be explained away, it seems to me, by references to the importance of the oral or the memorised over the written;

they should be taken as indications of the very nature of writing and author-ship. Only such chains of recitation could overcome the inevitable absence of the author within the text. Given the ambiguous nature of writing, which was not merely a flaw in particular texts but something essential, as we saw, to the way in which words acquire their force, a mute and private reading could never recover the author's meaning, never restore the author's presence. The entire practice of Arab scholarship revolved around the prob-lem of overcoming the absence in writing of the author's unequivocal meaning.

Ibn Khaldun wrote in a period of political crisis in the Arab world, as I mentioned, which was also a period of crisis in the problem of authorial absence. This relationship between political weakness and the weaknesses of written scholarship was no coincidence for Ibn Khaldun. He addressed one in terms of the other. The connection is evoked even in the title of his work, the 'Book of *ibar*'. As Muhsin Mahdi has shown, the term *ibar* is ambigu-ous, both referring to and illustrating the ambiguity of language. The word can mean the 'lessons' to be learnt from historical texts, but in a wider sense suggests both the expression of meaning and its concealment.[58] The fuller title continues this link between writing and history, for the work is further entitled 'the record of the subject and the predicate' in the history of the Arabs and others. The first sixty or seventy pages of the text are then con-cerned with the problem of writing, showing how texts are corrupted and misread, how the techniques of discipleship have broken down and the chains of authority have been severed. The purpose of the work is to bring a remedy to the political crisis by overcoming this breakdown in writing. The remedy Ibn Khaldun offers is entirely new. It stands out from the four-teenth century as a unique attempt to overcome the essential weaknesses of writing. But the remedy is not that of a theory of representation.

His solution is to attempt to set down for the first time the grounds of interpretation, principles which are to govern the future reading of texts. The grounds are in the form of the essential 'context' or 'circumstances' (*ahwal*) of human social life. He offers in the *Muqaddima* an elaborate state-ment of the ordinary limits of human community, explaining the process in which communities are formed, grow, flourish and decay. These contextual limits are to circumscribe the possible interpretation of all written works, to keep the reading of history, given the corruption of texts and the normal ambiguity of writing, within the bounds of historical probability. His work was an enormous effort to provide the interpretive limits that would help to overcome the absence of authors of the past, and thus make it possible to imitate what was useful from the historical record.

This perhaps explains the enormous interest in the work in nineteenth-century Egypt, where scholars faced a similar crisis, and where men like

Marsafi understood the crisis very much as a crisis in the use of words, to be resolved by a teaching of a proper understanding of writing. From around the time of Marsafi, however, the entire practice of writing had begun to change. Words were to lose their power, their ability to proliferate in meaning, their tendency to echo and reverberate with other words and set in movement a play of resemblance and difference. Or at least this tendency was to be denied, circumscribed as an exception, confined by names such as poetry. Their essence was to become the mechanical process of communication. The entire problem of authority to which Ibn Khaldun addressed himself was to be overcome, by a forgetting of the problematic nature of writing in the face of the apparent certainty – the effect of an unambiguous meaning – made possible by the modern methods of representation. How might such a transformation have occurred? Within the limits of this work I can only suggest an answer. The introduction and spread of printing was the most obvious factor, but the change can be seen in new kinds of writing, in particular the enormous state-sponsored pedagogic literature, and the new journalism with its 'telegraphic' style.

The telegraph and the printing press were among several kinds of new machinery and technique appearing in Egypt that introduced a modern practice of communication. (It was an Egyptian employee of one of the European telegraph companies, Abdullah Nadim, who had begun producing Egypt's first popular nationalist newspaper in the summer and autumn of 1881.)[59] The Egyptian army, as we saw, had adopted the new techniques of signalling, which made it possible to assemble and control the enormous modern armies of the nineteenth century. The operation of the new Egyptian railways, which as I mentioned were among the most extensive in the world in relation to the country's size and population, depended on an elaborate system of signals and codes. A general aim of the British was 'the improvement of communications, traffic and general commerce'.[60] The gradual spread of government schooling involved new techniques of instruction and new methods of classroom obedience. These kinds of development all demanded, during the decades of the later nineteenth century, that language be employed not in the 'proliferating' manner examined above, but as a precise system of signs, in which words are handled as though they were the unambiguous representatives of singular meanings. The aim was to use words in the ordinary manner of Europeans, who were observed in the streets of Paris, as we saw in chapter 2, to use words only as 'necessary to do business'.

The linguistic transformation was a part of the process of ordering, in armies and schools, architecture and railways, irrigation projects and the production of statistics, which, like the world exhibition, began to produce what seemed a structure standing apart from things themselves, a separate realm of order and meaning. This new realm, I propose to argue from the parallel with writing, would appear not only as the realm of meaning but also as the realm of intentionality – of authority or political certainty. With the older kind of writing, exemplified by Ibn Khaldun, the presence of an author's intention or meaning in the words of a text was, as we just saw, essentially problematic. The problem of the author's presence in writing corresponded to the problem of the presence of authority in political life. The new mode of writing and communication made the re-presenting of an author's meaning appear an essentially unproblematic mechanical process. The unproblematic presence of an author in writing would now correspond, in all the other realms of ordering that characterise the world-as-exhibition, to the production of an essentially unproblematic and mechanical presence of authority in political life.

This political authority, produced in the modern state the way a modern text produces the unambiguous effect of an author, would appear continuously and mechanically present. At the same time, like an author's meaning, this authority would somehow stand mysteriously apart. Just as meaning does not exist in the 'material' of the words themselves, but seems to belong to a separate mental or conceptual realm that words only ever re-present, political authority would now exist apart as something metaphysical, which in the material world is only ever re-presented. Authority would become something both mechanical and mysterious: as certain and straightforward as the process of meaning, and equally metaphysical.

To conclude this chapter, I want to offer some evidence that this transformation in the nature of authority took place, in a manner that parallels the transformation in the nature of the author, of the author's meaning in a text. The evidence I will offer is a common image of the nature and place of authority, the image of the community as a body. I want to demonstrate, in effect, a transformation that occurred in parallel, in three different aspects: in the notion of writing, of the body, and of politics.

The machinery of government

The description of the political community as a body can be found throughout the history of Arabic literature. In the new political writings of the 1860s and 1870s it remained the most common image to which writers turned when explaining the harmony and hierarchy of social life, even when introducing new themes such as nationalism and education. 'There can be no doubt that the nation is like a body', wrote Tahtawi in the opening pages of the *Manahij*, and that individuals and groups form its limbs or members.[61] Marsafi in *Eight Words* relied upon the body in the same way, whenever he wished to explain how the community was composed of interacting parts. In discussing education, he said that its purpose was to teach the student 'that his community is a body, of whose organs and limbs he is a part'.[62]

Jamal al-Din al-Afghani, the Iranian-born scholar and political activist who was teaching in Egypt at the same time as Marsafi, also used the living body to express the nature of social life. Every organ and limb corresponded to a particular profession or trade, the social groupings to which individuals all belonged. Government, which was one such profession, could be considered the brain, ironsmithing the upper arms, agriculture the liver, seamanship the legs, and so on.[63] This provided a powerful expression of the order of the social world and the authority of different groups within it, and its power was employed frequently in political debate. When Afghani was invited in 1870 to give an address in Istanbul at the inauguration of the new university, he argued for the importance in society of philosophical thought by suggesting that the bodily location of philosophy as a profession was alongside prophecy, in the position of the soul. This attempt to give the practice of philosophy an authoritative position in the social order, expressed in terms of the parts of the body, provoked a storm in Istanbul's scholarly and religious establishment, and Afghani was expelled from the country.[64]

The image of the body was powerful because it provided the separate elements of the human world with their intelligibility, revealing the meaningful relations between them. The living body was an image that expressed an order of things that was given in the nature of human existence, from which could be deduced how the social world should be arranged. It demonstrated hierarchies of task and position, by showing the connections linking different groups into a continuous whole. 'Just as every limb and organ of the body has a function to perform by nature, and one part does not consider its task honorable nor another contemptible but each simply performs that for which it was created . . . so the individuals of the community each have a function they must perform.'[65] Like the circle of eight words mentioned earlier, this continuous whole was not an order conceived in the image, common to us today, of an inside versus an outside, a material world versus its structure, or a physical body versus a mental entity called 'the mind'. Thus the rulers corresponded simply to a particular organ of the body. Just as writing was not thought of in the simple terms of the metaphysical presence of an author's meaning in a physical text, in the image of the body there was no abstract authority, no invisible interior source of power governing a physical exterior.

Even among the writers of the 1870s, however, the body as a metaphor was beginning to show symptoms of stress. The body was spoken of, but usually to say that some vital organ was absent,[66] or that some limb was diseased and should be removed.[67] Teachers were to teach their students in the new government schools that they were the limbs and organs of a body, but if they failed to do so the body itself would fail – the community would not be realised.[68] New political practices were making this image of the body inappropriate. The organisation of schooling, the expanding military order, the rebuilding of the country's capital and other towns and villages, and all the other new methods of order I have discussed in earlier chapters, were all processes introducing a new imagery of the body and at the same time a new effect of political authority. By the last decades of the nineteenth century, the old image of the body was seldom used in political writing. Where the body does appear, it is in a wholly new sense.

Unseen but none the less real

The image appears, for example, in Muhammad Majdi's *Eighteen Days in Upper Egypt*, an account of his trip up the Nile in 1892 on a Thomas Cook steamer. The context is indicative of the changes taking place in Egypt. Majdi was an official in the Egyptian Court of Appeal, and travelled as a tourist on a boat that carried mail, colonial officials, and officers of the army of occupation. The year 1892 was Majdi's first opportunity to tour Upper Egypt since the nationalist uprising of 1880–82, for, as I mentioned in the last chapter, it had taken the British ten years to suppress provincial resistance to the occupation.[69] As he boarded the steamer and set off from Cairo, he described the country as a body, whose heart was its capital city.

Whenever I leave Cairo I think of it as our country's heart, in which we ourselves are like the spherical particles of blood. We accumulate there, and form into lines in order to get out, proceeding just like the fluid of life. It is as though we are impelled by a regulated movement, on which the life of the body depends.[70]

This image of society as a body is very different from the earlier usage. The body is no longer something composed of social groups forming its various limbs and organs. It exists apart from people themselves, as a sort of machinery. The one organ mentioned, the heart, which corresponds to the new colonial capital, is a pump driving the machine. Individuals are not parts of the body, but uniform particles that flow within it. The body's mechanical parts serve to channel, regulate and set in motion these moving particles.

A second example is provided by an article published in March 1900 in one of Egypt's new daily newspapers, *al-Liwa'*, discussing the political need for organised education. The article compared the country's system of schooling to the nervous system of the body. Each school, it said, could be considered an individual nerve-ending, and the nerve-endings were connected back to the body's central nervous system. The system was controlled and regulated by its brain, the Ministry of Education. Orders were sent out from the brain to the schools at the nerve-endings, which sent back impulses registering the reaction of the school as it made contact with the outside. Although the body in this image still seems to refer to the way in which parts are interconnected, it has become something utterly different. The connection it refers to is not the interaction of separate members that form a whole, but the relationship of an exterior to an interior. Previous images of the parts of the body never referred in this way to an outside, and hence the body was never an inside. The body has now become not only a mechanical object, but an object with an outward surface. Its relationship to an exterior makes it into an interior. This interior forms a political apparatus, whose furthest extension is the school. Seeming to exist apart from a world 'outside', the apparatus of politics and schooling must touch this exterior world, send back messages about it, and work upon it. Notions of this sort the old imagery of the body was never thought to express.

These examples suggest how the political image of the body had changed, in accordance with new political practices. The body as a harmony of inter-acting parts has been replaced with the body as an apparatus, known as politics, schooling, government, or the state. It is thought of as a structure within which particles move, or else as an internal mechanism working upon something external to it, namely the people, Egyptian society, the outside world. Like the process of writing, the political process was now to be thought of more and more in terms of this kind of mechanical, internal/external apparatus. Perhaps nothing would seem more straightforward and less metaphysical than the idea of a machine – just as nothing seems more straightforward than the mechanical process of representation by which we understand the nature of meaning. But a machine never occurs by itself. What is mystifying, so to speak, about machinery is that thinking of something as a mere machine always implies something else apart from the machine; just as what is mystifying about the exhibition, as I suggested in chapter 1, is the effect it produces of a real world outside, a place beyond the process of representation. The image of the machine makes possible certain fundamental yet seemingly obvious separations in the understanding of the political world: between the machinery and the 'raw material' outside, and also between the mechanism and its operator. It is these separations, which pass unnoticed, that turn out to be problematic. I will illustrate this with a final example.

Just as the new machinery of war and communication, as we saw at the start of this chapter, was essential to Britain's colonial occupation of Egypt, the machine was a favourite metaphor among British colonial administrators. In Cromer's *Modern Egypt* the system of colonial power is described again and again as a machine, indeed as 'one of the most complicated political and administrative machines the world has ever known'. Chapters of Cromer's work are devoted to the 'nature of the machinery' and to describing the 'parts of the machine'. To explain the ideal of colonial government, explicit comparisons are made to steam machinery, where 'the rate at which each wheel turns is regulated to a nicety'. Safety-valves and 'a variety of other checks and counterchecks' are required as 'guarantees against accident'. In general, each portion of the machinery is to operate under 'perfect control'.[71] Cromer's text can be considered one of the first major works of modern political science, and it foreshadows in its vocabulary the kind of idiom which political science was required to develop. Politics is conceived mechanically, in terms of equilibrium and control, input and output – or in Cromer's terms, raw material and finished article. The colonial official, he wrote, 'will soon find that the Egyptian, whom he wishes to mould into something really useful . . . is merely the rawest of raw material'. The tools with which he worked would determine 'the excellence of the finished article'.[72] The political is a machinery, working upon an external world, a world in which the lives of Egyptians occur as 'raw material'.

This image of the political process corresponds both to the new, mechanical image of the body and to the new understanding of writing. Writing too was now to be understood as a mere apparatus or instrument, like the body and hence like the machinery of politics, an apparatus of communication which reacts to or works upon a world external to it. Like this understanding of the text, the politics of the world-as-exhibition would now presuppose its own unproblematic exterior, the raw world outside itself forming its great referent. Yet although writing, the body and the political process were each now understood mechanically, each seemed to share a similar physical/metaphysical nature. Just as the mechanical understanding of the body now presupposed the 'mind', the non-mechanical (non-physical) operating consciousness whose orders and intentions the body mechanically relayed, so writing would now presuppose an operating consciousness. A text would be the representation of an author, in our modern sense, of whose intentions and meanings it was likewise merely the machine. Just as the body was now thought of as a vehicle through which a mind communicates with the world, so writing was to be thought of from now on as a mere vehicle of communication which makes an author's mind or truth present in the world. Politics, in turn, would be understood as a mysterious machine that makes present the ideal realm of an authority, the state, within the material world of society.

After four chapters of *Modern Egypt* describing the various parts of the political machine, Cromer comes to describe himself, the Consul-General. The passage in which he introduces himself illustrates this new notion of authority. His power is mechanical, we are told, like the power of other parts of the colonial apparatus, yet, as we will read, it is unseen. It is something real, but invisible, operating through the machine and yet existing apart from it. To express this strange idea the metaphor switches, at a certain moment in the writing, between the machine and the body. 'An endeavour has been made in the four preceding chapters to give some idea of the machinery of Government in Egypt . . .', Cromer begins.

This description is however incomplete; indeed in some respects it is almost misleading; for allusion has so far only been made to those portions of the State machinery whose functions can be described with some degree of precision. There are, however, other portions of that machinery whose functions are incapable of exact definition, but whose existence is none the less real. Whether, in fact, the whole machine works well or ill depends in no small degree upon the action of those parts of the machinery which, to a superficial observer, might appear unnecessary, if not detrimental to its efficient working. In the Egyptian body politic, the *unseen* is often more important than the seen. Notably, of late years a vague but preponderant power has been vested in the hands of the British Consul-General . . . [73]

Cromer has discussed the power and functioning of each part of the political apparatus over several chapters without once, as far as I know, employing the image of the body. At the moment when he turns to discuss power itself – the vague, invisible, preponderant power of the 'British representative', who 'represents' colonial authority itself – the machine metaphor is suddenly associated with the body. In terms of the 'body politic' one can speak of the 'unseen'. To the physical apparatus of the body can be added a separate entity, the non-physical, non-visible realm of authority itself. Colonial authority appears as this unseen, yet 'none the less real', metaphysical power. Although the metaphor switches from the machine to the physical body, there is no contradiction. The body is now thought of like a machine, and a machine, like a physical body, always implies a non-mechanical power separate from itself. There is always apart from the machine an operator or a 'motive force', as Cromer says, the working of an unseen will.

What matters about this language is not how well it represents the working of colonial authority. What is interesting is the kind of imagery to which writings like *Modern Egypt* must resort in order to echo and correspond to the strange effects of colonial power. The question that matters is what kind of thing colonial or modern power might be, if it must be depicted in the form of a machine. The machine always implies an operator apart from itself, just as writing is now distinguished from its author's meaning and the physical body from its mind. In each case there is an absolute separation between a visible, material apparatus and an intention, meaning or truth continuously presented from within it. The world divided into two realms that I have been describing in these pages is a world where political power, however microphysical in its methods, operates always so as to appear as something set apart from the real world, effecting a certain, metaphysical authority.

Chapter 6

The philosophy of the thing

Marshal Lyautey was the colonial governor of French-occupied Morocco during the early part of the twentieth century. Near the end of his period in power, on the occasion of the opening of the Casablanca–Rabat Standard Gauge Railway, Lyautey led a group of French engineers and journalists on a tour of Rabat, the newly built colonial capital. The writer André Maurois was among the guests and he recorded the Marshal's words, words which can introduce the conclusions I want to draw in this final chapter.

'I shall explain to you the philosophy of the thing', Lyautey began, as they got off the train at Rabat and entered the new capital. 'The buildings as a whole form a fan. At the centre of the fan, in the mounting – those are the Administration. Beyond them, where it broadens out, are the Government Ministries placed in the logical order. You understand? For example, here, Public Works. Next to it: Roads and Bridges, and then Mines. Next to Agriculture, Forests. This, here, is the gap for Finance. The building has not yet been built, but it will be intercalated in its logical place.' One of the guests interrupts with a question: 'Monsieur le Maréchal', he asks, 'what is this kiosk for?' To which Lyautey replies: 'That? That is for the sale of maps.'[1]

The colonial city was to be unambiguously expressive. Its layout and its buildings were to represent, in the words of the architect who built Rabat, 'the genius for order, proportion and clear reasoning' of the French nation.[2] As a system of political expression, each building in the city seemed to stand for something further. Lyautey's language in naming the buildings actually named instead this something further: 'Here, Public Works. Next to it, Roads and Bridges . . . ' The method of building and naming made present to the visitor the order and the institutions of colonial authority. Later on when they entered 'Forests', there seemed to hang in the air 'the faint smell of cedar', so perfectly did the building represent the larger abstraction for which it stood. With the colonial governor as our guide, it is as though we have re-entered the world exhibition.

The similarity between the world exhibition and the new cities of the Middle East and North Africa was nothing accidental, nor did it go unnoticed by local writers. Both the exhibition and the city were built as

161

political expressions, didactic in style, and both demanded the individual to be an awed and curious spectator, a tourist in need of a political guide and a map. There were many particular similarities. In the case of Istanbul, the first Middle Eastern capital to construct a large Europeanised quarter, the new city was expressly intended to be a 'model' for the rest of the Ottoman world – and its construction was supervised by Sadatlu Kamil Bey, who had acquired his experience by supervising the construction of the Ottoman exhibit at the Paris World Exhibition.[3]

The similarity between cities like Rabat and the world exhibition was not something limited to the buildings of the French colonial administration, just as what was exhibited was not simply colonial power. Inside the German Consulate at Casablanca, for example, one found 'the elements of a remarkable commercial organisation: samples of everything the Reich could produce, which the Consulate was charged with offering to Moroccan merchants; and also samples of products desired by Morocco, which were sent to manufacturers in Germany capable of producing them'. Beyond such official buildings, moreover, were the European cafés, and the retail establishments with their display of European commodities, their advertisements, their postcards of the 'Arab city' for sale. An Egyptian writer at the turn of the century complained that Europe was converting the entire East into an 'exhibition', at which every kind of European commercial product was on display.[4] Lyautey himself claimed the title 'chief commercial traveller of the protectorate', and in 1915 after seeing what had been done with the German Consulate he organised a commercial exhibition at Casablanca, and the following year a trade fair at Fez. The effect of such commercial displays on the natives, we are told, was quite extraordinary:

> One of the rebel chieftains on the northern front, who was keeping up a stubborn resistance to General Henrys, heard a description of the exhibition and was seized with an irresistible curiosity. He requested a truce, and permission to go there and then resume his post of warfare against us. As strange and unacceptable as such a request appeared, it was granted. He was warmly welcomed, and after his visit he and his tribe made submission.[5]

To submit and become a citizen of such an exhibitional world was to become a consumer, of commodities and of meanings.

The need for the Oriental

In the order of an exhibitional world, such as Lyautey's Rabat, each building and each object appeared to stand for some further meaning or value, and these meanings appeared to stand apart as a realm of order and institutions, indeed as the very realm of the political. The effect of meaning, however, as we might expect from the discussion of language in the previous chapter, actually arose not from each building or object in itself but out of the continuous weave of buildings and objects in which an individual item occurred. So although 'Finance' had not yet been built, it already existed as a 'logical place' in the process of intercalation. To create the effect of a realm of meaning, this differential process was to mark every space and every gap. It was to extend across the whole city, as continuous as a system of disciplinary power, to include even the 'native town' portrayed on the European postcards.

At first sight the older, indigenous quarters of the city appeared to be excluded from the new colonial order. When Lyautey's guests are shown the main street of Casablanca it seems to them unbalanced, with low, irregular houses on one side and tall buildings on the other. 'Precisely!' replies Lyautey. 'On the left you have the façade of the native town . . . On the right, the façade of the European town, large properties in the French style.'[6] In Cairo during the colonial period, French experts discussing the *esthétique* of the modern quarters insisted on a similar exclusion of the older part of the city. There could be no reorganisation of the older part, and if anything were to be rebuilt there, they said, 'it must be Oriental'. The Arab town, it was explained,

> must be preserved to show to future generations what the former city of the Caliphs was like, before there was built alongside it an important cosmopolitan colony completely separate from the native quarter . . . There are two Cairo's, the modern, infinitely the more attractive one, and the old, which seems destined to prolong its agony and not to revive, being unable to struggle against progress and its inevitable consequences. One is the Cairo of artists, the other of hygienists and modernists.[7]

Thus although the new order seemed at first to exclude the Arab town, in a larger sense it included it. Colonialism did not ignore any part of the city, but divided it in two, one part becoming an exhibition and the other, in the same spirit, a museum.[8]

This 'preservation' of a picturesque 'Cairo of artists', it should be noted, was advocated after the population of the city had increased by seventy per cent in the first twenty-five years of colonial rule. More than two-thirds of this increase was caused by in-migration, including the movement of the poor from the towns and villages of the countryside to Cairo, where the rate of population growth was almost twice that of the country as a whole.[9] There was also a movement of population within the city, as the arrival of European settlers, the Europeanisation of the quarters in which they purchased property, and rising rents pushed the poor more and more into the crowded streets of the so-called 'old city'. As poverty, malnutrition and unemployment increased, this 'Oriental' quarter and other backstreets where the poor found room to live became rapidly more cramped and more decrepit. 'The poorer classes are being more and more crowded into "slums" of the worst type', wrote the *Egyptian Gazette* in an editorial of February 1902. 'No new houses are being built for their accommodation and the rising rent roll is constantly limiting the numbers that are still within their reach. Hence, in the byways and backstreets of all quarters of the town, as well as in the suburbs, there is an ever enlarging number of houses in which families are packed together in numbers and under conditions that render these places the exact counterpart of the slums of Europe and America.'[10] Under these circumstances, the argument that the native town must remain 'Oriental' did not mean preserving it against the impact of the colonial order. The Oriental was a creation of that order, and was needed for such order to exist. Both economically and in a larger sense, the colonial order depended upon at once creating and excluding its own opposite.

In a well-known passage in *The Wretched of the Earth*, Frantz Fanon describes the colonial world as 'a world divided into compartments, . . . a world cut in two'. His description of the division of the colonial city into the European and the native quarters can illuminate the larger sense in which the colonial depends upon its Oriental opposite.

The settler's town is a strongly-built town, all made of stone and steel. It is a brightly-lit town; the streets are covered with asphalt, and the garbage-cans swallow all the leavings, unseen, unknown and hardly thought about. The settler's feet are never visible, except perhaps in the sea; but there you're never close enough to see them. His feet are protected by strong shoes although the streets of his town are clean and even, with no holes or stones. The settler's town is a well-fed town, an easy-going town; its belly is always full of good things. The settler's town is a town of white people, of foreigners.

The town belonging to the colonised people, or at least the native town, the negro village, the medina, the reservation, is a place of ill fame, peopled by men of evil repute. They are born there, it matters little where or how; they die there, it matters not where, nor how. It is a world without spaciousness; men live there on top of each other, and their huts are built one on top of the other. The native town is a hungry town, starved of bread, of meat, of shoes, of coal, of light. The native town is a crouching village, a town on its knees, a town wallowing in the mire. It is a town of niggers and dirty arabs. The look that the native turns on the settler's town is a look of lust, a look of envy; it expresses his dreams of possession – all manner of possession: to sit at the settler's table, to sleep in the settler's bed, with his wife if possible.[11]

Fanon's writing captures the effect of colonial segregation by shifting between two vocabularies and two perspectives. Each zone is described using the language and viewpoint of those outside it. The colonisers' town is seen through the eyes of those who have suffered colonisation, those to whom the settler is a person never seen in bare feet. The native town is described in terms of the fears and prejudices of the colonisers, who represent those whom they exclude as the negatives of their own self-image: the natives are crowded together like animals, they are crouching or kneeling like slaves, they are without sexual restraint. Describing the process of exclusion through the eyes of those who do the excluding imitates, in the very style of writing, something of its nature. The identity of the modern city is created by what is keeps out. Its modernity is something contingent upon the exclusion of its own opposite. In order to determine itself as the place of order, reason, propriety, cleanliness, civilisation and power, it must represent outside itself what is irrational, disordered, dirty, libidinous, barbarian and cowed. The city requires this 'outside' in order to present itself, in order to constitute its singular, uncorrupted identity. It is this technique of establishing one's identity over and in terms of another that Edward Said has analysed, in a larger intellectual and political context, as 'Orientalism'. It is in this larger sense that the native town 'must be Oriental'.

To represent itself as modern, the city is dependent upon maintaining the barrier that keeps the other out. This dependence makes the outside, the Oriental, paradoxically an integral part of the modern city. The order of the city does not stop at the limit of the modern town, as Lyautey's guests were led to think. The limit is something the city maintains within itself, by means of a continuous ordering that is the source of its own ordered identity. Yet it appears as the boundary of order itself. The city, in this analysis, can be taken to exemplify a paradox at work in the maintenance of any modern political order, any modern self-identity.

A large definition

In the same period as the construction of divided colonial capitals, a similar separation was being made on a global scale, in the form of a cultural and historical 'break' dividing the modern West, as the place of order, reason, and power, from the outside world it was in the process of colonising and seeking to control.[12] 'As long as we know anything that deserves the name of history', declared the President of the International Congress of Orientalists held in London in 1892, 'that break exists.'[13] Professor Tylor, in his inaugural address as the President of the Congress's new Anthropological Section, explained more precisely that 'in the large definition adopted by this congress, the Oriental world reaches its extreme limits. It embraces the continent of Asia, stretching through Egypt over Africa, and into Europe over Turkey and Greece . . . '[14] The proceedings of the Congress were reported in the local periodical press in Egypt. Professor Tylor's definition of the Orient was reproduced in full, and an astonished Egyptian editor added his comment: 'It is as if the world were divided in two.'[15]

The world's division into two was an essential part of the larger process of its incorporation into the European world economy and the European political order. The President's audience included, among the vice-presidents of the Congress, William Gladstone, whose government had carried out the invasion and occupation of Egypt, Lord Dufferin, the first architect of Britain's colonial policy in the country, and many others – 'so many practical men,' as the President warmly remarked, 'so many statesmen, and rulers, and administrators of Eastern countries'.[16] It was to these colonial administrators and policy makers that the ordering of Orientalism was addressed. 'It is simply dazzling to think of the few thousands of Englishmen ruling the millions of human beings in India, in Africa, in America, and in Australia', said the President. After thanking for their generosity the nine Indian rajas and maharajas who had put up the money for the Congress, he called for a much closer cooperation between those who studied and those who administered the Orient. While it was one thing to conquer Eastern nations, he said, 'to understand them is quite another'. Greater understanding of the Orient, he concluded, would secure 'the commercial supremacy of England' and enable 'the young rulers and administrators who are sent every year to the East' to establish 'intimate relations with the people whom they are meant to rule'.[17]

What Orientalism offered was not just a technical knowledge of Oriental languages, religious beliefs and methods of government, but a series of absolute differences according to which the Oriental could be understood as the negative of the European. These differences were not the differences within a self, which would be understood as an always-divided identity; they were the differences between a self and its opposite, the opposite that makes possible such an imaginary, undivided self. The Orient was backward, irrational, and disordered, and therefore in need of European order and authority: the domination of the West over the non-Western world depended on this manner of creating a 'West', a singular Western self-identity. Like the 'Arab town', the Orient was created as the apparent exterior of the West; as with the colonial city, what is outside is paradoxically what makes the West what it is, the excluded yet integral part of its identity and power.

Further examples of this paradoxical method of order could be mentioned. It helps to produce, for instance, the identity and authority of an 'individual' nation-state. One could think of a particular case in the modern Middle East, of a state whose existence is contingent upon maintaining a radical difference between itself and the identity of those outside it. The outside must be represented as negative and threatening, as the method of maintaining meaning and order within. The outside, in this sense, is an aspect of the inside. On closer inspection, moreover, the same opposition is found at work within the state, between what belongs to the outside and what belongs within. The authority and self-identity of the nation-state, like that of the city and the colonial world, are not stable, circumscribed conceptions but internal boundaries of hierarchical separation which must constantly be policed.

The paradox I have been describing is not something unique to colonial or modern politics. On the contrary, the indigenous modes of order that I tried to describe in chapter 2 illustrated the same paradox. In Pierre Bourdieu's ethnography of the Kabyle house we found oppositions such as interior/exterior and male/female that tended continually to reverse and to collapse upon themselves. So-called segmentary political systems could be explained in terms of the same paradox: the identity of a political group is not fixed as a rigid boundary containing those inside. The inside is contingent upon the designation of an exterior, and exists only in relation to particular exteriors. Political identity, therefore, never exists in the form of an absolute, interior self or community, but always as an already-divided relation of self/other. Political identity, this means to say, is no more singular or absolute than the identity of words in a system of writing. Just as the particularity of words, as we saw, is merely an effect of the differences that give rise to language, so difference gives rise to political identity and existence.[18] There are no political 'units', no atomistic, undivided selves; only relations or forces of difference, out of which identities are formed as something always self-divided and contingent.

What difference, then, does colonialism bring? What distinguishes its modern political order? Clearly the answer is not, in itself, the division into selves and others. Rather, it is the effect of seeming to exclude the other absolutely from the self, in a world divided absolutely into two. The establishing of this seemingly absolute difference is in fact an overcoming, or an overlooking, of difference. As with the example of the colonial city, by establishing a boundary that rigorously excludes the Oriental, the other, from the self, such a self acquires its apparent cleanliness, its purity, its uncorrupted and undivided identity. Identity now appears no longer self-divided, no longer contingent, no longer something arranged out of differences; it appears instead as something self-formed, and original. What is overlooked, in producing this modern effect of order, is the dependence of such identity upon what it excludes. It is forgotten that the boundary of the outside, as we have just seen, in this sense is something integral, something inside. How is such an overlooking, a forgetting, in the colonial order achieved?

A first answer might be that modern colonialism was constructed upon a vastly increased power of representation, a power which made possible an unprecedented fixing and policing of boundaries – an unprecedented power of portraying what lay 'outside'. During the colonial occupation of Egypt in 1882, as I mentioned in chapter 5, railways, steamships, telegraphs, newspaper correspondents, official reports, photographers, artists, and postcards from the front were all brought into coordination. The coordination made it possible to produce and relay back to Europe a continuous image of British imperial power, and an equally effective image of the disordered and backward Egyptians. In this manner, the enormous truth of colonialism – both its description and its justification – could be ordered up, put into circulation, and consumed. The truth of colonialism was congruous with the existing reality-images of the East elaborated in the popular and scholarly literature of nineteenth-century Orientalism, which I discussed in chapter 1. These images in turn referred back to the great *Description de l'Egypte* produced during Egypt's earlier period of European occupation, under Napoleon. By the end of the nineteenth century, as Said has shown, knowledge of the Orient had become an expertise institutionalised in the centres of colonial administration, in government ministries, and in universities. This expertise, combined with images of the Orient in popular writing, entertainment, the press, government reports, guide books, travelogues and the memoires of colonial officials, came to form a broad discursive field, a vast theatre or exhibition of the real. Within this theatrical machinery, elaborate representations of the 'objects' of colonial authority could be produced.

Before pursuing further my question about what distinguishes the order and self-identity of modern politics, it may be worth mentioning something of the penetration of these mechanisms of reality, by recalling the extent to which the truths of Orientalism were reproduced under the British in political debate within Egypt. I have already discussed, in chapter 4, how such Orientalist representations as the Egyptian character, the place of women in Islam and the power of custom and superstition were taken up in Egyptian writing and in the strategies of modern schooling as fundamental political issues. I have also mentioned the process by which the writings of some of the more popular and racist European Orientalists, such as Gustave Le Bon, made their way into Egyptian political life. The British themselves were active in encouraging and financing the spread of Orientalist ideas in Egypt. They worked in particular with writers drawn from the Christian communities of Lebanon, educated by American missionaries in Beirut, who tended to believe the only way to rival the West was to learn from it and for this and other reasons preferred European colonialism to local Turkish rule. The British secretly subsidised a daily and monthly Arabic press in Egypt, edited by such writers, and also organised the production of textbooks for the new government schools. The result, as I will briefly describe, was a steady penetration of Orientalist themes into the writings of the Middle East.

Our present backwardness

'How have we come to be regarded as part of the Orient?' asked a reader who wrote to the Egyptian journal *al-Muqtataf* in 1888. 'Are we not closer to Europe than to China or North Africa?' It had happened, replied the editor, because those who study us 'call themselves Orientalists'.[19] But his scepticism did not last. Five years later, when he had come to know personally some of the leading Orientalists of his day, the editor was willing to accept the Orient as a self-image. 'It is we who have placed ourselves in this position. There is one thing that unites us all in the Orient: our past greatness and our present backwardness.'[20]

The manner in which this kind of Oriental self-conception was spread can be illustrated with the case of the writer Jurji Zaydan, a Lebanese Christian who lived in Egypt during the period of British occupation. Zaydan was commissioned to produce two textbooks for use in the new government secondary schools, a *Modern History of Egypt* (1889) and a *Universal History* (1890).[21] He was also the author of a five-volume *History of Islamic Civilisation*, based on a wide reading of pre-modern Arab historians but also, by his own account, on half a dozen European studies of Islam, the first among which was *La civilisation des arabes* by Gustave Le Bon. Working from these sources, Zaydan explained that 'the history of Islamic Civilisation . . . constitutes the history of the civilised world in the Middle Ages'.[22] Describing the period of the first four caliphs as the highest phase of Islamic civilisation, Zaydan represented every subsequent period, from the Umayyad and Abbasid caliphates onward, as a successive stage of decline. The purpose of the work was to show for each stage the 'political' causes of decline, and its cultural consequences.

This view of history as a unilinear development in which Islam represented only a 'connecting link' in the medieval formation of an object called the West had direct political implications. Writing in the journal he had founded, *al-Hilal*, on the Indian uprisings of 1857 against the British, Zaydan warned Egyptians of the social disruption that faced them if they did not follow the steady course of development whose stages had been marked out by the West. The Indian revolt against colonialism had failed because India had not yet reached the historical stage in its development that made possible an independent political life. The Indian people had not acquired a knowledge of 'science and administration', or an understanding of their obligations to the state. Similarly, discussing the nationalist revolution of 1880–82 in Egypt, Zaydan described the country's political disorder as the consequence of a 'premature' demand for change, by a people that had not properly followed the laws of social development.[23]

Zaydan's Orientalist historiography was strongly criticised by certain intellectual groups within Egypt.[24] Yet he was subsequently invited, although a Christian, to become the first Egyptian professor of Islamic history at the new national university. Support for Zaydan was strongest from European Orientalists, many of whom he knew as acquaintances or friends.[25] One of these friends, D. S. Margoliouth, the Laudian Professor of Arabic at Oxford, translated the fourth volume of Zaydan's history of Islamic civilisation into English. It covered the period of the Umayyad and Abbasid caliphates, on which there was no scholarly work in English yet written.[26] Thus English scholarship began to repeat, via Arabic, the ideas of men like Gustave Le Bon.

The influence of Orientalism on Egyptian learning was not confined to the writing of Egypt's political history as a part of the history of the West. All of Arabic literature was now to be organised and studied in the same way, as subject to the principle of a unilinear historical development. Already in the 1890s Hasan Tawfiq, a student of Husayn al-Marsafi, had returned from study in Germany and the influence of the Orientalist Brockelmann to produce the first *History of Arabic Literature*.[27] Zaydan himself turned to the subject in response to a request from the new university for a textbook to use in teaching Arabic literature. He produced the four-volume *Ta'rikh adab al-lugha al-arabiyya* (1910–14) which covered all aspects of intellectual life, explaining its history once again in terms of the rise and long decline of Islam.[28]

Such Orientalism reached a wide audience. Besides its propagation through the university and through the textbooks used in schools, it was widely circulated in journals like Zaydan's monthly *al-Hilal*. Moreover, from 1891 Zaydan was engaged in an enormous effort to spread his ideas among the newspaper-reading population, by writing the history of Islamic civilisation in a series of popular historical novels. Over the course of two decades he produced a sequence of seventeen novels encompassing the history of Islam from its beginnings to the age of the Mamluks. The novels circulated widely, for they were distributed free among the subscribers to *al-Hilal*, which had the widest circulation of all Middle Eastern periodicals of its time. They made the new understanding of history both popular and entertaining. Taha Husayn wrote of being captivated by these books, which would keep him away from his studies at al-Azhar whenever he read one, and attributed to them a major influence on modern Arabic letters.[29]

The example of Zaydan's work illustrates how extensive were the historical representations out of which colonial authority was built. The absolute opposition between the order of the modern West and the backwardness and disorder of the East was not only found in Europe, but began to repeat itself in Egyptian scholarship and popular literature, just as it was replicated in colonial cities. Through its textbooks, school teachers, universities, newspapers, novels and magazines, the colonial order was able to penetrate and colonise local discourse.[30] This colonising process never fully succeeded, for there always remained regions of resistance and voices of rejection. The schools, universities and the press, moreover, like the military barracks, were always liable to become centres of some kind of revolt, turning the colonisers' methods of instruction and discipline into the means of organised opposition. (Hence the rise after the First World War of disciplinary political movements opposed to European occupation, such as the Muslim Brotherhood in Egypt, whose leaders were almost invariably school teachers.) Nevertheless the power of colonialism was itself a power that sought to colonise: to penetrate locally, spreading and establishing settlements not only in the shape of cities and barracks, but in the form of classrooms, journals and works of scholarship. Colonialism – and modern politics generally – distinguished itself in this colonising power. It was able at the most local level to reproduce theatres of its order and truth.

Colonialism was distinguished by its power of representation, whose paradigm was the architecture of the colonial city but whose effects extended themselves at every level. It was distinguished not just by representation's extent, however, but by the very technique. The order and certainty of colonialism was the order of the exhibition, the certainty of representation itself. Other kinds of political order, however harmonious, tended to be dynamic and indecidable, liable to reverse and to collapse upon themselves in ways that were already understood in the writings of Ibn Khaldun. Such orders arose out of the opposing play of differences. To return to my earlier question, how did the new order appear to overcome internal difference, and set up the different as something outside? How did it seem to establish an absolute boundary, between West and non-West, between modernity and its past, between order and disorder, between self and other? The answer, I think, lies in recalling the connections between all the different ways in which the world now seemed divided in two. Modern politics was to reside within a reality effect, a technique of certainty, order and truth, by which the world seemed absolutely divided into self and other, into things themselves and their plan, into bodies and minds, into the material and the conceptual. It is with the connections between these different divisions that I want to conclude.

The philosophy of the thing

'I shall explain to you the philosophy of the thing', Lyautey's tour of Rabat
had begun. It had ended at the kiosk selling maps. There was nothing before
the visitors' eyes except, as in any city, a certain distributing of surfaces and
spaces. Yet the regularity of their distribution and the distance maintained
between the surfaces and the eye resolved this distributing into what seemed
to the observer two distinct entities, one spatial and material, the other non-
spatial and conceptual: on the one hand the buildings themselves, and on the
other a plan. What was before them appeared divided into the 'thing' and its
'philosophy', the city and its map – as though cities and maps belonged to
two different categories of being.

The division of the world into the material and the conceptual seems
something obvious and commonsensical. Surely, it will still be said, the
nature of the world and of personhood has always been understood in terms
of some sort of distinction between the material and the immaterial. Perhaps
so. To understand what was novel about the distinction between things
themselves and their plan we must recall the encounter with the world
exhibition. What characterised those exhibitions was not just their accuracy
and extent of representation, but the absolute distinction between the representation and 'reality'. The exhibit of an Egyptian street, of the City of
Paris, of the Progress of Industry, was always merely an exhibit, clearly dis-
cernable, or so it seemed, from the original street, the real city, the actual
industrial progress to which it referred. This discernability, between a representation and the original object or idea to which it refers, is the principle
on which exhibitions exist. It is the method by which our effect of an original
'reality' is achieved.

The same principle was at work, moreover, outside the exhibition. It was
at work in museums and zoological gardens, in Orientalist congresses and
libraries, in statistics and legal codes, in works of art and Alpine scenery, in
the commerce of department stores and in the architecture of the city.
Everywhere one went in the modern world, 'things' seemed more and more
to be built, arranged, handled or consumed as 'signs of' something further.
A certain street, a particular view, a book, an advertisement or a commodity
appeared as a mere object or arrangement that somehow always stood, as in
an exhibition, for some more original idea or experience. The arrangement
of buildings seemed to express the institutions and authority of a political
power, Alpine scenery became an experience of nature, articles in museums
conveyed the presence of history and culture, words in Oriental languages
represented an exotic past, animals in zoos an exotic present. Life was more
and more to be lived as though the world itself were an exhibition, an

exhibition of the exotic, of experience, of the original, the real. What this meant was that the absolute discernability which was the principle of exhibitions was to be the principle of the world beyond as well. As in the exhibition, the careful ordering of buildings, views, displays and experiences around the individual sought to make everything into a mere representation of something more real beyond itself, something original outside. The reality-effect of the West lay in effecting this absolute distinction between mere 'things in themselves', as the Westerner could say, and the 'real' meaning, purpose or plan for which they stood.

However, if the world outside the exhibition was in this sense not a simple original, not reality itself, but a further series of representations, then the distinction between an exhibit and the real thing was not, after all, something absolute. The clear discernability between a representation and an original, promised by the exhibition, actually consisted only of representations standing for representations. Life was to be lived as though the world were an exhibition of reality; but the exits from the exhibition led not to reality itself, but only to further exhibitions. The real outside was never quite reached. It was only ever represented.

The exhibition, I hope, can serve as a motif for the kind of order and certainty we consider natural and commonsensical while remaining oblivious to its mysterious nature. With the help of this motif, such order can be seen no longer as something natural but as a particular historical practice in which we are still caught up. My aim has not been to describe its history, even in relation to the Middle East, but to isolate it and understand its peculiarity and power. To assist in its isolation, in chapter 2 I tried to suggest what other kinds of order there may have been, in the case of the Middle Eastern or Mediterranean world, which the order of the exhibition sought to replace. I did so with the reservation that such other kinds of order risk seeming, as a consequence of this sort of analysis, simply the opposite of our own; and as such, something total and self-contained. These consequences, as I said then, are unintended.

Borrowing some examples from the work of Pierre Bourdieu, I argued that the order of this world does not appear as a fixed correspondence between material objects and the concepts they represent – between a realm of things in themselves and their meaning or plan. There is nothing symbolic in such a world, in our own strange sense of that term. Its order, therefore, is not something analogous to a picture, a text or an exhibit. It does not form a single, enframed totality, set up before an observing or reading subject and representing to this subject a 'meaning'. Order does not occur, in this sense, in relation to the idealised position of an observer (or reader) situated outside itself. Rather, order occurs as a play of correspondence and difference between things, or perhaps better, between forces; and always

173

as a particular order, contingent upon a point or person formed out of this play.

As with the exhibition, my purpose was to take Bourdieu's Kabyle village as an instance that enables us to think about the larger world to which it belonged. To do so overlooks, of course, the enormous differences between a North African village and, say, the city of Cairo, as well as those between different social groups within such a city (including the learned and the unlearned), and between different periods in its history. It overlooks in particular the major economic and social transformations already under way in cities like Cairo in the eighteenth century and earlier. Nevertheless, to the extent that the example of the village makes it possible to conceive of a kind of ordering which is not that of the exhibition, and to do so without the usual recourse to notions of magic, religion or culture, it can be of use.

The kind of ordering which can be conceived with this example is not that of a structure, a text or a code. In such a world nothing pretends to stand apart as an inert spatial or conceptual framework. Thus there is no simple or absolute distinction, for example, between a city and its 'structure', nor, it follows, between the inside and its outside . As I suggested later on in chapter 2, a city such as pre-colonial Cairo was not divided into an exterior, public part and a private, enframed interior. It consisted of a series of more or less open enclosures, whose opening and closing was contingent upon such things as the time of day and the relationship between those entering and those within. These dynamics of spatial and personal relation provide a way of understanding not just the order of the house and the city, but wider notions of geographical and political order – none of which were conceived in terms of a fixed and separate framework. Order as a framework or structure, however, should not be mentioned simply as something absent; for its 'presence', in the contrasting case of the colonial city, was seen just now to be somewhat problematic. The absolute division between a modern city and its Oriental exterior, for example, which seemed to form the very identity of the colonial city, was found to be only a structural effect; on closer examination, the identity of the city could be understood to include its excluded exterior. The pre-colonial city, it follows, lacked not an actual framework establishing such divisions as exterior and interior, but rather the mysterious effect of such a framework.

In nineteenth-century Egypt the methods of creating such apparent distinctions between conceptual frameworks and the material they enframed provided a new technology of power. I discussed these technologies in chapters 2, 3 and 4, illustrating how they sought to work directly upon the bodies of individuals. I examined this 'disciplinary power', as Michel Foucault has called it, first of all in the New Order of the Egyptian army and in the attempt to form a parallel system of rural discipline and surveillance. I then showed how the same kind of disciplinary order, or *nizam*, was envisioned for the civilian population as a whole, in the form of a nationally organised programme of schooling. By its careful control of the body's movements, gestures, sounds, posture and cleanliness, education was to generate an authority no longer concentrated in the personal command of a master, but 'systematically diffused over the whole school . . . without diminution', producing in the pupil a habit of 'implicit obedience'.

The politics of the modern state were modelled on this method of replacing a power concentrated in personal command, and always liable to diminish, with powers that were systematically and uniformly diffused. The diffusion of control required mechanisms that were measured rather than excessive and continuous rather than sporadic, working by invigilation and the management of space. Besides schooling and the army, these mechanisms included such civilising innovations as the supervision of hygiene and public health, a military-style system of permanent rural policing, the building of model villages on new, privately-owned agricultural estates, the construction of networks to channel and control the movement of commodities, Nile waters and tourists, the surveillance of workers on irrigation projects, on the railways and in factories, the opening up of towns and cities to continuous inspection with wide thoroughfares, street lighting and police forces, and the organisation of a system of criminal courts, prisons and insane asylums.[31] 'The waters of the Nile are now utilised in an intelligent manner', wrote Lord Cromer in summing up the achievements of the British occupation, ' . . . The soldier has acquired some pride in the uniform which he wears. He has fought as he has never fought before. The sick man can be nursed in a well-managed hospital. The lunatic is no longer treated like a wild beast. The punishment awarded to the worst criminal is no longer barbarous. Lastly, the schoolmaster is abroad, with results which are as yet uncertain, but which cannot fail to be important.'[32] Within the language of improvement and civilisation reside the strategies of order that provided an unprecedented hold upon the bodies of individuals.

At the same time as they were extended, these strategies were to become increasingly unnoticeable. Lord Cromer, who liked to describe colonial control as a process of continuous 'tutoring', envisaged the ideal colonial official in the form of an omnipotent yet silent school teacher: 'he was to exercise supreme authority over his pupil, and at the same time . . . his authority was to be unfelt'.[33] Yet while the new methods of order were to make the mechanisms of power increasingly unnoticeable, at the same time the truth of political power was to become something increasingly certain. This was because the new methods of creating the effect of frameworks or structures worked not only to hold and coordinate the individual subject's physical body. They were also to work upon a non-physical interior, the individual mind.

Schooling was again the practice in which this working upon the mind was most readily envisioned and put into practice. The discipline and coordination of schooling was to produce not only the implicit obedience of the body, but also a well-formed character. The most important trait of this character, as we saw in chapter 4, was its industriousness. The individual was to be produced, and was to be produced as, essentially, a producer. Character was something to be examined, to improve it and also to know how to rule it and control it. Such examination, as men like Lord Cromer made clear, was to be an essential part of the process of political control.

There was more to the question of the mind, however. The division of the political subject into an external body and a mental interior corresponded to the other divisions I have been examining, between representation and reality and between things and their structure, each of which was a method of effecting the same internal/external and material/conceptual dualities. This correspondence provides the connection between the disciplinary mechanisms that I examined in chapters 2, 3 and 4 and the questions about representation I raised in chapters 1 and 5. There might at first seem to be a contradiction rather than a correspondence: in discussing representation, I have examined the ways in which political authority or sovereignty was made visible, whereas in discussing disciplinary power I have stressed, following Foucault, that such power became more and more unnoticeable. Foucault in fact has argued that the new disciplinary power was something 'absolutely incompatible' with the notion of the authority or sovereignty of the state. The theory of sovereignty, he argues, was retained merely as an ideology, 'to be superimposed upon the mechanisms of discipline in such a way as to conceal its actual procedures'.[34]

My own response to this apparent contradiction is that discipline and representation are two aspects of the same novel strategies of power, linked by the notion of enframing. Disciplinary powers acquire their unprecedented hold upon the body by methods of distributing and dividing that create an order or structure in which individuals are confined, isolated, combined together and kept under surveillance. This 'order' is, in effect, a framework that seems to precede and exist apart from the actual individuals or objects ordered. The framework, appearing as something pre-existent, non-material and non-spatial, seems to constitute a separate, metaphysical realm – the realm of the conceptual. It is such 'order' that the modern and colonial state claimed to have introduced into Egypt; what was introduced, with this order, was the effect of the world's division into two realms, the material and the conceptual. In the same way as it divided the world, this division separated the human person into two distinct parts, a body and a mind. The

power of representation worked in terms of this correspondence between
the division of the world and the division of the person. Lyautey, once more,
is the man to illustrate the correspondence.

Marshal Lyautey's tour of the colonial capital had been followed, in the
evening, by a dinner at the New Residence for the visiting journalists and
engineers. In his after-dinner speech, Lyautey discussed the formation of
his own political ideas, recalling from his youth his discovery of the work of
Descartes. 'I was at the *lycée* in Dijon, starting to study philosophy. That
morning we had been given the *Discours de la méthode* in a small student
edition. I kept that book for many years . . . Anyhow, that night, in bed, I
began reading this new book. Ah! I was fascinated. Such tidiness. Such
order.'[35] Lyautey, one might say, conceived of the nature of colonial order
in the same terms as Descartes conceived of the nature of the human subject.
The colonial city was to be constructed, like a world exhibition, as a representation set up before the mind of an observing subject. The Cartesian
mind was conceived, in a similar way, as an interior space in which representations of external reality are inspected by an internal eye – in other words,
again, like an exhibition set up before an observer.

Native scholars in the country Lyautey was seeking to colonise did not
share this conception of human personhood. They did not conceive of the
person as possessing a mind in this sense – that strange myth of a separate,
non-spatial entity within which occur the 'mental processes' of representation.[36] They shared with other Muslim scholars what used to be the common scholarly conception of personhood throughout the Mediterranean
world, going back to Aristotle. They conceived of the person as possessing
reason, a power or faculty. Reason was the power of grasping universals
amid particulars, the unchanging sameness amid differences.[37] It was one
among numerous human faculties, albeit the most important since it was the
mark or resemblance within human beings connecting them with the universal and the unchanging. For Muslim scholars, knowledge was a question
of increasing this power of reason, deepening the grasp of universals. For
Descartes, on the other hand, knowledge became the quest for certainty,
understood as the correct modelling of an 'external reality' in the internal
exhibit of the mind.

For the Muslim scholar, it follows, there was no corresponding mind/
body dichotomy. The conceptual/material distinction was a distinction, at
most, only between different human faculties rather than between different
parts of the person. The faculty of reason, moreover, was concerned with
distinguishing the trace of universal within the particular, rather than the
conceptual from the material. It was only with Cartesian thought and, in the
case of the Middle East, nineteenth-century politics that the human person

came to be treated as something divided into two parts, on the one hand an external physical apparatus and on the other an interior mechanism of representation.

The exhibition motif can indicate the connections between a Cartesian notion of the mind and the politics of colonial order. The kind of political order epitomised in the world exhibition addresses, and demands, a political subject who must learn that reality is simply that which is capable of representation. Colonial or modern politics will seek to create for this subject a continuous theatre of certainty, unknown to pre-colonial politics. Such certainty rests, as we have seen, on accepting a series of essential distinctions, between mere representations and an 'external reality' beyond the play of representation, between models, texts or copies and an absolute 'original' to which they refer, and generally between a realm of the conceptual and the 'real world' outside. With a Cartesian conception of the subject, these distinctions come to inhabit the very nature of personhood, as something self-evident and unquestionable.

Lyautey's passion for the *Discourse on the Method* was not, perhaps, surprising. It was in the *Discourse* that European philosophy broke with the method of scholarship it had shared with the Islamic world. Such scholarship understood learning as a process that moved from text to text, as we saw with the learning of al-Azhar, constructing interpretation upon interpretation, one reading resting upon another like the buildings of a pre-modern city. What was wrong with such 'book-learning', as Descartes called it, was what was wrong with pre-modern cities. Descartes announced the West's rejection of the scholastic tradition by comparing it to 'those old cities' which 'are as a rule badly laid out, as compared with those towns of a regular pattern that are laid out by a designer'. The buildings of old cities, he explained, give no indication of such a designer, of the mind and intention that planned them. 'In view of their arrangement – here a large one, there a small – and the way they make the streets twisted and irregular, one would say that it was chance that placed them so, not the will of men who had the use of reason.'[38] Just as the person was now understood as composed of mind and material body, the material world was to be arranged in such a way as to reveal this mind, this pre-existent plan or framework, this intention or will. The practice of colonial politics would be based on the same strategy of arranging, of ordering everything up so as to reveal a pre-existent plan, a political authority, a 'meaning', a truth.

In the colonial order, in other words, the effect created of a framework would always appear as though it were a 'conceptual structure', as we say. It would appear, that is to say, as an order of meaning or truth existing somehow before and behind what would now be thought of as mere 'things in themselves'. Political authority itself would now more and more reside in this effect of a prior, ordering truth. The reorganisation of towns and the laying out of new colonial quarters, every regulation of economic or social practice, the construction of the country's new system of irrigation canals, the control of the Nile's flow, the building of barracks, police stations and classrooms, the completion of a system of railways – this pervasive process of 'order' must be understood as more than mere improvement or 'reform'. Such projects were all undertaken as an enframing, and hence had the effect of re-presenting a realm of the conceptual, conjuring up for the first time the prior abstractions of progress, reason, law, discipline, history, colonial authority and order.

These abstractions were no more than effects, and yet the very possibility and power of such effects was something new. They were created by the techniques that now divided the world into its two realms, the realm of mere things and the realm of order. The realm of order, of what was signified, was the new realm of authority, of the certainty of political power. Such political authority presides, as what is seemingly prior and superior. And yet it presides without ever quite being present. In the white mythology, it is that which stands apart from the world itself, as the meaning that things themselves represent. This political method is the essence of the modern state, of the world-as-exhibition. The certainty of the political order is to be everywhere on exhibit, yet nowhere quite accessible, never quite touchable. Like reality at the world exhibition, the world's political truths are never presented, they are only ever represented. But we remain certain they exist – outside.

Notes

1 Egypt at the exhibition

1 Muhammad Amin Fikri, *Irshad al-alibba' ila mahasin Urubba* (Cairo, 1892), p. 128.
2 *ibid.* pp. 128–36.
3 R. N. Crust, 'The International Congresses of Orientalists', *Hellas* 6 (1897): 351.
4 *ibid.* p. 359.
5 Rifa`a Rafi` al-Tahtawi, *al-A`mal al-kamila*, vol. 2: *al-Siyasa wa-l-wataniyya wa-l-tarbiya*, p. 76.
6 Rifa`a Rafi` al-Tahtawi, *Qala'id al-mafakhir fi gharib awa'id al-awa'il wa-l-awakhir* (1883), p. 86.
7 Bernard Lewis, *The Muslim Discovery of Europe* (London: Weidenfeld and Nicolson, 1982), p. 299.
8 Tahtawi, *al-A`mal al-kamila*, 2: 177, 119–20; Alain Silvera, 'The first Egyptian student mission to France under Muhammad Ali', *Modern Egypt: Studies in Politics and Society*, ed. Elie Kedourie and Sylvia G. Haim (London: Frank Cass, 1980), p. 13.
9 Georges Douin, *Histoire du règne du Khédive Ismaïl*, 2: 4–5.
10 *The Times*, 16th June 1846; Aimé Vingtrinier, *Soliman-Pacha, Colonel Sève: Généralissime des armées égyptiennes; ou, Histoire des guerres de l'Egypte de 1820 à 1860* (Paris: Didot, 1886), pp. 500–1.
11 Ali Mubarak, *Alam al-Din* (Alexandria, 1882), p. 816.
12 Lewis, *Muslim Discovery*, pp. 299–301.
13 Tahtawi, *al-A`mal al-kamila*, 2: 121.
14 Of the eight works published in Cairo during the last ten years of the nineteenth century describing the countries and ideas of Europe, five were accounts of a trip to an Orientalist congress or a world exhibition: Dimitri ibn Ni`mat Allah Khallat, *Sifr al-safar ila ma`rad al-hadar*, an account of the Paris world exhibition of 1889 (Cairo: Matba`at al-Muqtataf, 1891); Mahmud Umar al-Bajuri, *al-Durar al-bahiyya fi al-rihla al-urubawiyya*, an account of a journey to the Exposition Universelle in Paris, and the Eighth International Congress of Orientalists, Stockholm, 1889 (Cairo, 1891); Muhammad Amin Fikri, *Irshad al-alibba' ila mahasin Urubba*, an account of the same journey; Ahmad Zaki, *al-Safar ila al-mu'tamar, wa hiya al-rasa'il allati katabaha ala Urubba*, an account of a journey to the Ninth International Congress of Orientalists,

London 1892 (Cairo, 1893), and *al-Dunya fi Baris*, an account of the Paris world exhibition (Cairo, 1900). In the preceding decade (the 1880s), the two major works on Europe had included accounts of the Paris Exhibition of 1878 and the Milan Exhibition of 1881 in Muhammad Bayram, *Safwat al-i`tibar bi-mustawda` al-amsar wa-l-aqtar*, 5 vols. (Cairo, 1302–1311h, 1884/5–1893/4), 3: 54, 73–81, and of a fictional Congress of Orientalists in Paris in Ali Mubarak, *Alam al-Din*, pp. 1153–79. On Egyptian writing about Europe in the nineteenth century, see Ibrahim Abu-Lughod, *Arab Rediscovery of Europe*, and Anouar Louca, *Voyageurs et écrivains égyptiens en France au XIXe siècle*.

15 Asa Briggs, *The Age of Improvement, 1783–1867*, rev. ed. (London: Longmans, 1979), p. 398.

16 International Congress of Orientalists, *Transactions of the Ninth Congress, London, 5–12 September 1892*, ed. E. Delmar Morgan, 2 vols. (London, International Congress of Orientalists, 1893), 1: 34.

17 Cited Edward W. Said, *Orientalism*, p. 165.

18 Theodor Adorno, *Minima Moralia: Reflections From a Damaged Life*, trans. E. F. N. Jephcott (London: Verso, 1978), p. 116; on the theatre, see for example Muhammad al-Muwailihi, *Hadith Isa ibn Hisham, aw fatra min al-zaman*, p. 434; on the public garden, Muhammad al-Sanusi al-Tunisi, *al-Istitla`at al-barisiyya fi ma`rad sanat 1889* (Tunis, 1309h), p. 37.

19 International Congress of Orientalists, *Transactions*, 1: 35.

20 Martin Heidegger, 'The age of the world picture' in *The Question Concerning Technology and Other Essays*, p. 127.

21 al-Sanusi, *al-Istitla`at*, pp. 243–4.

22 Clovis Lamarre and Charles Fliniaux, *L'Egypte, la Tunisie, le Maroc et l'exposition de 1878*, in the series, *Les pays étrangers et l'exposition de 1878*, 20 vols. (Paris: Libraire Ch. Delagrave, 1878), p. 123.

23 al-Sanusi, *al-Istitla`at*, p. 242.

24 Lamarre and Fliniaux, *L'Egypte, la Tunisie, le Maroc et l'exposition de 1878*, p. 133.

25 Edmond About, *Le fellah: souvenirs d'Egypte* (Paris: Hachette, 1869), pp. 47–8.

26 On this labyrinth see Jacques Derrida, *Speech and Phenomena, and other Essays on Husserl's Theory of Signs*, p. 104, as well as his subsequent writings, all of which, he once remarked, 'are only a commentary on the sentence about a labyrinth': 'Implications: Interview with Henri Ronse', in *Positions*, trans. Alan Bass (Chicago: University of Chicago Press, 1981), p. 5.

27 Susan Lee Yeager, 'The Ottoman Empire on exhibition: the Ottoman Empire at international exhibitions 1851–1867, and the sergi-i umumi osmani, 1863' (Ph.D. dissertation, Columbia University, 1981), p. 168.

28 David Harvey, *Consciousness and the Urban Experience: Studies in the History and Theory of Capitalist Urbanization* (Baltimore: The Johns Hopkins University Press, 1985), p. 118.

29 Cited Walter Benjamin, 'Paris, capital of the nineteenth century', in *Reflections: Essays, Aphorisms, Autobiographical Writings*, pp. 146–7.

30 Mubarak, *Alam al-Din*, p. 818.

31 Idwar Bey Ilyas, *Mashahid Uruba wa-Amirka* (Cairo, 1900), p. 268.

32 Mubarak, *Alam al-Din*, pp. 829–30.

33 Tahtawi, *al-A`mal al-kamila*, 2: 55–6; for another example see Mubarak, *Alam al-Din*, p. 817.

34 The phrase 'organisation of the view' occurs in Mubarak, *Alam al-Din*, p. 817. The zoo is described in Sanusi, *al-Istitla`at*, p. 37, the theatre in Tahtawi, *al-A`mal al-kamila*, 2: 119–20, the model farm outside Paris in Mubarak, *Alam al-Din*, pp. 1008–42, the visual effect of the street in *ibid.* pp. 448, 964, and in Ilyas, *Mashahid*, p. 268, the new funicular at Lucerne and the European passion for panoramas in Fikri, *Irshad*, p. 98.

35 See Heidegger, 'The age of the world picture'.

36 The best accounts of nineteenth-century Egypt are to be found in Jacques Berque, *Egypt: Imperialism and Revolution*, Albert Hourani, *Arabic Thought in the Liberal Age, 1798–1939*, Roger Owen, *The Middle East in the World Economy 1800–1914*, and, for the first half of the century, Afaf Lutfi Al-Sayyid Marsot, *Egypt in the Reign of Muhammad Ali*.

37 Benjamin, 'Paris, capital of the nineteenth century', pp. 146, 152; Tahtawi, *al-A`mal al-kamila*, 2: 76. The reflection of these changes in European and American writings of the period is explored in Rachel Bowlby, *Just Looking: Consumer Culture in Dreiser, Gissing and Zola* (New York: Methuen, 1985).

38 See André Raymond, *Artisans et commerçants au Caire au XVIIIe siècle*, 1: 173–202; Roger Owen, *The Middle East in the World Economy 1800–1914*; and Charles Issawi, *An Economic History of the Middle East and North Africa*.

39 Roger Owen, *Cotton and the Egyptian Economy* (Oxford: Oxford University Press, 1969), p. 307.

40 On the Saint-Simonists in Egypt, see Anouar Abdel-Malek, *Idéologie et renaissance nationale: l'Egypte moderne*, pp. 191–7; on Chevalier see J. M. Carré, *Voyageurs et écrivains français en Egypte*, 2: 326, and Benjamin, 'Paris, capital of the nineteenth century', p. 152.

41 *The Times*, 13th October 1851.

42 Cited Benjamin, 'Paris, capital of the nineteenth century', p. 151.

43 Sulayman al-Harayri, *Ard al-bada'i` al-amm* (Paris, 1867).

44 Yeager, 'Ottoman Empire on exhibition', pp. 120–2.

45 Mary Rowlatt, *A Family in Egypt* (London: Robert Hale, 1956), p. 42. On the rebuilding of Cairo see Janet Abu-Lughod, *Cairo: 1001 Years of the City Victorious*, pp. 98–113; on similar projects for the rebuilding of Istanbul, see Zeynep Çelik, *The Remaking of Istanbul: Portrait of an Ottoman City in the Nineteenth Century* (Seattle: University of Washington Press, 1986).

46 Benjamin, 'Paris, capital of the nineteenth century', pp. 151–2.

47 Karl Marx, *Capital*, 1: 163–77.

48 Benjamin, 'Paris, capital of the nineteenth century', p. 152.

49 Marx, *Capital*, 1: 173.

50 *ibid.* pp. 173, 283; Karl Marx, *Selected Writings*, ed. David McLellan (Oxford: Oxford University Press, 1977), p. 455.

51 See Jean Baudrillard, *The Mirror of Production*, pp. 21–51.

52 Marx, *Selected Writings*, pp. 455–6.
53 Cited Yeager, 'Ottoman Empire on exhibition', p. 39.
54 *The Times*, 13th October 1851. Yeager, 'Ottoman Empire on exhibition', p. 8.
55 Charles Edmond, *L'Egypte à l'exposition universelle de 1867* (Paris: Dentu, 1867).
56 Marx, *Selected Writings*, p. 456. See Stefania Pandolfo, 'The voyeur in the old city', mimeo, October 1983, for the following argument.
57 On the exhibition as the origin of the tourist industry, see C. R. Fay, *Palace of Industry, 1851: A Study of the Great Exhibition and its Fruits* (Cambridge: Cambridge University Press, 1951), pp. 76, 94.
58 Gustave Flaubert, *Flaubert in Egypt: A Sensibility on Tour*, p. 79.
59 Mubarak, *Alam al-Din*, p. 308.
60 Gérard de Nerval, *Oeuvres*, vol. 1: *Le voyage en Orient* (1851), p. 400, n. 104.
61 Flaubert, *Flaubert in Egypt*, p. 23.
62 Cited Kenneth P. Bendiner, 'The portrayal of the Middle East in British painting, 1825–1860' (Ph.D. dissertation, Columbia University, 1979), p. 314.
63 The phrase belongs to Eliot Warburton, author of *The Crescent and the Cross: or Romance and Realities of Eastern Travel* (1845), describing Alexander Kinglake's *Eōthen, or Traces of Travel Brought Home from the East* (London, 1844; reprint ed., J. M. Dent, 1908). Cf. *Oxford Companion to English Literature*, 5th ed. (Oxford: Oxford University Press, 1985).
64 Edward Lane, *An Account of the Manners and Customs of the Modern Egyptians* (London, 1835), pp. vii, xvii; Stanley Lane-Poole, 'Memoir', in Edward Lane, *An Arabic–English Lexicon, derived from the best and most copious Eastern sources* (London: William and Norgate, 1875; reprint ed., Beirut: Libraire du Liban, 1980), 5: xii.
65 Leila Ahmed, *Edward W. Lane: A Study of His Life and Work, and of British Ideas of the Middle East in the Nineteenth Century*; John D. Wortham, *The Genesis of British Egyptology, 1549–1906* (Norman, Oklahoma: University of Oklahoma Press, 1971), p. 65. The camera lucida was the invention of Edward Lane's friend Dr Wollastone (Lane, *Arabic–English Lexicon*, 5: xii).
66 Bendiner, 'The Middle East in British painting', pp. 13–18.
67 Dolf Sternberger, *Panorama of the Nineteenth Century*, Trans. Joachim Neugroschel (New York: Urizen Books, 1977), pp. 188–9; Benjamin, 'Paris, capital of the nineteenth century', p. 150.
68 Cited Ahmed, *Edward Lane*, p. 26.
69 Gérard de Nerval, *Oeuvres*, 1: 281–90.
70 Muhammad al-Muwailihi, *Hadith Isa ibn Hisham, aw fatra min al-zaman*, pp. 405–17.
71 Jeremy Bentham, 'Panopticon', in *The Complete Works of Jeremy Bentham*, ed. John Bowring, 4: 65–6.
72 Malek Alloula examines the voyeurism of the European photographer as a mode of colonial presence in *The Colonial Harem*.
73 *Handbook for Travellers in Lower and Upper Egypt* (London: John Murray, 1888), p. 12.

183

74 Carré, *Voyageurs et écrivains*, 1: 272.
75 Ibrahim Abduh, *Tatawwur al-sahafa al-misriyya, 1798–1951*, pp. 242–4.
76 Cited Carré, *Voyageurs et écrivains*, 2: 191; cf. Said, *Orientalism*, pp. 160–1, 168, 239.
77 Cited Lane, *Arabic–English Lexicon*, 5: vii.
78 Gérard de Nerval, *Oeuvres*, 1: 172–4.
79 Said, *Orientalism*, pp. 160–4.
80 Pierre Bourdieu, *Outline of a Theory of Practice*, pp. 2, 96. On the critique of 'visualism' in anthropology, see also Johannes Fabian, *Time and the Other* (New York: Columbia University Press, 1983), pp. 105–41, and James Clifford, 'Partial truths', in *Writing Culture: The Poetics and Politics of Ethnography*, ed. James Clifford and George E. Marcus (Berkeley: University of California Press, 1986), pp. 11–12.
81 Carré, *Voyageurs et écrivains*, 2: 200.
82 Ahmed, *Edward Lane*, p. 9; Bendiner, 'The Middle East in British painting', pp. 35–48.
83 Gérard de Nerval, *Oeuvres*, 1: 878–9, 882, 883.
84 Kinglake, *Eōthen*, p. 280; Théophile Gautier, *Oeuvres complètes*, vol. 20, *L'Orient*, 2: 187; Flaubert, *Flaubert in Egypt*, p. 81.
85 Cited Bendiner, 'The Middle East in British painting', p. 6.
86 Gautier, *L'Orient*, 2: 91–122.
87 Gérard de Nerval, *Oeuvres*, 1: 862, 867.
88 Said, *Orientalism*, pp. 176–7.
89 *Goodbye to All That* (Harmondsworth: Penguin Books, 1960), p. 265.
90 See in this respect James Clifford, 'Review of Orientalism', *History and Theory* 19 (1980): 204–23.
91 Herman Melville, *Journal of a Visit to the Levant, October 11 1856–May 1857*, ed. Howard C. Horsford (Princeton: Princeton University Press, 1955), pp. 79, 114.
92 See Stefania Pandolfo, 'The voyeur in the old city: two postcards from French Morocco', paper presented at the Department of Anthropology, Princeton University, October 1983.
93 Gérard de Nerval, *Oeuvres*, 1: 1276.
94 Cited Alain Silvera, 'Edme-François Jomard and the Egyptian reforms of 1839', *Middle East Studies* 7 (1971): 314; on Lambert see Carré, *Voyageurs et écrivains*, 1: 264–73.
95 'J.B. au Pacha', 16th April 1828. Bentham archives, University College, London.

2 Enframing

1 Bayle St John, *Village Life in Egypt*, 2 vols. (London, 1852), 1: 35; Helen Rivlin, *The Agricultural Policy of Muhammad Ali in Egypt*, pp. 89–101; on Egyptian politics in general in this period, see Afaf Lutfi al-Sayyid Marsot, *Egypt in the Reign of Muhammad Ali*, pp. 100–61.

2 Jean Deny, *Sommaire des archives turques du Caire* (Cairo, 1930), pp. 126–9; Rivlin, *Agricultural Policy*, pp. 79, 89–101.

3 See Daniel Crecelius, *The Roots of Modern Egypt: A Study of the Regimes of `Ali Bey al-Kabir and Muhammad Bey Abu al-Dhahab, 1760–1775*; on intellectual changes in this earlier period, see Peter Gran, *Islamic Roots of Capitalism, 1769–1840*. I am grateful to Peter Gran for his comments on an earlier version of some of the chapters of this book.

4 Albert Hourani analyses the nature of these households and their power, and their nineteenth-century transformation, in 'Ottoman reform and the politics of notables', in *Beginnings of Modernization in the Middle East: the Nineteenth Century*, ed. William R. Polk and Richard L. Chambers, pp. 41–68.

5 Michel Foucault, 'Two lectures', in *Power/Knowledge: Selected Interviews and Other Writings 1972–1977*, pp. 78–108, and *Discipline and Punish: The Birth of the Prison*. The following pages owe much of their analysis to the paths of enquiry opened up by Foucault. The phrase 'productive powers' is found in 'Report on Egypt and Candia' by John Bowring, the friend of Jeremy Bentham, who served as an advisor to the Egyptian government.

6 Jeremy Bentham's panoptic principle was devised in factories run by his brother Samuel on the Potemkin estates, land colonised by Russia after the defeat of the Ottomans in 1768–74. See Mathew S. Anderson, 'Samuel Bentham in Russia', *The American Slavic and East European Review* 15 (1956): 157–72.

7 On the formation of this landowning class see F. Robert Hunter, *Egypt Under the Khedives, 1805–1874: From Household Government to Modern Bureaucracy*, pp. 109–21.

8 See D. Farhi, 'Nizam-i cedid: military reform in Egypt under Mehmed `Ali', *Asian and African Studies* 8 (1972): 153.

9 André Raymond, *Grandes villes arabes à l'époque ottomane*, pp. 69–78; Crecelius, *Roots of Modern Egypt*, pp. 15–24.

10 Justin McCarthy, 'Nineteenth-century Egyptian population', *Middle Eastern Studies* 12 (October 1978): 37, n. 77; if the National Guard of the early 1840s is included, the Egyptian military may have been much larger still. Rivlin, *Agricultural Policy*, p. 351, n. 28.

11 Amin Sami, *al-Ta`lim fi Misr fi sanatay 1914–1915, wa-bayan tafsili li-nashr al-ta`lim al-awwali wa-l-ibtida' bi-anha' al-diyar al-misriyya*, p. 8.

12 Judith E. Tucker, *Women in Nineteenth-Century Egypt*, pp. 135–7.

13 See Stanford J. Shaw, *Between Old and New: The Ottoman Empire Under Selim III, 1789–1807* (Cambridge: Harvard University Press, 1971), pp. 86–179.

14 Bernard Lewis, *The Emergence of Modern Turkey*, 2nd ed. (London: Oxford University Press, 1968), p. 57.

15 Rivlin, *Agricultural Policy*, p. 251. The introduction of the *nizam jadid* in Tunisia began a decade later: see L. Carl Brown, *The Tunisia of Ahmed Bey, 1837–55* (Princeton: Princeton University Press, 1974), pp. 261–321. In Morocco, men began to write about the innovation of *nizam* in the 1830s: see Abdallah Laroui, *Les origines sociales et culturelles du nationalisme marocain (1830–1912)* (Paris: Maspero, 1977), pp. 272–84.

16 Amin Sami, *al-Ta`lim*, p. 8.

17 Mustafa Reshid Celebi Effendi, 'An explanation of the nizam-y-gedid', in William Wilkinson, *An Account of the Principalities of Wallachia and Moldavia Including Various Political Observations Relating to Them* (London: Longman *et al.*, 1820), appendix 5, p. 234. A baccal is a greengrocer.

18 Mustafa Reshid, 'Nizam-y-gedid', pp. 236–7.

19 Compare with the Mamluk *furusiyya* exercises described by Ayalon, where military training was a parade, a game, a public entertainment, and a mark of individual honour, in which the cavalryman displayed and developed his bodily prowess, his agility, his skill with horse and lance, his chivalry: David Ayalon, 'Notes on the furusiyya exercises and games in the Mamluk Sultanate', in *The Mamluk Military Society: Collected Studies* (London: Variorum Reprints, 1979), ch. 2. Although European artillery experts were employed in Egypt in the 1770s, they made little impact on the tactics of the army, which continued to rely on the charge of the individual cavalier as the preferred form of attack. See Crecelius, *Roots of Modern Egypt*, pp. 77–8, 175.

20 *Military Instructions of the Late King of Prussia, etc.*, fifth English edition, 1818, p. 5, cited in J. F. C. Fuller, *The Decisive Battles of the Western World and Their Influence Upon History*, 3 vols. (London: Eyre & Spottiswoode, 1955), vol. 2: *From the Spanish Armada to the Battle of Waterloo*, p. 196.

21 Fuller, *Decisive Battles*, 2: 192–215. V. J. Parry, on the other hand, describes this change in European practice, which the *nizam jadid* was an attempt to adopt, as 'not so much a new departure as an elaboration of accepted, indeed of "traditional" practice': 'La manière de combattre', in *War, Technology and Society in the Middle East*, ed. by V. J. Parry and M. E. Yapp (London: Oxford University Press, 1975), p. 240. It is true that drill had been systematised and routinely practised by European armies for over two hundred years, since the innovations of Maurice of Nassau. Only in the later eighteenth century, however, were simultaneous breakthroughs made in drill, signalling and command, embodying the new thought about what an army was and how it could be created, that resulted in armies doubling their speed of manoeuvre, tripling their firing rate, and quadrupling their manageable size.

22 Abd al-Rahman al-Jabarti, *Ta'rikh muddat al-faransis bi-Misr*, edited by S. Moreh and published with a translation as *Al-Jabarti's Chronicle of the First Seven Months of the French Occupation of Egypt, Muharram–Rajab 1213 (15 June–December 1798)*, p. 21.

23 Mustafa Reshid, 'Nizam-y-gedid', pp. 268–9. The elaboration and significance of these techniques in eighteenth- and nineteenth-century Europe are discussed by Foucault, *Discipline and Punish*, pp. 135–69.

24 Fuller, *Decisive Battles*, 2: 192–215; Foucault, *Discipline and Punish*, pp. 162–3.

25 Mustafa Reshid, 'Nizam-y-gedid', p. 268. The British military advisor attached to the Turkish forces that fought the French considered the Ottomans excellently armed and supplied, lacking only the new system of discipline. 'They have fine men,' he wrote, 'excellent horses, good guns, plenty of ammunition and provisions and forage, and in short great abundance of all the materials

required to constitute a formidable army, but they want order and system.' (General Koehler, British military advisor to the regular Ottoman army during the Egyptian campaign, in despatch to London, 29th January 1800. FO 78/28, cited in Shaw, *Between Old and New*, p. 136.)

26 Mustafa Reshid, 'Nizam-y-gedid', p. 269; cf. Foucault, *Discipline and Punish*, p. 163.

27 Mustafa Reshid, 'Nizam-y-gedid', p. 242.

28 *ibid.* pp. 166–7.

29 Ahmad Izzat Abd al-Karim, *Ta'rikh al-ta`lim fi asr Muhammad Ali* (Cairo, 1938), pp. 82–92; James Heyworth-Dunne, *An Introduction to the History of Education in Modern Egypt*, pp. 115–80.

30 A.-B. Clot Bey, *Mémoires*, ed. Jacques Tagher (Cairo: Institut Français d'Archéologie Orientale, 1949), p. 325.

31 Heyworth-Dunne, *Education in Modern Egypt*, pp. 185, 195. The *kurbaj* is a leather whip.

32 *ibid.* p. 197.

33 John Bowring, 'Report on Egypt and Candia', p. 49.

34 As reported by the British Consul-General, Colonel Patrick Campbell: FO 78/4086, cited Rivlin, *Agricultural Policy*, p. 211.

35 Deny, *Sommaire des archives turques du Caire*, pp. 150–3.

36 Rivlin, *Agricultural Policy*, pp. 89, 102–3.

37 These paragraphs were republished one month after the issuing of the booklet under the title 'Qanun al-filaha' (The Agricultural Code). Hiroshi Kato, 'Egyptian village community under Muhammad `Ali's rule: an annotation of Qanun al-filaha', *Orient* 16 (1980): 183.

38 Rivlin, *Agricultural Policy*, pp. 78, 89–98.

39 *ibid.* pp. 105–36, 200–12.

40 Bowring, 'Report on Egypt and Candia', p. 49; Afaf Lutfi Al-Sayyid Marsot, *Muhammad Ali*, pp. 132–6; on the political nature of such revolt see Fred Lawson, 'Rural revolt and provincial society in Egypt, 1820–24', *International Journal of Middle East Studies* 13 (1981): 131–53.

41 Bowring, 'Report on Egypt and Candia', pp. 5–6.

42 Tucker, *Women in Nineteenth-Century Egypt*, p. 135; on the British intervention, and its effect on Egypt's nascent, military-based industrialisation, see Marsot, *Muhammad Ali*, pp. 232–57.

43 Original translation from the British Foreign Office records: FO 78/502, 24th May 1844, in Rivlin, *Agricultural Policy*, appendix 3, p. 271.

44 Original translation from the British Foreign Office records: FO 78/231, 16th March 1833, cited in Rivlin, *Agricultural Policy*, pp. 276–7.

45 On the comparison with contemporary European methods, see Marsot, *Muhammad Ali*, p. 129.

46 Cited Moustafa Fahmy, *La révolution de l'industrie en Egypte et ses conséquences sociales au 19e siècle (1800–1850)* (Leiden: E. J. Brill, 1954), p. 19.

47 Rivlin, *Agricultural Policy*, pp. 65–70; Marsot, *Muhammad Ali*, pp. 157–60, 250–1.

48 Kenneth Cuno traces the origin of this system and its antecedents in 'The origins of private ownership of land in Egypt: a reappraisal', *International Journal of Middle Eastern Studies* 12 (1980): 245–75.

49 D'Arnaud, 'Reconstruction des villages de l'Egypte', p. 280; see also Ali Mubarak, *al-Khitat al-jadida li-Misr al-qahira wa-muduniha wa-biladiha al-qadima wa-l-shahira*, 15: 7.

50 St John, *Village Life*, 1: 104.

51 On space as a system of magnitudes, and the 'neutrality of order', see Lewis Mumford, *Technics and Civilization*, pp. 20, 326. The term 'enframing' is borrowed from Martin Heidegger, *The Question Concerning Technology*, pp. 20–1.

52 See Pierre Bourdieu and Abdelmalek Sayed, *Le déracinement: la crise de l'agriculture traditionnelle en Algérie* (Paris: Editions de Minuit, 1964). For a further discussion of the 'discipline of space' see Michael Gilsenan, *Recognizing Islam: Religion and Society in the Modern Arab World*.

53 Bowring, 'Report on Egypt and Candia', p. 3.

54 P. S. Girard, 'Mémoire sur l'agriculture, l'industrie, et le commerce de l'Egypte', *Description de l'Egypte, état moderne*, 2 vols. (Paris, 1809–22), vol. 1, part 1, p. 688, cited Charles Issawi, ed., *The Economic History of the Middle East 1800–1914: A Book of Readings* (Chicago: University of Chicago Press, 1966), p. 376.

55 Bowring, 'Report on Egypt and Candia', pp. 3–4.

56 D'Arnaud, 'Reconstruction des villages', p. 279.

57 Although Bourdieu's essay 'The Kabyle house or the world reversed' is a structuralist interpretation, his later *Outline of a Theory of Practice* offers what might be called a post-structuralist reading of the same material. For an attempt to describe the life of the pre-colonial village in Egypt, see Jacques Berque, *Histoire sociale d'un village égyptien au XXe siècle* (Paris: Mouton, 1957), and *Egypt: Imperialism and Revolution*, pp. 45–59, 65–9.

58 Michael T. Taussig, *The Devil and Commodity Fetishism in South America* (Chapel Hill: University of North Carolina Press, 1980), p. 7.

59 Bourdieu, *Outline*, p. 90; 'Kabyle house', pp. 135–6.

60 Bourdieu, *Outline*, pp. 90–1.

61 Bourdieu, 'Kabyle house', p. 138; *Outline*, p. 116.

62 Bourdieu, 'Kabyle house', p. 139.

63 Brinkley Messick, 'Subordinate discourse: women, weaving and gender relations in North Africa', *American Ethnologist* 14/2 (1987): 20–35.

64 Cf. Mushin Mahdi, *Ibn Khaldun's Philosophy of History* (Chicago: University of Chicago Press, 1957; Phoenix ed., 1964), pp. 184–7.

65 This is not to deny, of course, that there were regular, carefully ordered constructions in pre-nineteenth-century Arab cities (often laid out as the core of newly founded dynastic capitals) – just as the Kabyle house can be understood as a carefully ordered construction. The point is not the regularity of the building in modern cities, which in itself is nothing new, but the new distinction between the materiality of the city and its non-material structure. It is interesting

to note the remark of al-Jahiz on the circular palace-complex (misleadingly referred to as the 'round city') constructed in the year 762 by the Caliph al-Mansur: 'It is as though it were poured into a mould and cast'. The regularity of the building is evoked by referring to the process of construction, and not in terms of any distinction between the materiality of the city and its 'structure'. Cited J. Lassner, 'The Caliph's personal domain: the city plan of Baghdad re-examined', in Albert Hourani and S. M. Stern, eds., *The Islamic City*, p. 103.

66 Bourdieu, 'Kabyle house', p. 145; *Outline*, pp. 111, 126.

67 S. D. Goitein, *A Mediterranean Society: The Jewish Communities of the Arab World as Portrayed in the Documents of the Cairo Geniza*, 4 vols. (Berkeley: University of California Press, 1967–85), 4: 64–74; David King, 'Architecture and astronomy: the ventilators of Cairo and their secrets', *Journal of the American Oriental Society* 104 (1984): 97–133.

68 King, 'Architecture and astronomy'.

69 Raymond, *Grandes villes arabes*, p. 186.

70 Roberto Berardi, 'Espace et ville en pays d'Islam', in D. Chevallier, ed., *L'Espace sociale de la ville arabe*, p. 106.

71 'The whole shows very clearly the appearance of their private life. The architecture portrays their necessities and customs, which do not result only from the heat of the climate. It portrays extremely well the political and social state of the Muslim and Oriental nations: polygamy, the seclusion of women, the absence of all political life, and a tyrannical and suspicious government which forces people to live hidden lives and seek all spiritual satisfaction within the private life of the family.' Alexis de Tocqueville, 'Notes du voyage en Algérie de 1841', *Oeuvres complètes*, gen. ed. J. P. Mayer, vol. 5, *Voyages en Angleterre, Irlande, Suisse et Algérie*, ed. J. P. Mayer and André Jardin (Paris: Gallimard, 1958), part 2, p. 192.

72 Melvin Richter, 'Tocqueville on Algeria', *Review of Politics* 25 (1963): 369–98; on the floating hotel, see Charles-Henri Favrod, *La révolution algérienne*, cited William B. Quandt, *Revolution and Political Leadership: Algeria 1954–68* (Cambridge: MIT Press, 1969), p. 3.

73 P. M. Holt, Ann K. S. Lambton, and Bernard Lewis, eds., *The Cambridge History of Islam*, 2 vols. (Cambridge: Cambridge University Press, 1970), 2: 256–7.

74 'It is not with the material, topographical aspects of the Islamic city that I wish to deal, but with its inner structure. I should like to suggest that one of the most essential characteristics of the Islamic city is the looseness of its structure, the absence of corporate municipal institutions.' S. M. Stern, 'The constitution of the Islamic city', in Hourani and Stern, eds., *The Islamic City*, p. 26.

75 Oleg Grabar, 'The illustrated *maqamat* of the thirteenth century: the bourgeoisie and the arts', in Hourani and Stern, eds., *The Islamic City*, p. 213; Goitein, *Mediterranean Society*, 4: 34.

76 Muhammad al-Sanusi al-Tunisi, *Istitla`at al-barisiyya fi ma`rad sanat 1889* (Tunis, 1309h), p. 242.

77 Cf. Jacques Derrida, 'The double session', in *Dissemination*, p. 191.

78 Bourdieu, *Outline*, pp. 109–58; cf. Michel Foucault, *The Order of Things: An Archaeology of the Human Sciences*, pp. 17–30; Jean Baudrillard, *The Mirror of Production*, pp. 53–67. Similarly, with the jars of grain used for cooking: to tell the quantity of grain they held, these jars have holes down the side, so that the grain itself can indicate its level. The quantity is not measured by some measuring device, or represented on an abstract scale whose arbitrary divisions would 'stand for' a certain amount. Nothing is arbitrary in that sense. The grain indicates its own level by a direct reference or repetition.

79 Derrida, 'The double session', p. 191.

80 Max Weber, ' "Objectivity" in social science and social policy', in *The Methodology of the Social Sciences*, p. 81, emphasis in original, translation modified.

81 Max Weber, 'Science as a vocation', *From Max Weber: Essays in Sociology*, trans. H. H. Gerth and C. Wright Mills (New York: Oxford University Press, 1946), p. 139.

3 An appearance of order

1 Ali Mubarak, *al-Khitat al-jadida li-Misr al-qahira wa-muduniha wa-biladiha al-qadima wa-l-shahira*, 9: 49–50.

2 Ali Mubarak, *Alam al-Din*, pp. 446–7.

3 *ibid.* pp. 816–18, 962–3, 447.

4 The government's acquisition of this property marked at the same moment Egypt's successful break with the authority of Istanbul. The palace had been the Egyptian residence of the Khedive's half-brother Mustafa Fadil, who had served as finance minister to the Ottoman Sultan in Istanbul and schemed to become Isma`il's successor. The schemes had failed, Mustafa Fadil had fled to Paris, and Isma`il and his direct descendents had been recognised as the future rulers of Egypt. Şerif Mardin, *The Genesis of Young Ottoman Thought* (Princeton: Princeton University Press, 1962), pp. 42–8, 276.

5 Mubarak, *al-Khitat*, 9: 50.

6 See Janet Abu-Lughod, *Cairo: 1001 Years of the City Victorious*, pp. 98–113; Jacques Berque, *Egypt: Imperialism and Revolution*, pp. 91–2, 94.

7 Abbate-Bey, 'Questions hygiéniques sur la ville du Caire', *Bulletin de l'Institut égyptien*, 2nd series, 1 (1880): 69.

8 Abu-Lughod, *Cairo*, p. 113.

9 Edwin De Leon, *The Khedive's Egypt* (London: Sampson Low & Co., 1877), p. 139.

10 William H. McNeill, *Plaques and Peoples* (New York: Doubleday, 1976), pp. 266–78.

11 Abbate-Bey, 'Questions hygiéniques', pp. 59, 61, 64.

12 Muhammad Amin Fikri, *Jughrafiyyat Misr* (Cairo: Matba`at Wadi al-Nil, 1879), p. 53.

13 The only government schools in existence were a military school, set up in 1862 and closed again in 1864, a naval school, and a much-neglected medical school at Qasr al-Aini. One other group of new schools that existed were those estab-

lished by the communities of resident foreigners in Egypt and by European and American missionaries, mostly in the period of Sa'id Pasha (1854–63). James Heyworth-Dunne, *An Introduction to the History of Education in Modern Egypt*, pp. 323, 340.

14 Amin Sami, *Taqwim al-Nil, wa-asma' man tawallaw amr Misr ma'a muddat hukmihim alayha wa mulahazat ta'rikhiyya an ahwal al-khilafa al-amma wa shu'un Misr al-khassa*, 3: 16–17; Heyworth-Dunne, *Education in Modern Egypt*, pp. 185, 225, 347.

15 Khedival Order of 13 Jumadi II, 1284 h., in Sami, *Taqwim al-Nil*, 3: 722.

16 Ahmad Izzat Abd al-Karim, *Ta'rikh al-ta'lim fi asr Muhammad Ali*, pp. 200–5.

17 Joseph Lancaster, 'The Lancasterian system of education' (1821), in Carl F. Kaestle, ed., *Joseph Lancaster and the Monitorial School Movement: A Documentary History*, pp. 92–3.

18 Joseph Lancaster, 'Improvements in education as it respects the industrious classes of the community . . . ' (1805), in Kaestle, ed., *Joseph Lancaster*, p. 66.

19 R. R. Tronchot, 'L'enseignement mutuel en France', cited Michel Foucault, *Discipline and Punish: The Birth of the Prison*, p. 315, n. 5, translation modified. The mutual improvement school was introduced from England into France in 1814. By the 1820s, when Egyptians went there are observed methods of schooling, there were 1200 such schools (Kaestle, ed., *Joseph Lancaster*, pp. 30–1).

20 Lancaster, 'The Lancasterian system of education', p. 91.

21 *ibid.* pp. 94, 95–6.

22 Abd al-Karim, *al-Ta'lim fi asr Muhammad Ali*, pp. 201–3.

23 Kaestle, ed., *Joseph Lancaster*, pp. 29–34. Lancaster model schools were introduced in the same period in Istanbul. See Niyazi Berkes, *The Development of Secularism in Turkey* (Montreal: McGill University Press, 1964), pp. 102–6.

24 Abd al-Karim, *al-Ta'lim fi asr Muhammad Ali*, p. 209.

25 Sixty-six students were sent to study at the school. Besides Isma'il Pasha and Ali Mubarak, they included: Ali Ibrahim, later Director of the Government Primary School under Isma'il, and Minister of Education and Minister of Justice under Tawfiq; Muhammad Sharif, later Minister of Foreign Affairs under Sa'id, President of the Legislative Assembly and Minister of Education under Isma'il, and Prime Minister several times under Tawfiq; Sulayman Najjati, Director of the Military School under Sa'id, an administrator of the military schools under Isma'il, and later a judge of the Mixed Courts; Uthman Sabri, Director of the School for Princes established by Tawfiq, and later a judge of the Mixed Courts and President of the Mixed Court of Appeal; Shahata Isa, Director of the Military Staff College under Isma'il; Muhammad Arif, holder of several government posts and founder of the Society of Knowledge for the Diffusion of Useful Books (Jam'iyyat al-Ma'arif li-Nashr al-Kutub al-Nafi'a), and its press Matba'at al-Ma'arif (see below); Nubar the Armenian, later Minister of Public Works and of Foreign Affairs under Isma'il, and three times Prime Minister under Tawfiq; Sa'id Nasr, holder of numerous administrative posts in education under Isma'il, and appointed Judge of the Mixed Courts in 1881 and Honorary President of the Mixed Courts in 1903; Mustafa

Mukhtar, appointed Inspector of Upper Egypt, and later of Lower Egypt; Sadiq Salim Shanan, later Director of the Government Primary School, of the Government Preparatory School, and finally of the School of Engineering – and many others. Heyworth-Dunne, *Education in Modern Egypt*, pp. 253–9; Umar Tusun, *al-Bi`that al-ilmiyya fi ahd Muhammad Ali thumma fi ahday Abbas al-awwal wa-Sa`id*, pp. 226–366.

26 Umar Tusun, *al-Bi`that al-ilmiyya*, pp. 176–9.

27 Heyworth-Dunne, *Education in Modern Egypt*, p. 246.

28 Heyworth-Dunne, *Education in Modern Egypt*, p. 246.

29 Cf. Foucault, *Discipline and Punish*, pp. 135–228.

30 Abd al-Karim, *al-Ta`lim fi asr Muhammad Ali*, p. 210.

31 Ahmad Izzat Abd al-Karim, *Ta'rikh al-ta`lim fi Misr min nihayat hukm Muhammad Ali ila awa'il hukm Tawfiq, 1848–1882*, 1: 177–81, 3: 1–14; Fritz Steppat, 'National education projects in Egypt before the British occupation', in William R. Polk and Richard L. Chambers, eds., *Beginnings of Modernization in the Middle East: The Nineteenth Century* (Chicago: University of Chicago Press: 1968), p. 282; Gilbert Delanoue, *Moralistes et politiques musulmans dans l'Egypte du XIXe siècle (1798–1882)*, pp. 405–8.

32 Mubarak, *Khitat*, 9: 48.

33 Nubar Pasha, letter of 8th October 1866, cited in Angelo Sammarco, *Histoire de l'Egypte moderne depuis Mohammad Ali jusqu'à l'occupation britannique (1801–1882)* vol. 3: *Le règne du khédive Ismaïl de 1863 à 1875*, p. 137.

34 François de Salignac de la Mothe-Fénelon, *Les aventures de Télémaque*, cited in Israel Altman, 'The political thought of Rifa`ah Rafi` al-Tahtawi' (Ph.D. dissertation, University of California, Los Angeles, 1976), p. 152.

35 *Mawaqi` al-aflak fi waqa'i` Tilimak* (Beirut: al-Matba`a al-Suriyya, 1867). Tahtawi's other writings of the period were clearly influenced by this work (cf. Delanoue, *Moralistes et politiques*, 2: 405).

36 F. Robert Hunter, *Egypt Under the Khedives*, p. 53.

37 Nubar Pasha, letter of 8th October 1866, cited Sammarco, *Histoire de l'Egypte moderne*, 3: 137.

38 Abd al-Rahman al-Rafi`i, *Asr Isma`il*, 2 vols, 2: 93.

39 Sami, *Taqwim al-Nil*, 2: 732–3; *al-Ta`lim fi Misr fi sanatay 1914–15*, p. 21.

40 Sami, *Ta`lim*, pp. 21–2; Heyworth-Dunne, *Education in Modern Egypt*, pp. 362–69.

41 Sami, *Ta`lim*, p. 40.

42 V. Edouard Dor, *L'Instruction publique en Egypt*, p. 216.

43 Rifa`a Rafi` al-Tahtawi, *al-A`mal al-kamila*, 2: 387–8.

44 Rifa`a Rafi` al-Tahtawi, *al-Murshid al-amin li-l-banat wa-l-banin*, p. 45.

45 Tahtawi, *al-A`mal al-kamila*, 2: 388–9.

46 Dor, *Instruction publique*, pp. 245, 359, 368.

47 *ibid*. p. 235.

48 *ibid*. pp. 231–2, 268.

49 Sami, *Ta`lim*, pp. 23–32, and appendix 4.

50 Dor, *Instruction publique*, pp. 231–2.
51 Cf. Foucault, *Discipline and Punish*, pp. 141–9.
52 Dor, *Instruction Publique*, p. 235.
53 *ibid.* p. 240.
54 *ibid.* pp. 166, 170.
55 Ahmad al-Zawahiri, *al-Ilm wa-l-ulama wa-nizam al-ta`lim*, pp. 90–3.
56 Pierre Arminjon, *L'Enseignement, la doctrine et la vie dans les universités musul-manes d'Egypte*, p. 85.
57 Dor, *Instruction publique*, p. 170; Arminjon, *Enseignement*, p. 81.
58 Dor, *Instruction publique*, pp. 166–7.
59 *ibid.* pp. 77, 83.
60 Cf. Foucault, *Discipline and Punish*, p. 147.
61 See Ibn Khaldun, *The Muqaddimah*, for a discussion of learning in the mosque as the practice of a *sina`a* (2: 426–35) and for the textual sequence discussed below (2: 436–3: 103). On the teaching mosque as a centre of law, see Richard W. Bulliet, *The Patricians of Nishapur: A Study in Medieval Islamic Social History* (Cambridge: Harvard University Press, 1972), pp. 47–60; and George Makdisi, *The Rise of the Colleges: Institutions of Learning in Islam and the West* (Edinburgh: Edinburgh University Press, 1981), where it is shown that general references in the medieval sources to studying and teaching in the mosque (terms such as *madrasa, dars, darras, tadris* and *mudarris*) always referred to *fiqh*, the law (p. 113).
62 Arminjon, *Enseignement*, pp. 253–4.
63 See Mustafa Bayram, *Ta'rikh al-Azhar* (Cairo, n.d., c. 1902), pp. 35–8; and (for a much earlier period) Makdisi, *Rise of the Colleges*, pp. 13–19.
64 Cf. Michael M. J. Fischer, *Iran: From Religious Dispute to Revolution*, Harvard Studies in Cultural Anthropology, no. 3 (Cambridge: Harvard University Press, 1980), pp. 61–76.
65 See Mubarak, *Khitat*, 9: 37–8, and *Alam al-Din*, pp. 242ff.; Jacques Berque, *Egypt: Imperialism and Revolution*, pp. 76–83; Afaf Lutfi al-Sayyid Marsot, 'The `ulama' of Cairo in the eighteenth and nineteenth centuries', in Nikki R. Keddie, ed., *Scholars, Saints, and Sufis: Muslim Religious Institutions in the Middle East since 1500* (Berkeley: University of California Press, 1972); Daniel Crecelius, 'Nonideological responses of the Egyptian ulama to modernization', in Keddie, ed., *Scholars, Saints and Sufis*; Haim Shaked, 'The biographies of `ulama' in Mubarak's *Khitat* as a source for the history of the `ulama' in the nineteenth century', *Asian and African Studies* 7 (1971): 59–67. For the life and learning of a Moroccan scholar and the impact of political and social changes in the colonial period, see Dale F. Eickelman, *Knowledge and Power in Morocco: The Education of a Twentieth-Century Notable* (Princeton: Princeton University Press, 1985).
66 For an analysis of the idiom of exposure, its relation to notions of honour and modesty, and the way these conceptions invest social practice and relations of power, see Lila Abu-Lughod, *Veiled Sentiments: Honor and Poetry in a Bedouin*

Society. The work's analysis is drawn from the life of an Egyptian Bedouin community, but its theoretical insights have wide relevance for Egypt and the Mediterranean world.

67 Michael Gilsenan, *Recognizing Islam: Religion and Society in the Modern Arab World*, p. 16.

68 Ahmad Amin, *Qamus al-adat wa-l-taqalid wa-l-ta`abir al-misriyya* (Cairo, 1953), p. 308; Heyworth-Dunne, *History of Education*, pp. 5–6.

69 Cf. Winifred S. Blackman, *The Fellahin of Upper Egypt* (London: Frank Cass, 1968), pp. 109–17, 256, 259.

70 Tahtawi, *al-A`mal al-kamila*, 2: 387.

71 *ibid.* 1: 298.

72 Sami, *Taqwim al-Nil*, 3: 779.

73 Tahtawi, *al-A`mal al-kamila*, 2: 169. Tahtawi published at the same time a translation of a work by Georg Depping, in which he had met the following sentence: '[For the inhabitant of ancient Greece] les exercices du corps . . . faisaient partie chez lui de l'éducation nationale.' The word 'nation' he could handle, but 'education' required a circumlocution: 'Riyadat al-budun . . . hiya maslaha qad ya`udu naf`aha ala sa'ir al-watan' (The exercise of the body . . . is a good whose benefit may redound generally upon the nation). Rifa`a al-Tahtawi, *Qala'id al-mafakhir fi gharib awa'id al-awa'il wa-l-awakhir* (Bulaq, 1833), p. 52; a translation of Georg Bernhard Depping, *Aperçu historique sur les moeurs et coutumes des nations*, p. 107.

74 Tahtawi, *al-A`mal al-kamila*, 2: 18.

75 *ibid.* 2: 159, 770.

76 In his lexicographical work, published in 1881, Dozy gave the meaning of *tarbiya* as 'to bring up' or 'to breed', but added the following gloss on the word, citing sources most of which had been written or published in Cairo in the previous fifty years: 'On emploie ce mot dans le sens d'*ordre, arrangement, disposition,* et dans les phrases où l'on s'attendrait plutôt à trouver le mot *tartib*'. R. Dozy, *Supplément aux dictionnaires arabes* (Leiden: E. J. Brill, 1881), 1: 506.

77 Tahtawi, *al-Murshid al-amin*, p. 33.

78 *ibid.* pp. 28–9.

79 Abd al-Aziz Jawish, *Ghunyat al-mu'addibin fi turuq al-hadith li-l-tarbiya wa-l-ta`lim*, p. 4; Anwar al-Jindi, *Abd al-Aziz Jawish* (Cairo: al-Dar al-Misriyya li-l-Ta'lif wa-l-Tarjama, 1965), pp. 43–165.

80 Husayn al-Marsafi, *Risalat al-kalim al-thaman*, pp. 30–1.

81 Similar ideas were central to the thought of Abduh's mentor, al-Afghani, and Abduh's disciple, Rashid Rida. Cf. Rashid Rida, 'al-Jara'id: waza'if ashabiha', *al-Manar* 1 (1898): 755.

82 Abd al-Rahman al-Rafi`i, *Asr Isma`il*, 1: 242–4.

83 Ibrahim Abduh, *Ta'rikh al-Waqa'i` al-Misriyya, 1828–1942* (Cairo: al-Matba`a al-Amiriyya, 1942), p. 29.

84 Cited Sami, *Taqwim al-Nil*, 3: 454.

85 Heyworth-Dunne, *Education in Modern Egypt*, p. 345

86 See Henry Habib Ayrout, *The Egyptian Peasant*, rev. ed., trans. John Alden Williams (Boston: Beacon Press, 1963), pp. 114–15.
87 Bourdieu discusses at length how this kind of polarisation renders every action within the house and every movement in relation to it a re-enactment, and thereby an implicit inculcation, of the practical principles in terms of which everyday life is improvised. *Outline of a Theory of Practice*, pp. 87–95.
88 Ayrout, *The Egyptian Peasant*, p. 130.

4 After we have captured their bodies

1 Charles Richard, *Etude sur l'insurrection du Dahra (1845–1846)*, in Michael Gilsenan, *Recognizing Islam: Religion and Society in the Modern Arab World*, p. 142, cited from Pierre Bourdieu and Abdelmalek Sayad, *Le déracinement: la crise de l'agriculture traditionelle en Algérie* (Paris: Editions de Minuit, 1964), p. 15.
2 Great Britain, Foreign Office, *Further Correspondence Respecting the Affairs of Egypt*, no. 34, July–September 1890 (London: Foreign Office, 1890), pp. 19–20.
3 Baron de Kusel, *An Englishman's Recollections of Egypt, 1863 to 1887* (London: John Lane, The Bodley Head, 1915), pp. 19–20.
4 Great Britain, *Further Correspondence*, no. 38, January–June 1892 (1893), p. 72.
5 The Earl of Cromer, *Modern Egypt*, 2: 311, 313; Charles Issawi, *An Economic History of the Middle East and North Africa*, pp. 54–5; Zachary Lockman, 'Class and nation: the emergence of the Egyptian workers' movement' (Ph.D. dissertation, Harvard University, 1983), p. 41.
6 Cromer, *Modern Egypt*, 2: 482.
7 Jacques Berque, *Egypt: Imperialism and Revolution*, pp. 127–35; Great Britain, *Further Correspondence*, no. 31, October–December 1889 (1890), p. 42; and no. 32, January–March 1890 (1890), p. 19.
8 Cromer, *Modern Egypt*, 2: 87; cf. M. E. Howard, 'The armed forces', *The New Cambridge Modern History*, vol. 11: *Material Progress and World-wide Problems, 1879–1898*, ed. F. H. Hinsley (Cambridge: Cambridge University Press, 1962), p. 225.
9 Great Britain, *Further Correspondence*, no. 37, July–December 1891 (1892), pp. 7–8; no. 38, January–June 1892 (1893), p. 72; and no. 42, January–June 1894 (1895); Robert Tignor, *Modernization and British Colonial Rule in Egypt, 1882–1914* (Princeton: Princeton University Press, 1966), pp. 184–5, 207; Berque, *Egypt*, p. 135.
10 Cf. Michel Foucault, *Discipline and Punish: The Birth of the Prison*, pp. 135–228.
11 Gabriel Baer, *Studies in the Social History of Modern Egypt*, p. 138.
12 Ali Mubarak, *Alam al-Din*, pp. 160–2.
13 Baer, *Social History of Modern Egypt*, p. 138.

14 As early as the 1830s Rifa`a al-Tahtawi, who was working as a translator at the government's military hospital, produced books in Arabic on European medicine. The first work of general interest to be printed on the new Arabic printing presses was Tahtawi's translation of a French book written for children on the 'manners and customs' of different nations, which included sections on 'False beliefs, heresies and superstitions', stressing that 'such errors are greater in the village than in the city'. Tahtawi, *Qala'id al-mafakhir fi gharib awa'id al-awa'il wa-l-awakhir*, p. 85; cf. Salih Majdi, *Hilyat al-zaman bi-manaqib khadim al-watan: sirat Rifa`a al-Tahtawi* (Cairo, n.d., c. 1874), pp. 33, 35.

15 Abd al-Rahman Isma`il, *Tibb al-rukka* (Cairo: 2 vols., 1892–94; serialised earlier in *al-Adab*), partial translation by John Walker, *Folk Medicine in Modern Egypt, Being the Relevant Parts of the Tibb al-Rukka or Old Wives' Medicine of `Abd al-Rahman Isma`il* (London: Luzac and Co., 1934), pp. 7, 9. The second volume was printed in the name of the Tenth International Congress of Orientalists, held in Geneva in September 1894.

16 Abd al-Rahman Isma`il, *al-Taqwimat al-sihhiyya an al-awa'id al-misriyya* (Cairo: n.p., 1895); and *al-Tarbiya wa-l-adab al-shar`iyya li-l-makatib al-misriyya* (Cairo, 1896). On the Ministry of Education's sponsorship, see *al-Muqtataf* 20 (April 1896): 269; on the author, see Isma`il, *Folk Medicine*, p. 32.

17 Isma`il, *Folk Medicine*, p. 16.

18 *ibid.* pp. 79, 112.

19 Cited Angelo Sammarco, *Histoire de l'Egypte moderne depuis Mohammed Ali jusqu'à l'occupation britannique (1801–1882)*, 3: 256.

20 Amin Sami, *al-Ta`lim fi Misr fi sanatay 1914–1915*, pp. 47–8.

21 Abd al-Aziz Jawish, *Ghunyat al-mu'addibin fi turuq al-hadith li-l-tarbiya wa-l-ta`lim*, pp. 17–19, 42; cf. Anwar al-Jindi, *Abd al-Aziz Jawish* (Cairo: al-Mu'assasa al-misriyya al-amma li-l-ta'lif wa-l-anba' wa-l-nashr, 1965).

22 Rifa`a Rafi` al-Tahtawi, *al-A`mal al-kamila*, 1: 517.

23 *ibid.*

24 Ellious Bochthor, *Dictionnaire française–arabe*, 3rd ed. (Paris, 1864).

25 Butrus al-Bustani, *Muhit al-muhit* (Beirut, 1870).

26 Tahtawi, *al-A`mal al-kamila*, 1: 5.

27 *ibid.* 1: 511.

28 *ibid.* 1: 512.

29 Cromer, *Modern Egypt*, pp. 569–70.

30 V. Edouard Dor, *L'Instruction publique en Egypte*, p. 36.

31 *ibid.* pp. 5, 10–11, 16, 22. The same concern with the 'oriental character' is found in a report on Egyptian education presented to the French Minister of Public Instruction in 1868: Octave Sachot, 'Mission en Egypte: Rapport addressé à Victor Duruy, ministre de l'Instruction Publique, sur l'état des sciences en Egypte dans la population indigène et dans la population européenne' (Paris, June 1868) cited in Gilbert Delanoue, 'Réflexions et questions sur la politique scolaire des vice-rois réformateurs', in *L'Egypte au XIXe siècle* (Paris: CNRS, 1982), p. 326.

32 Dor, *Instruction publique*, p. 36.

33 Edward Lane, *An Account of the Manners and Customs of the Modern Egyptians*, pp. 302–3, 338–9.
34 Georg Bernhard Depping, *Evening Entertainments* (London, 1812; Philadelphia: David Hogan, 1817), pp. vi, 303, 331–5.
35 Georg Bernhard Depping, *Aperçu historique sur les moeurs et coutumes des nations: Contenant le tableau comparé chez les divers peuples anciens et modernes, des usages et des cérémonies concernant l'habitation, la nourriture, l'habillement, les marriages, les funérailles, les jeux, les fêtes, les guerres, les superstitions, les castes, etc., etc.* (Paris: L'Encyclopedie Portative, 1826).
36 Rifa`a Rafi` al-Tahtawi, *Qala'id al-mafakhir fi gharib awa'id al-awa'il wa-l-awakhir* (Bulaq: Dar al-Taba`a, 1833). Among Tahtawi's other translations from Paris were parts of a similar work by Conrad Malte-Brun (1775–1826), *Précis de la géographie universelle*, 8 vols. (Paris: F. Buisson, 1810–29), which were also later published in Cairo. In contrast, two manuscripts of translations from works on Natural Law by Jean Jacques Burlamaqui (1694–1748), *Principes du droit naturel et politique* (Geneva, 1747), and *Principes ou éléments du droit politique* (Lausanne, 1784), were never published. Tahtawi, *al-A`mal al-kamila*, 1: 72–4; see also Alain Silvera, 'The first Egyptian student mission to France under Muhammad Ali', in *Modern Egypt: Studies in Politics and Society*, ed. Elie Kedourie and Sylvia Haim (London: Frank Cass, 1980), pp. 1–22.
37 Israel Altman, 'The political thought of Rifa`a Rafi` al-Tahtawi' (Ph.D. dissertation, University of California, Los Angeles, 1976), p. 24.
38 François de Salignac de la Mothe-Fénelon, *Les Aventures de Télémaque*, pp. 45, 69; Arabic translation pp. 26, 63.
39 Tahtawi, *Manahij al-albab al-misriyya, fi mabahij al-adab al-asriyya*, p. 120.
40 Tahtawi, *al-A`mal al-kamila*, 1: 518.
41 *Self-Help, with Illustrations of Conduct and Perseverence*, introduction by Asa Briggs, 72nd impression (London: John Murray, 1958), translated into Arabic by Ya`qub Sarruf as *Sirr al-Najah* (Beirut, 1880).
42 Smiles, *Self-Help*, p. 36, Arabic translation p. 4.
43 *ibid.* p. 36, Arabic translation p. 5.
44 *ibid.* pp. 35, 315–16.
45 Nadia Farag, 'al-Muqtataf 1876–1900: a study of the influence of Victorian thought on modern Arabic thought', p. 169.
46 Cromer, *Modern Egypt*, 1: 4–8; cf. Ronald Robinson and John Gallagher, *Africa and the Victorians: The Official Mind of Imperialism* (London: Macmillan, 1961), pp. 274–5; Roger Owen, 'The influence of Lord Cromer's Indian experience on British policy in Egypt, 1883–1907' in Albert Hourani, ed., *Middle Eastern Affairs No. 4* (London: Oxford University Press, 1965), pp. 109–39; Tignor, *Modernization and British Colonial Rule*, pp. 48–93. A century later, in 1986, a new edition of *Self-Help* was published in Britain, with an introduction by the government's Minister of Education.
47 Farag, 'al-Muqtataf', p. 169.
48 Speech at the school prize-giving, cited in *Majallat al-Liwa'*, 15 November 1900.

49 Ali Fahmi Kamil, *Mustafa Kamil fi arba`a wa-thalathin rabi`an: siratuhu wa-a`maluhu min khutab wa-ahadith wa-rasa'il*, 11 vols. (Cairo: Matba`at al-Liwa', 1908), pp. 108–9.

50 Asa Briggs, 'Introduction' to Smiles, *Self-Help*, p. 7.

51 *al-Liwa'*, 25th January 1900.

52 *ibid.* 4th January 1900.

53 Mahmud Salama, *al-Liwa'*, 11th February 1900. Besides those I will discuss later, other books discussing the problem of mentality included: the influential work by Ahmad Hafiz Awad, *Min walid ila waladihi* (Cairo: Matba`at al-Bashlawi, 1923), consisting of letters written before the First World War; Ali Efendi Fikri, *Adab al-fatah* (Cairo, 1898); Abd al-Rahman Isma`il, *al-Tarbiya wa-adab al-shar`iyya* (Cairo, 1896); Salih Hamdi Hammad, *Tarbiyat al-banat*, a translation of Fénelon's *L'Education des filles* (Cairo: Matba`at Madrasat Walidat Abbas al-Awwal, 1909); Rafiq al-Azm, *Tanbih al-afham ila matalib al-haya al-jadida wa-l-islam* (Cairo: Matba`at al-Mawsu`at, 1900); Muhammad al-Saba`i, *al-Tarbiya*, a translation of Herbert Spencer's essay on Education (Cairo: Matba`at al-Jarida, 1908).

54 Mustafa Kamil, *al-Shams al-mushriqa* (Cairo: Matba`at al-Liwa', 1904), pp. 11, 176–8.

55 Mahmud Salama, *al-Liwa'*, 11th February 1900.

56 Farag, 'al-Muqtataf', p. 309.

57 Ahmad Fathi Zaghlul, *Sirr taqaddum al-inkliz al-saksuniyyin* (Cairo: Matba`at al-Ma`arif, 1899), a translation of Edmond Demolins, *A quoi tient la supériorité des Anglo-Saxons* (Paris: Librairie de Paris, 1897).

58 Demolins, *Anglo-Saxons*, p. iv.

59 *ibid.* p. 92, Arabic translation, p. 75.

60 *ibid.* p. 93; Arabic translation, p. 76.

61 *ibid.* p. 98.

62 *ibid.* p. 410; Arabic translation, p. 333.

63 Ahmad Fathi Zaghlul, *Sirr taqaddum*, p. 20.

64 *ibid.* pp. 24–30.

65 See Hasan Tawfiq al-Dijwi's introduction to *al-Tarbiya al-haditha* (Cairo: Matba`at al-Taraqqi, 1901), p. 7.

66 Ahmad Lutfi al-Sayyid, cited Husayn Fawzi Najjar, *Ahmad Lutfi al-Sayyid: ustadh al-jil* (Cairo: al-Mu'assasa al-Misriyya al-Amma, 1965), p. 86.

67 Albert Metin, *La transformation de l'Egypte*, cited in Henri Pérès, 'Les origines d'un roman célèbre de la littérature arabe moderne: "Hadith `Isa ibn Hisham" de Muhammad al-Muwailihi', *Bulletin des études orientales* 10 (1944): 101–18.

68 Hasan Tawfiq al-Dijwi, *al-Tarbiya al-haditha*.

69 Cromer, *Modern Egypt*, 2: 538–9.

70 On the transformation of women's lives in nineteenth-century Egypt, see Judith Tucker, *Women in Nineteenth-Century Egypt*. On the writings on this subject at the turn of the century, see Juan Ricardo Cole, 'Feminism, class and Islam in turn-of-the-century Egypt', *International Journal of Middle East Studies* 13 (1981): 387–407.

71 Harry Boyle, 'Memorandum on the British Occupation of Egypt' (1905), in Clara Boyle, *Boyle of Cairo: A Diplomatist's Adventures in the Middle East* (Kendal: Titus Wilson and Son, 1965), p. 56.

72 Qasim Amin, *al-Mar'a al-jadida*, p. 11.

73 Qasim Amin, *Les égyptiens* (Cairo: Jules Barbier, 1894); Duc d'Harcourt, *L'Egypte et les égyptiens* (Paris: Plon, 1893).

74 Harcourt, *L'Egypte*, pp. 1, 3–6, 218, 247–8, 262.

75 Qasim Amin, *Les égyptiens*, pp. 45–7, 243.

76 *ibid.* pp. 100–10.

77 Cited Walter Benjamin, 'On some motifs in Baudelaire', *Illuminations*, ed. Hannah Arendt (New York: Harcourt Brace and World, 1968), p. 167.

78 *ibid.*

79 Muhammad al-Muwailihi, *Hadith Isa ibn Hisham, aw fatra min al-zaman*, 2nd ed. (Cairo: al-Maktaba al-Azhariyya, 1911), pp. 15–20.

80 *ibid.* p. 314.

81 *ibid.* pp. 389, 434–5.

82 For example by the novelist Mahmud Taymur. See Henri Pérès, 'Les origines d'un roman célèbre de la littérature arabe moderne: "Hadith `Isa ibn Hisham" de Muhammad al-Muwailihi', *Bulletin des études orientales* 10 (1944): 101.

83 For the book's publishing history and the expurgated parts, see Roger Allen, 'Hadith `Isa ibn Hisham: the excluded passages', *Die Welt des Islams* 12 (1969): 74–89, 163–81.

84 Roger Allen, *A Study of 'Hadith `Isa ibn Hisham': Muhammad al-Muwaylihi's View of Egyptian Society During the British Occupation* (New York: State University of New York Press, 1974), p. 165.

85 Alexander Schölche, *Egypt for the Egyptians: The Socio-Political Crisis in Egypt, 1878–1882*, p. 327, n. 53. Afaf Lutfi al-Sayyid Marsot, *Egypt in the Reign of Muhammad Ali*, pp. 45, 60; Berque, *Egypt*, pp. 116–17.

86 Qasim Amin, *Les égyptiens*, p. 45; Ahmad Fathi Zaghlul, *Sirr taqaddum al-inkliz al-saksuniyyin*, p. 75.

87 Roger Allen, 'Writings of members of the Nazli circle', *Journal of the American Research Center in Egypt*, 8 (1969–70): 79–84.

88 Henri Pérès, 'Les origines d'un roman célèbre', p. 105; for the preceding decade Mubarak gives the figures of 1,067 cafés and 467 bars, a total of 1,543 establishments (Ali Mubarak, *al-Khitat al-jadida li-Misr al-qahira wa-muduniha wa-biladiha al-qadima wa-l-shahira*, 1: 238).

89 Ali Mubarak, *Alam al-Din*, pp. 453–4.

90 Muhammad Umar, *Hadir al-misriyyin aw sirr ta'akhkhurihim* (Cairo: Matba`at al-Muqtataf, 1902). English translation of the title given on the Arabic title page.

91 *ibid.* p. 230.

92 *ibid.* pp. 267–9.

93 *ibid.* pp. 235, 114–15.

94 Abd al-Hamid al-Zahrawi, *al-Jarida*, 2nd July 1907; for his biography see Umar Rida Kahhala, *Mu`jam al-mu'allifin: tarajim musannifi al-kutub al-*

arabiyya, 15 vols. (Damascus: Matba`at al-Taraqqi, 1957–61), 5: 104, and George Antonius, *The Arab Awakening: the Story of the Arab National Movement* (Philadelphia: Lippincott, 1939), pp. 117, 189. Why wealthy urban-based landowners in the Ottoman-ruled parts of the Arab world turned from Ottomanism to Arab nationalism in this period is explored in Philip S. Khoury, *Urban Notables and Arab Nationalism: the Politics of Damascus, 1860–1920* (Cambridge: Cambridge University Press, 1983).

95 Umar, *Hadir al-misriyyin*, pp. 117–24.
96 *ibid.* pp. 43–4.
97 *ibid.* pp. 166–7.
98 Cf. Benedict Anderson, *Imagined Communities: Reflections on the Origins and Spread of Nationalism* (London: Verso, 1983), for a critical exploration of the themes discussed in this section.
99 On the intellectual formation of Egyptian nationalism, including the central theme of 'political education', see Albert Hourani, *Arabic Thought in the Liberal Age, 1798–1939*, pp. 103–221.
100 Tahtawi, *Manahij al-albab*, p. 6.
101 Tahtawi, *al-A`mal al-kamila*, 1: 516.
102 *ibid.* 1: 519.
103 al-Muwailihi, *Hadith Isa ibn Hisham*, p. 29.
104 *ibid.* p. 30.
105 Durkheim, *The Rules of Sociological Method*, p. 5.
106 For this critique of liberalism, see Uday Mehta, 'The anxiety of freedom: John Locke and the emergence of political subjectivity' (Ph.D. dissertation, Princeton University, 1984).
107 Emile Durkheim, *Education and Sociology*, trans. S. D. Fox, with an Introduction by Talcott Parsons (Glencoe: The Free Press, 1956), p. 123.
108 Cited Steven Lukes, *Emile Durkheim, His Life and Work: A Historical and Critical Study* (Harmondsworth: Penguin Books, 1973), pp. 112, 117, 123.
109 *al-Mu'ayyad*, 18th December 1910, by the anonymous author of the paper's 'Yawmiyyat al-ahad' column. Ahmad Fathi Zaghlul, *Ruh al-ijtima`* (Cairo: Matba`at al-Sha`b, 1909), a translation of Gustave Le Bon, *Psychologie des foules* (Paris: Felix Alcan, 1895); translated into English as *The Crowd: A Study of the Popular Mind* (New York: Macmillan, 1896).
110 On the Dinshawai incident see Afaf Lutfi al-Sayyid, *Egypt and Cromer: A Study in Anglo-Egyptian Relations* (London: John Murray, 1968), pp. 169–73.
111 Ahmad Lutfi al-Sayyid, *al-Jarida*, 13th April 1913, reprinted in his *Ta'ammulat fi al-falsafa wa-al-adab wa-al-siyasa wa-al-ijtima`*, 2nd ed. (Cairo: Dar al-Ma`arif, 1965), pp. 84–5. According to Lutfi al-Sayyid, Fathi Zaghlul's translations of Le Bon, and also of Demolins, Bentham, Spencer and Rousseau, 'were the start of Egypt's intellectual renaissance along political lines' (Afaf Lutfi al-Sayyid, *Egypt and Cromer*, p. 152).
112 Ahmad Fathi Zaghlul, *Sirr tatawwur al-umam* (Cairo: Matba`at al-Ma`arif, 1913), a translation of Le Bon's *Lois psychologiques de l'évolution des peuples*, 12th ed. (Paris: Alcan, 1916), translated into English as *The Psychology of Peoples*

(New York: Macmillan, 1898); Taha Husayn, *Ruh al-tarbiya* (Cairo: Dar al-Hilal, 1922), a translation of Le Bon's *Psychologie de l'éducation* (Paris: Flammarion, 1904; nouvelle edition, 1912, 'augmenté de plusieurs chapitres sur les méthodes d'éducation en Amérique et sur l'enseignement donné aux indigènes des colonies'); Ahmad Fathi Zaghlul also translated Le Bon's *Aphorisms du temps présent* (Paris: Flammarion, 1913), published posthumously as *Jawami` al-kalim* (Cairo: al-Matba`a al-Rahmaniyya, 1922). Cf. Carl Brockelmann, *Geschichte der arabischen Literatur*, supplement 3: 287, 326.

113 Gustave Le Bon, *La civilisation des Arabes* (Paris: Firmin-Didot, 1884), translated in installments in *al-Mufid* (see Rashid Khalidi, '`Abd al-Ghani al-Uraisi and *al-Mufid*; the press and Arab nationalism before 1914', in Martin R. Buheiry, ed., *Intellectual Life in the Arab East, 1890–1939* (Beirut: American University of Beirut Press, 1981), p. 41); and *Les premières civilisations* (Paris: Marpon et Flammarion, 1889), trans. Muhammad Sadiq Rustum, *al-Hadara al-misriyya* (Cairo: al-Matba`a al-Asriyya, n.d.).

114 Gordon Allport, *The Handbook of Social Psychology*, ed. Gardner Lindzey and Elliot Aronson, 2nd ed. (Reading, Mass: Addison-Wesley, 1968), 1: 41; for Freud's use of 'Le Bon's deservedly famous work' see *Group Psychology and the Analysis of the Ego* (New York: Norton, 1959), ch. 2; see also George Rudé, *The Crowd in History* (New York: Wiley, 1964) and Georges Lefebvre, *La Grande peur de 1789* (Paris: Colin, 1932). On the work of Le Bon in general see Susanna Barrows, *Distorting Mirrors: Visions of the Crowd in Late Nineteenth-Century France* (New Haven: Yale University Press, 1981).

115 Barrows, *Distorting Mirrors*. See also Alice Widener, *Gustave Le Bon: The Man and His Works* (Indianapolis: Liberty Press, 1979), pp. 23, 40.

116 Emile Durkheim, *The Division of Labour in Society*, trans. W. D. Halls, Contemporary Social Theory series (London: Macmillan, 1984), pp. 18, 19, 89.

117 Barrows, *Distorting Mirrors*, p. 164.

118 Le Bon, *The Psychology of Peoples*, pp. 4–5, 13.

119 On Le Bon's influence on Durkheim, see Mary Douglas, *Purity and Danger: An Analysis of the Concepts of Pollution and Taboo* (New York: Praeger, 1966), p. 20.

120 Le Bon, *The Psychology of Peoples*, pp. xix, 6, 37.

121 *ibid*. pp. 199–200, 231.

122 *ibid*. pp. 211–12.

123 The translation was published in instalments in *al-Mufid*, one of the most influential daily newspapers in the entire Arab east in this period. See Khalidi, '`Abd al-Ghani al-Uraisi', p. 41.

124 Le Bon was away, so Abduh left his card and a small, amicable correspondence ensued (Anouar Louca, *Voyageurs et écrivains égyptiens en France au XIXe siècle*, p. 142). On Abduh, the influence of French social science, and his influence in turn on Arab political thought, see Albert Hourani, *Arabic Thought in the Liberal Age, 1789–1939*, especially pp. 139–40.

125 Cf. Barrows, *Distorting Mirrors*, p. 72.

126 Le Bon, *The Crowd*, p. 36; Freud, *Group Psychology*, ch. 2.

127 Durkheim, *Rules*, pp. 8, 30.

5 The machinery of truth

1 Baron de Kusel, *An Englishman's Recollections of Egypt, 1863 to 1887* (London: John Lane, The Bodley Head, 1915), p. 199.
2 The Earl of Cromer, *Modern Egypt*, 1: 296–8.
3 Col. J. F. Maurice, *Military History of the Campaign of 1882 in Egypt*, prepared in the intelligence branch of the War Office (London: HMSO, 1887), p. 96.
4 Maurice, *Military History*, p. 105.
5 *ibid.* p. 6.
6 Husayn al-Marsafi, *Risalat al-kalim al-thaman* (1881). The eight Arabic terms are: *umma, watan, hukuma, adl, zulm, siyasa, hurriyya, tarbiya*. There is only a passing reference to the book in the major work of the Urabi Revolution: Alexander Schölch, *Agypten der Agyptern! Die politische und gesellschaftliche Krise der Jahre 1878–1882 in Agypten* (Freiburg: Atlantis, 1972), p. 361; the reference is omitted from the English translation. On Marsafi and his relationship with the nationalists see Muhammad Abd al-Jawad, *Al-Shaykh al-Husayn ibn Ahmad al-Marsafi: al-ustadh al-awwal li-l-ulum al-adabiyya bi-Dar al-Ulum* (Cario: al-Ma'arif, 1952), pp. 40–2, and Ahmad Zakariya al-Shilq, *Ru'ya fi tahdith al-fikr al-misri: al-shaykh Husayn al-Marsafi wa-kitabuhu 'Risalat al-kalim al-thaman'* (Cairo: al-Hay'a al-Misriyya al-Amma li-l-Kutub, 1984), p. 25.
7 'Arabi's account of his life and of the events of 1881–1882' in Wilfred Scawen Blunt, *Secret History of the English Occupation of Egypt, Being a personal narrative of events*, 2nd ed. (London: T. Fisher Unwin, 1907), appendix 1, p. 482; 'Programme of the National Party', in Blunt, *Secret History*, appendix 5, p. 558.
8 Alexander Schölch, *Egypt for the Egyptians: The Socio-Political Crisis in Egypt 1878–1882*, pp. 181–2.
9 Abd al-Rahman al-Jabarti, *Ta'rikh muddat al-faransis bi-Misr*, pp. 7–17.
10 Abu al-Futuh Radwan, *Ta'rikh Matba'at Bulaq* (Cairo: al-Matba'a al-Amiriyya, 1953), pp. 446–79.
11 Radwan, *Ta'rikh*, pp. 56–74.
12 Marsafi, *al-Kalim al-thaman*, pp. 31–2.
13 Tahtawi, *Manahij al-albab al-misriyya, fi mabahij al-adab al-asriyya*, p. 231. For the same theme in Ottoman political writing, see Şerif Mardin, *The Genesis of Young Ottoman Thought* (Princeton: Princeton University Press, 1962), pp. 95–102.
14 Abd al-Rahman Ibn Khaldun, *Muqaddimat Ibn Khaldun*, ed. E. Quatremère, 1: 65; cf. *The Muqaddimah: An Introduction to History*, trans. Franz Rosenthal, 1: 81–2.
15 Ibn Khaldun, *Kitab al-ibar wa-diwan al-mubtada' wa-l-khabar* etc., ed. Nasr al-Hurini, 7 vols. (Bulaq, 1867). Volume 1 ('The Muqaddima') and volumes 6 and 7 (dealing with the history of North Africa) had appeared in print slightly earlier, in editions published by French scholars in the 1850s. Volume 1 is translated into English in three volumes by Franz Rosenthal as *The Muqqadimah: An Introduction to History*.

16 Ahmad Taymur, *Tarajim a'yan al-qarn al-thalith ashar wa-awa'il al-rabi' ashar* (Cairo: Matba'at Abd al-Hamid Ahmad Hanafi, 1940), p. 148; Anouar Abdel-Malek, *Idéologie et renaissance nationale: l'Egypte moderne*, p. 388.

17 Ibn Khaldun, *Muqaddimat Ibn Khaldun*, ed. E. Quatremère, p. 65.

18 His students wrote the textbooks of Arabic literature and grammar that were to be used in government schools for more than a generation; his lectures were compiled into two multi-volume works, *al-Wasila al-adabiyya ila al-ulum al-arabiyya*, 2 vols. (Cairo: vol. 1, Matba'at al-Madaris al-Malikiyya, 1872–75; vol. 2, Matba'at Wadi al-Nil, 1875–79), and 'Dalil al-mustarshid fi fann al-insha'' (Cairo, 1890), the manuscript of which was completed just before the author's death but never published; and he was an important influence on the writer Abdullah Fikri (who was later Minister of Education and delegate to the Stockholm Orientalist Congress) and on a number of major Egyptian poets, including al-Barudi, Ahmad Shawqi and Hafiz Ibrahim (Abd al-Jawad, *Marsafi*, pp. 82–91, 117–19; Carl Brockelmann, *Geschichte der Arabischen Literatur* (Leiden, 1943–49), supplement 2: 727).

19 See Charles Pellat, 'Variations sur le thème de l'adab', in his *Etudes sur l'histoire socio-culturelle de l'Islam* (London: Variorum Reprints, 1976).

20 Marsafi, *al-Kalim al-thaman*, p. 140.

21 *ibid.* p. 3.

22 *ibid.* pp. 85–6, 131, for references to French authors.

23 *ibid.* pp. 75–9.

24 *ibid.* pp. 16, 112, 116, 126, 140.

25 *ibid.* pp. 112–13, 142, 122–3.

26 *ibid.* pp. 125–8.

27 Salim Khalil al-Naqqash, *Misr li-l-misriyyin*, 9 vols. (vols. 1 to 3 never published) (Alexandria: Matba'at Jaridat al-Mahrusa, 1884), 7: 444–5.

28 *Encyclopaedia of Islam*, new edition, 5 vols., prepared by a number of leading Orientalists (Leiden: E. J. Brill, London: Luzac and Co., 1960–), 3: 514.

29 Michel Foucault, *The Order of Things: An Archaeology of the Human Sciences*, pp. 217–343.

30 Friedrich Max Müller, *Lectures on the Science of Language* (London: Longman, 1861), pp. 25–6.

31 Ernest Renan, 'De l'origine du langage' (1848), *Oeuvres complètes*, 8: 11.

32 William Dwight Whitney, *Oriental and Linguistic Studies*, 2 vols. (New York: Scribner, Armstrong and Co., 1873), 2: 347.

33 International Congress of Orientalists, *Transactions of the Ninth Congress, London, 5–12 September 1892*, ed. E. Delmar Morgan, 1: 9.

34 Renan, *Oeuvres complètes*, 8: 37–8.

35 Michel Bréal, *Essai de sémantique; Science des significations* (Paris: Hachette, 1899; 1st ed. 1897) p. 279; cf. Hans Aarsleff, 'Bréal vs. Schleicher: Reorientations in linguistics in the latter half of the nineteenth century' in *From Locke to Saussure: Essays on the Study of Language and Intellectual History* (Minneapolis: University of Minnesota Press, 1982), p. 296.

36 Michel Bréal, 'Les idées latentes du langage' (1868), in *Mélanges de mythologie*

et de linguistique (Paris: Hachette, 1877), p. 321; cf. Aarsleff, 'Bréal vs. Schleicher', pp. 306–7.

37 Michel Bréal, 'De la forme et fonction des mots', in *Mélanges*, p. 249, cited Aarsleff, 'Bréal vs. Schleicher', p. 297.

38 Cf. Aarsleff, 'Bréal vs. Schleicher'.

39 Michel Bréal, 'La langage et les nationalités', *Revue des deux mondes* 108 (1st December 1891): 619, cited Aarsleff, 'Bréal vs. Schleicher', p. 384.

40 Bréal, 'Les idées latentes', in *Mélanges*, p. 322.

41 Gilbert Delanoue, *Moralistes et politiques musulmans dans l'Egypte du XIXe siècle (1798–1882)*, 2: 371.

42 Marsafi, *al-Kalim al-thaman*, p. 4. For the following discussion, see Monçef Chelli, *La parole arabe: une théorie de la relativité des cultures*, pp. 46–67.

43 Geoffrey Hartman, *Saving the Text: Literature/Derrida/Philosophy* (Baltimore: Johns Hopkins University Press, 1981), p. xxi.

44 Ferdinand de Saussure, *Course in General Linguistics*, trans. Wade Baskin (New York: Philosophical Library, 1959), pp. 66–7.

45 Jacques Derrida, *Of Grammatology*, trans. Gayatri Chakravorty Spivak (Baltimore: The Johns Hopkins University Press, 1974).

46 Jacques Derrida, *Speech and Phenomena, and other essays of Husserl's Theory of Signs*; Terry Eagleton, *Literary Theory* (Oxford: Basil Blackwell, 1983), pp. 127–8.

47 Derrida, *Speech and Phenomena*, p. 50; and 'Differance', in *Margins of Philosophy*, pp. 1–27.

48 Derrida, *Speech and Phenomena*, p. 52.

49 Chelli, *La parole arabe*, pp. 35–45.

50 Cf. Jacques Derrida, 'Signature event context', in *Margins of Philosophy*, pp. 307–30.

51 Ibn Khaldun, *Muqaddimah*, trans. Rosenthal, 2: 356.

52 Cf. Ibn Khaldun, *Muqaddimat Ibn Khaldun*, ed. Quatremère, 3: 242 line 5, 243 lines 3–4.

53 Cf. Ibn Khaldun, *Muqaddimah*, trans. Rosenthal, 3: 55–75.

54 *ibid.* 3: 316.

55 *ibid.* 3: 316.

56 *ibid.* 3: 292.

57 cf. Richard W. Bulliet, *The Patricians of Nishapur: A Study in Medieval Islamic Social History* (Cambridge: Cambridge University Press, 1972), pp. 49, 57.

58 Muhsin Mahdi, *Ibn Khaldun's Philosophy of History* (Chicago: University of Chicago Press, 1957; Phoenix ed., 1964).

59 Schölch, *Egypt for the Egyptians*, pp. 181, 348.

60 The Earl of Cromer, in Great Britain, Foreign Office, *Further Correspondence Respecting the Affairs of Egypt* no. 35, October–December 1890 (London: Foreign Office, 1891), p. 22.

61 Tahtawi, *al-A`mal al-kamila*, 1: 247; see also 1: 520.

62 Marsafi, *al-Kalim al-thaman*, pp. 11, 93, 142.

63 Rashid Rida, *Ta'rikh al-ustadh al-imam Muhammad Abduh*, 1: 30–1.

64 Homa Pakdaman, *Djamal ed-Din Assad Abadi dit Afghani* (Paris: Maisonneuve et Larose, 1969), pp. 46–7, 49.

65 Marsafi, *al-Kalim al-thaman*, p. 93.

66 See for example al-Afghani, cited in Pakdaman, *Djamal ed-Din*, p. 47.

67 See for example Tahtawi, *al-A`mal al-kamila*, 1: 247.

68 Marsafi, *al-Kalim al-thaman*, p. 93.

69 Muhammad Majdi, *Thamaniyata ashar yawman bi-sa`id Misr, sanat 1310* (Cairo: Matba`at al-Mawsu`at, 1319h), p. 42.

70 *ibid.* p. 50.

71 Cromer, *Modern Egypt*, 2: 257, 260.

72 *ibid.* 2: 131.

73 *ibid.* 2: 321, emphasis added.

6 The philosophy of the thing

1 André Maurois, *Lyautey*, pp. 319–20.

2 Janet L. Abu-Lughod, *Rabat: Urban Apartheid in Morocco* (Princeton: Princeton University Press, 1980), p. 152.

3 Steven T. Rosenthal, 'Municipal reform in Istanbul 1850–1870: the impact of tanzimat on Ottoman affairs' (Ph.D. dissertation, Yale University, 1974), pp. 52–66.

4 Muhammad Farid Wajdi, *al-Islam wa-l-madaniyya, aw, tatbiq al-diyana al-islamiyya ala nawamis al-madaniyya* (Cairo: 2nd ed., n.p., 1904; 1st ed., al-Matba`a al-Uthmaniyya, 1898), p. 4.

5 Maurois, *Lyautey*, pp. 252–3.

6 *ibid.* p. 316.

7 Henri Pieron, 'Le Caire: Son esthétique dans la ville arabe et dans la ville moderne', *L'Egypte Contemporaine* 5 (January 1911): 512.

8 See the discussion of this theme in Michael Gilsenan, *Recognizing Islam: Religion and Society in the Modern Arab World*, pp. 192–214, and in Abu-Lughod, *Rabat*, pp. 131–95.

9 According to Janet Abu-Lughod, during the first decade of the twentieth century only about thirty per cent of Cairo's growth was due to natural increase. Of the remainder, more than a third was due to rural in-migration and almost two-thirds to the influx of Europeans (*Cairo: 1001 Years of the City Victorious*, pp. 111–15); cf. Justin McCarthy, 'Nineteenth-century Egyptian population', *Middle East Journal* 12 (1976): 31.

10 Cited in Bent Hansen, 'Prices, wages, and land rents: Egypt 1895–1913', *Working Papers in Economics*, no. 131, Department of Economics, University of California, Berkeley, October 1979, pp. 34–5.

11 Frantz Fanon, *The Wretched of the Earth*, trans. Constance Farrington (Harmondsworth: Penguin Books, 1979) pp. 29–30.

12 See Edward W. Said, *Orientalism*.

13 International Congress of Orientalists, *Transactions of the Ninth Congress, London, 5–12 September 1892*, ed. E. Delmar Morgan, 1: 8.

14 *ibid.* 2: 805.
15 *Muqtataf* 17 (1893): 88, cited Nadia Farag, 'al-Muqtataf 1876–1900: a study of the influence of Victorian thought on modern Arabic thought', p. 243.
16 International Congress of Orientalists, *Transactions of the Ninth Congress*, 1: 35.
17 *ibid.* 1: 36–7.
18 As in chapter 5, these arguments are indebted to the work of Jacques Derrida.
19 *al-Muqtataf* 12 (1888): 316, cited Farag, 'al-Muqtataf', p. 243.
20 *al-Muqtataf* 17 (1893): 88; cf. Sadik Jalal al-`Azm, 'Orientalism and Orientalism in reverse', *Khamsin 8* (London: Ithaca Press, 1981), pp. 5–26.
21 Jurji Zaydan, *Ta'rikh Misr al-hadith* (Cairo: Matba`at al-Muqtataf, 1889); and *al-Ta'rikh al-amm* (Cairo: Matba`at al-Muqtataf, 1890), of which only the first volume, the ancient and modern history of Asia and Africa (dealing for all except two pages with Egypt) was ever published.
22 Jurji Zaydan, *Ta'rikh al-tamaddun al-islami*, 5 vols. (Cairo: Dar al-Hilal, 1901–6; reprint ed., 1958), 1: 12, 13–14. See also Lewis Ware, 'Jurji Zaydan: the role of popular history in the formation of a new Arab world view' (Ph.D. dissertation, Princeton University, 1973), pp. 181–92, 197–204.
23 *al-Hilal* 6: 109, 15: 18, cited Ware, 'Jurji Zaydan', pp. 109, 159.
24 Critical essays were collected and published by Rashid Rida in *Intiqad kitab ta'rikh al-tamaddun al-islami* (Cairo: Matba`at al-Manar, 1912).
25 See for example the review of his work by de Goeje in *Journal asiatique* 10: 3 (1904). Among his friends and acquaintances were the Orientalists Noldecke, Wellhausen, Goldzieher, Wright, MacDonald and Margoliouth. See Zaydan, *Ta'rikh al-tamuddun*, 1: 9, and D. S. Margoliouth, trans., *Umayyads and `Abbasids*, being the 4th part of Jurji Zaydan's history of Islamic civilisation (Leiden: E. J. Brill, 1907), p. xiv.
26 The only serious general history of Islam written by then in Europe was August Müller's *Der Islam in Morgen- und Abendland* (Berlin: Grote, 1885–87); Alfred von Kremer's *Culturgeschichte des Orients unter den Chalifen* (Vienna: W. Braumüller, 1875–77) had been used as a source by Zaydan but was not available in English. Serious works in English on Islamic history dealt only with the lives of Muhammad and the first four caliphs: D. S. Margoliouth, *Muhammad and the Rise of Islam* (1905); and Sir William Muir, *Life of Muhammad* (1861) and *Annals of the Early Caliphate* (London: Smith, Elder and Co., 1883).
27 *Ta'rikh adab al-lugha al-arabiyya*. See Muhammad Abd al-Jawad, *Al-Shaykh al-Husayn ibn Ahmad al-Marsafi: al-ustadh al-awwal li-l-ulum al-adabiyya bi-Dar al-Ulum* (Cairo: Dar al-Ma`arif, 1952), p. 81.
28 Jurji Zaydan, *Ta'rikh adab al-lugha al-arabiyya*, 1: 8.
29 Thomas Philipp, *Gurgi Zaydan: His Life and Work* (Beirut: Orient-Institut der Deutshe Morgenländ Gesellschaft, 1979), p. 44.
30 Bernard Cohen discusses a similar process of penetration in colonial India, and relates it in a similar way to the larger process of organising an exhibition of colonial authority: 'Representing authority in Victorian India' in Eric

Hobsbawm and Terence Ranger, eds., *The Invention of Tradition* (Cambridge: Cambridge University Press, 1983), pp. 165–209.

31 On insane asylums see the thesis by Marilyn Mayers, 'A century of psychiatry: the Egyptian mental hospital' (Ph.D. dissertation, Princeton University, 1982).

32 The Earl of Cromer, *Modern Egypt*, 2: 556–7. 'The schoolmaster is abroad' was the famous phrase of the Benthamite reformer Lord Brougham, whose projects 'for the diffusion of useful knowledge' I have referred to in earlier chapters.

33 Cromer, *Modern Egypt*, 2: 280.

34 Michel Foucault, 'Two Lectures' in *Power/Knowledge: Selected Interviews and Other Writings, 1972–1977*, pp. 104–5.

35 Maurois, *Lyautey*, p. 320.

36 For the following discussion, see Richard Rorty, *Philosophy and the Mirror of Nature*.

37 Cf. Ibn Khaldun, *Muqaddimat Ibn Khaldun*, ed. E. Quatremère.

38 'Discourse on the method', in Descartes, *Philosophical Writings*, trans. and ed. Elizabeth Anscombe and Peter Thomas Geach, rev. ed. (London: Thomas Nelson, 1970), pp. 15–16.

Select bibliography

`Abd al-Karīm, Ahmad `Izzat, *Ta'rīkh al-ta`līm fī `asr Muhammad `Alī*. Cairo: Matba`at al-Nahda al-Misriyya, 1938.
Ta'rīkh al-ta`līm fī Misr min nihāyat hukm Muhammad `Alī ilā awā'il hukm Tawfīq, 1848–1882. Cairo: Matba'at al-Nasr, 1945.
Abdel-Malek, Anouar, *Idéologie et renaissance nationale: l'Egypte moderne*. Paris: Anthropos, 1969.
`Abduh, Ibrāhīm, *Tatawwur al-sahāfa al-misriyya, 1798–1951*. Cairo: Maktabat al-Adāb, n.d.
Abu-Lughod, Ibrahim, *Arab Rediscovery of Europe*. Princeton: Princeton University Press, 1963.
Abu-Lughod, Janet, *Cairo: 1001 Years of the City Victorious*. Princeton: Princeton University Press, 1971.
Abu-Lughod, Lila, *Veiled Sentiments: Honor and Poetry in a Bedouin Society*. Berkeley: University of California Press, 1986.
Ahmed, Leila, *Edward W. Lane: A Study of His Life and Work, and of British Ideas of the Middle East in the Nineteenth Century*. London: Longmans, 1978.
Alloula, Malek, *The Colonial Harem*, trans. Myrna Godzich and Wlad Godzich, with an Introduction by Barbara Harlow, Theory and History of Literature, vol. 21. Minneapolis: University of Minnesota Press, 1986.
Arminjon, Pierre, *L'Enseignement, la doctrine et la vie dans les universités musulmanes d'Egypte*. Paris: Felix Alcan, 1907.
D'Arnaud, 'Reconstruction des villages de l'Egypte', *Bulletin de la Société de Géographie*, series 3, no. 52/53 (April/May 1848): 278–81.
Baer, Gabriel, *Studies in the Social History of Modern Egypt*. Chicago: University of Chicago Press, 1969.
Baudrillard, Jean, *The Mirror of Production*, trans. Mark Poster. St. Louis: Telos Press, 1975.
Bendiner, Kenneth P., 'The portrayal of the Middle East in British painting, 1825–1860'. Ph.D. dissertation, Columbia University, 1979.
Benjamin, Walter, 'Paris, capital of the nineteenth century', in *Reflections: Essays, Aphorisms, Autobiographical Writings*, ed. Peter Demetz. New York: Harcourt, Brace, Jovanovich, 1978.
Bentham, Jeremy, 'Panopticon', in *The Complete Works of Jeremy Bentham*, ed. John Bowring, 11 vols. Edinburgh and London: Tait, 1838–42.
Berardi, Roberto, 'Espace et ville en pays d'Islam', in D. Chevallier, ed., *L'Espace sociale de la ville arabe*. Paris: Maisonneuve et Larose, 1979.

Berque, Jacques, *Egypt: Imperialism and Revolution*, trans. Jean Stewart. London: Faber and Faber, 1972.

Bowring, John, 'Report on Egypt and Candia', in Great Britain, House of Commons, *Sessional Papers*, 1840, vol. xxi, pp. 1–227.

Bourdieu, Pierre, 'The Kabyle house or the world reversed', in *Algeria 1960*. Cambridge: Cambridge University Press, 1979, pp. 133–53.

Outline of a Theory of Practice. Cambridge: Cambridge University Press, 1977.

Bréal, Michel, *Essai de sémantique; science des significations*. Paris: Hachette, 1897; 2nd ed., 1899.

'Les idées latentes du langage' (1868), in *Mélanges de mythologie et de linguistique*. Paris: Hachette, 1877, pp. 295–322.

Brockelmann, Carl, *Geschichte der arabischen Litteratur*, 2 vols., den Supplementbänden angepasste Auflage. Leiden: E. J. Brill, 1937–49.

Carré, J. M., *Voyageurs et écrivains français en Egypte*, 2nd ed. Cairo: Institut Français d'Archéologie Orientale, 1956.

Chelli, Monçef, *La parole arabe: une théorie de la relativité des cultures*. Paris: Sindbad, 1980.

Crecelius, Daniel, *The Roots of Modern Egypt: A Study of the Regimes of `Ali Bey al-Kabir and Muhammad Bey Abu al-Dhahab, 1760–1775*. Minneapolis and Chicago: Bibliotheca Islamica, 1981.

Cromer, The Earl of, *Modern Egypt*, 2 vols. New York: Macmillan, 1908.

Delanoue, Gilbert, *Moralistes et politiques musulmans dans l'Egypte du XIXe siècle (1798–1882)*, 2 vols. Paris: Institut Français d'Archéologie Orientale, 1982.

Derrida, Jacques, 'The double session', *Dissemination*, trans. Barbara Johnson. Chicago: University of Chicago Press, 1981, pp. 173–285.

Margins of Philosophy, trans. Alan Bass. Chicago: University of Chicago Press, 1982.

Speech and Phenomena, and other Essays on Husserl's Theory of Signs, trans. David B. Allison, Northwestern Studies in Phenomenology and Existential Philosophy. Evanston: Northwestern University Press, 1973.

Dor, V. Edouard, *L'Instruction publique en Egypte*. Paris: A. Lacroix, Verboeckhoven et cie, 1872.

Douin, Georges, *Histoire du regne du Khedive Ismail*, 2 vols. Rome: Royal Egyptian Geographical Society, 1934.

Durkheim, Emile, *The Rules of Sociological Method*, 8th ed., trans. Sarah A. Solovay and John H. Mueller, ed. George E. G. Catlin. New York: The Free Press, 1938.

Eagleton, Terry, *Literary Theory*. Oxford: Basil Blackwell, 1983.

Farag, Nadia, 'al-Muqtataf 1876–1900: a study of the influence of Victorian thought on modern Arabic thought'. Ph.D. thesis, Oxford University, 1969.

Fikrī, Muhammad Amīn, *Irshād al-alibbā' ilā mahāsin Urūbbā*. Cairo: Matba`at al-Muqtataf, 1892.

Flaubert, Gustave, *Flaubert in Egypt: A Sensibility on Tour*, trans. and ed. Francis Steegmuller. London: Michael Haag, 1983.

Foucault, Michel, *Discipline and Punish: The Birth of the Prison*, trans. Alan Sheridan. New York: Pantheon, 1977.

The Order of Things: An Archaeology of the Human Sciences. New York: Random House, 1970.

'Two lectures', in *Power/Knowledge: Selected Interviews and Other Writings 1972–1977*, ed. Colin Gordon. New York: Random House, 1981, pp. 78–108.

Gautier, Théophile, *Oeuvres complètes*, 26 vols. Vol. 20, *L'Orient*. Paris: Charpentier, 1880–1903.

Gérard de Nerval, *Oeuvres*, ed. Albert Béguin and Jean Richer, 2 vols. Vol. 1: *Voyage en Orient* (1851), ed. Michel Jeanneret. Paris: Gallimard, 1952.

Gilsenan, Michael, *Recognizing Islam: Religion and Society in the Modern Arab World.* New York: Pantheon, 1982.

Gran, Peter, *Islamic Roots of Capitalism, 1769–1840.* Austin: University of Texas Press, 1979.

Heidegger, Martin, 'The age of the world picture', in *The Question Concerning Technology and Other Essays*, trans. William Lovitt. New York: Harper and Row, 1977, pp. 115–54.

Heyworth-Dunne, James, *An Introduction to the History of Education in Modern Egypt.* London: Luzac and Co., 1939.

Hourani, Albert, *Arabic Thought in the Liberal Age, 1798–1939*, 3rd ed. Cambridge: Cambridge University Press, 1983.

'Ottoman reform and the politics of notables', in *Beginnings of Modernization in the Middle East: the Nineteenth Century*, ed. William R. Polk and Richard L. Chambers. Chicago: University of Chicago Press, 1968, pp. 41–68.

and S. M. Stern, eds., *The Islamic City.* Oxford: Bruno Cassirer, and Philadelphia: University of Pennsylvania Press, 1970.

Hunter, F. Robert, *Egypt Under the Khedives, 1805–1874: From Household Government to Modern Bureaucracy*, Pittsburgh: University of Pittsburgh Press, 1984.

Ibn Khaldūn, 'Abd al-Rahmān, *Muqaddimat Ibn Khaldūn*, ed. E. M. Quatremère, 3 vols. Paris: Institut Impérial de France, 1858; reprint ed., Beirut: Maktabat Lubnān, 1970. English trans., *The Muqaddimah: An Introduction to History*, trans. Franz Rosenthal, 2nd ed., 3 vols. Princeton: Princeton University Press, 1967.

Ilyās, Idwār Bey, *Mashāhid Urūbā wa-Amīrkā.* Cairo: Matba'at al-Muqtataf, 1900.

International Congress of Orientalists, *Transactions of the Ninth Congress, London, 5–12 September 1892*, ed. E. Delmar Morgan, 2 vols. London, International Congress of Orientalists, 1893.

Ismā'īl, 'Abd al-Rahmān, *Tibb al-rukka*, 2 vols. Cairo, 1892–94. Partial translation, John Walker, *Folk Medicine in Modern Egypt, Being the Relevant Parts of the Tibb al-Rukka or Old Wives' Medicine of 'Abd al-Rahmān Ismā'īl.* London: Luzac and Co., 1934.

Issawi, Charles, *An Economic History of the Middle East and North Africa.* New York: Columbia University Press, 1982.

Jabartī, 'Abd al-Rahmān al-, *Ta'rīkh muddat al-faransīs bi-Misr*, ed. S. Moreh and published with a translation as *Al-Jabarti's Chronicle of the First Seven Months of the French Occupation of Egypt, Muharram-Rajab 1213 (15th June–December 1798).* Leiden: E. J. Brill, 1975.

Jawīsh, ʿAbd al-ʿAzīz, *Ghunyat al-muʾaddibīn fī turuq al-hadīth li-l-tarbiya wa-l-taʿlīm*. Cairo: Matbaʿat al-Shaʿb, 1903.

Kaestle, Carl F., ed., *Joseph Lancaster and the Monitorial School Movement: A Documentary History*. New York: Columbia University Teachers College Press, 1973.

Lamarre, Clovis, and Charles Fliniaux, *L'Egypte, la Tunisie, le Maroc et l'exposition de 1878*, in the series, *Les pays étrangers et l'exposition de 1878*, 20 vols. Paris: Libraire Ch. Delagrave, 1878.

Lane, Edward, *An Account of the Manners and Customs of the Modern Egyptians*. London: Charles Knight, 1835; Everyman Edition, London: J. M. Dent, 1908.

Le Bon, Gustave, *Les premières civilisations*. Paris: Marpon et Flammarion, 1889. Arabic trans. of the third part, Muhammad Sādiq Rustum, *al-Hadāra al-misriyya*. Cairo: al-Matbaʿa al-ʿAsriyya, n.d.

Lois psychologiques de l'évolution des peuples, 12th ed. Paris: Felix Alcan, 1916. English trans., *The Psychology of Peoples*. New York: Macmillan, 1898.

Psychologie des foules. Paris: Felix Alcan, 1895. English trans., *The Crowd: A Study of the Popular Mind*. New York: Macmillan, 1896.

Louca, Anouar, *Voyageurs et écrivains égyptiens en France au XIXe siècle*. Paris: Didier, 1970.

Marsafī, Husayn al-, *Risālat al-kalim al-thamān*. Cairo: Matbaʿat al-Jumhūr, 1903; 1st ed. 1881.

al-Wasīla al-adabiyya ilā al-ʿulūm al-ʿarabiyya, 2 vols. Vol. 1, Cairo: Matbaʿat al-Madāris al-Malikiyya, 1872–75; vol. 2, Matbaʿat Wadī al-Nīl, 1875–79.

Marsot, Afaf Lutfi Al-Sayyid, *Egypt in the Reign of Muhammad Ali*. Cambridge: Cambridge University Press, 1984.

Marx, Karl, *Capital*, trans. Ben Fowkes, 3 vols. Harmondsworth: Penguin, 1976.

Maurois, André, *Lyautey*. Paris: Plon, 1931.

Mubārak, ʿAlī, *ʿAlam al-Dīn*, Alexandria: Matbaʿat Jarīdat al-Mahrūsa, 1882.

al-Khitat al-jadīda li-Misr al-qāhira wa-mudunihā wa-bilādihā al-qadīma wa-l-shahīra, 20 vols. in 4. Bulaq, 1307h (1889/90); 1st ed. 1305h (1887/8).

Mumford, Lewis, *Technics and Civilization*. New York: Harcourt Brace and Co., 1934.

Mustafa Reshīd Celebi Effendi, 'An explanation of the nizam-y-gedid', in William Wilkinson, *An Account of the Principalities of Wallachia and Moldavia Including Various Political Observations Relating to Them*. London: Longman *et al.*, 1820, appendix 5.

Muwailihī, Muhammad al-, *Hadīth ʿIsā ibn Hishām, aw fatra min al-zaman*, 2nd ed. Cairo: al-Maktaba al-Azhariyya, 1911; 1st ed. 1907.

Owen, Roger, *The Middle East in the World Economy 1800–1914*. London: Methuen, 1981.

Pieron, Henri, 'Le Caire: son ésthetique dans la ville arabe et dans la ville moderne'. *L'Egypte contemporaine* 5 (January 1911): 511–28.

Qāsim Amīn, *Les égyptiens*. Cairo: Jules Barbier, 1894.

Radwān, Abū al-Futūh, *Ta'rīkh Matbaʿat Bulāq*. Cairo: al-Matbaʿa al-Amīriyya. 1953.

Select bibliography

Rāfiʿī, ʿAbd al-Rahmān al-, *ʿAsr Ismāʿīl*, 2nd ed., 2 vols. Cairo: Maktabat al-Nahda al-Misriyya, 1948.

Raymond, André, *Artisans et commerçants au Caire au XVIIIe siècle*, 2 vols. Damascus: Institut français de Damas, 1973.

Grandes villes arabes à l'époque ottomane. Paris: Sindbad, 1985.

Renan, Ernest, 'De l'origine du langage' (1848), *Oeuvres complètes*, ed. Henriette Psichari, 10 vols. Paris: Calmann-Lévy, 1947– .

Ridā, Rashīd, *Ta'rīkh al-ustādh al-imām Muhammad ʿAbduh*, 3 vols. Cairo: Matbaʿat al-Manār, 1324–50h (1906–31).

Rivlin, Helen, *The Agricultural Policy of Muhammad Ali in Egypt*. Cambridge: Harvard University Press, 1961.

Rorty, Richard, *Philosophy and the Mirror of Nature*. Princeton: Princeton University Press, 1979.

Said, Edward, *Orientalism*. New York: Pantheon, 1978.

St John, Bayle, *Village Life in Egypt*, 2 vols. London: Chapman and Hall, 1852; reprint ed., New York: Arno Press, 1973.

Sāmī, Amīn, *al-Taʿlīm fī Misr fī sanatay 1914–1915, wa-bayān tafsīlī li-nashr al-taʿlīm al-awwalī wa-l-ibtidāʾī bi-anhāʾ al-diyār al-misriyya*. Cairo: Matbaʿat al-Maʿārif, 1916.

Taqwīm al-Nīl, wa-asmāʾ man tawallaw amr Misr maʿa muddat hukmihim ʿalayhā wa mulāhazāt taʾrīkhiyya ʿan ahwāl al-khilāfa al-ʿāmma wa shuʾūn Misr al-khāssa. Cairo: Matbaʿat Dār al-Kutub al-Misriyya, 1936.

Sammarco, Angelo, *Histoire de l'Egypte moderne depuis Mohammad Ali jusqu'à l'occupation britannique (1801–1882)*, vol. 3: *Le règne du khédive Ismaïl de 1863 à 1875*. Cairo: Société Royale de Géographie d'Egypte, 1937.

Sanūsī al-Tunisī, Muhammad al-, *al-Istitlāʿāt al-bārisiyya fī maʿrad sanat 1889*. Tunis, 1309h.

Sarrūf, Yaʿqūb, *Sirr al-najāh*. Beirut, 1880. A translation of Samuel Smiles, *Self-Help, with Illustrations of Conduct and Perseverence*, 72nd impression, with an Introduction by Asa Briggs. London: John Murray, 1958; 1st ed. 1859.

Saussure, Ferdinand de, *Course in General Linguistics*, trans. Wade Baskin. New York: Philosophical Library, 1959.

Schölch, Alexander, *Egypt for the Egyptians: The Socio-Political Crisis in Egypt 1878–1882*. London: Ithaca, 1981. A translation of *Ägypten der Ägyptern! Die politische und gesellschaftliche Krise der Jahre 1878–1882 in Agypten*, Freiburg: Atlantis, n.d. (1972).

Taha Husayn, *Rūh al-Tarbiya*. Cairo: Dār al-Hilāl, 1922. A translation of Gustave Le Bon, *Psychologie de l'éducation*, 1st ed., 1904; 2nd ed., 'augmenté de plusieurs chapitres sur les méthodes d'éducation en Amérique et sur l'enseignement donné aux indigènes des colonies'. Paris: Flammarion, 1912.

Tahtāwī, Rifāʿa Rāfiʿ al-, *al-Aʿmāl al-kāmila*, 4 vols., vol. 1: *al-Tamaddun wa-l-hadāra wa-l-ʿumrān*, vol. 2: *al-Siyāsa wa-l-wataniyya wa-l-tarbiya*. Beirut: al-Muʾassasa al-ʿArabiyya li-l-Dirāsāt wa-l-Nashr, 1973.

Mawāqiʿ al-aflāk fī waqāʾiʿ Tīlīmak. Beirut: al-Matbaʿa al-Sūriyya, 1867.

Manāhij al-albāb al-misriyya, fī mabāhij al-ādāb al-'asriyya, 2nd printing. Cairo: Matba'at Shirkat al-Raghā'ib, 1912.

al-Murshid al-amīn li-l-banāt wa-l-banīn. Cairo: 1289h (1872/3).

Qalā'id al-mafākhir fī gharīb 'awā'id al-awā'il wa-l-awākhīr. Bulaq: Dār al-Tabā'a, 1833. A translation of Georg Bernhard Depping, *Aperçu historique sur les moeurs et coutumes des nations*. Contenant le tableau comparé chez les divers peuples anciens et modernes, des usages et des cérémonies concernant l'habitation, la nourriture, l'habillement, les marriages, les funérailles, les jeux, les fêtes, les guerres, les superstitions, les castes, etc., etc. Paris: L'Encyclopedie Portative, 1826.

Tocqueville, Alexis de, 'Notes du voyage en Algérie de 1841', *Oeuvres complètes*, gen. ed. J. P. Mayer, vol. 5, *Voyages en Angleterre, Irlande, Suisse et Algérie*, ed. J. P. Mayer and André Jardin. Paris: Gallimard, 1958.

Tucker, Judith E., *Women in Nineteenth-Century Egypt*. Cambridge: Cambridge University Press, 1985.

Tusūn, 'Umar, *al-Bi'thāt al-'ilmiyya fī 'ahd Muhammad 'Alī thumma fī 'ahday 'Abbās al-awwal wa-Sa'īd*. Alexandria: Matba'at Salāh al-Dīn, 1934.

'Umar, Muhammad, *Hādir al-misriyyīn aw sirr ta'akhkhurihim*. Cairo: Matba'at al-Muqtataf, 1902.

Weber, Max, ' "Objectivity" in social science and social policy', in *The Methodology of the Social Sciences*, trans. and ed. Edward A. Shils and Henry A. Finch. New York: The Free Press, 1949, pp. 49–112.

Zaghlūl, Ahmad Fathī, *Rūh al-ijtimā'*. Cairo: Matba'at al-Sha'b, 1909. A translation of Gustave Le Bon, *Psychologie des foules*. Paris: Felix Alcan, 1895.

Sirr taqaddun al-inklīz al-sāksūniyyīn. Cairo: Matba'at al-Ma'ārif, 1899. A translation of Edmond Demolins, *A quoi tient la supériorité des Anglo-Saxons*. Paris: Libraire de Paris, 1897.

Sirr tatawwur al-umam. Cairo: Matba'at al-Ma'ārif, 1913. A translation of Gustave Le Bon, *Lois psychologiques de l'évolution des peuples*, 12th ed. Paris: Felix Alcan, 1916.

Zawāhirī, Ahmad al-, *al-'Ilm wa-l-'ulamā' wa-nizām al-ta'līm*. Tantā: al-Matba'a al-'Umūmiyya, 1904.

Zaydān, Jurjī, *Ta'rīkh ādāb al-lugha al-'arabiyya*, 4 vols. Cairo: Dār al-Hilāl, 1914.

Ta'rīkh al-tamaddun al-islāmī, 5 vols. Cairo: Dār al-Hilāl, 1901–6; reprint ed. 1958.

Index

Abbas Pasha, 74
Abdullah Nadim, 153
Abu al-nazzara al-zarqa', 26
adab, 135–6
Adorno, Theodor, 7
Afghani, Jamal al-Din al-, 155, 194n81
agriculture, 34–5, 40–3, 75, 175; *see also*
   cotton cultivation, landownership, villages
Alexandria, 34, 109; bombardment of, 128
Ali Mubarak, 63–5, 68, 71, 74, 84–5, 93, 108
Alloula, Malek, 26
American University in Beirut, 108–9
army, 14, 35–40, 153, 174, 186n21
author, concept of, 144, 150–2, 154, 155,
   158; *see also* authority, writing
authority: new methods of, 15, 104, 128–9,
   154, 158–60, 171, 179; in school, 70, 175;
   textual, 15, 132–3, 135, 150–3
Ayrout, Henry Habib, 92–3
al-Azhar, 2, 80–5, 132–3, 135

Barudi, Mahmud Sami al-, 131
Benjamin, Walter, 15, 18, 114
Bentham, Jeremy, 24, 33, 40
Berardi, Roberto, 56
body: notion of, 14, 19, 95, 100–2, 154–9,
   171; and exercise of power, 93–4, 95–100;
   see also materiality, mind
Boyle, Harry, 112
Bourdieu, Pierre, 28, 48–51, 53, 55, 60–1,
   93, 167, 173–4, 195n87
Bowring, John, 40, 42, 46
Bréal, Michel, 140–1, 143
Brigandage Commissions, 97
Britain, occupation of Egypt by, 14, 15, 16,
   35, 95–6, 97–8, 100, 104, 109, 111–12,
   116, 117–18, 122, 128–31, 138, 156,
   157–9, 166, 168, 169, 175; *see also*
   colonialism
Brockelmann, Carl, 170

cafés, 1, 12, 117, 119, 162, 199n88
Cairo: attempts to represent, 1, 6, 27, 29–30;

pre-modern, 54–6, 174; modern, 17, 63,
   65–8, 115, 117–19, 156, 163–4, 205n9
capitalism, requirements of, 34–5, 40–3, 75,
   96–8, 135, 166; *see also* commerce, commodity fetishism, cotton cultivation,
   landownership
Casablanca, 161, 162, 163
certainty, 7, 13, 15, 23, 31, 51, 129–30, 150,
   171, 175, 177–9; *see also* authority, representation, truth
Chamber of Deputies, 75–6, 90
character, 101–2, 104–14, 168, 176, 196n13;
   see also industriousness, mind, self
cities: pre-modern, 53–6, 178, 188n65; and
   problem of representation, 27, 32–3, 56–9;
   and Descartes, 177–8; and colonial order,
   63, 65–8, 161–5, 171; *see also* Cairo, Rabat
Chelli, Monçef, 148–9
Chevalier, Michel, 16
colonialism: methods of, 15–16, 33, 126–7,
   157–9, 165–7, 167–8, 171, 175, 178–9; as
   essence of modern power, 13, 14, 35, 95,
   171; and exhibitions, 8–9; and liberalism,
   116; and Orientalism, 7, 138–40; and
   Tocqueville, 57–8; *see also* Britain,
   capitalism, discipline, order, power
commerce, transformation of, 10–12, 15,
   98–9, 116
commodity fetishism, 18–19
communication: and capitalism, 16; and
   imperial power, 129–30, 131; and nature
   of language, 140–1, 143–4, 150–1, 158
conceptual realm, effect of, 79, 126, 171,
   172–3, 177–9; in linguistic theory, 143–50;
   see also enframing, structure, materality,
   mind
cotton cultivation, promotion of, 15–16, 17,
   40–1, 96
Cromer, Earl of, 95–6, 97, 104, 111, 157–9,
   175, 176
crowds, 37–8, 40, 64, 114–17, 119–26; *see
   also* disorder
culture, concept of, 61–2, 101, 104–5; and

215